AMERICAN JESUS

VOLUME TWO:

THE NEW MESSIAH

MARK MILLAR
STORY
PETER GROSS
ART
JEANNE MCGEE
COLOR
CORY PETIT
LETTERING

MELINA MIKULIC
COLLECTION COVERS DESIGN AND PRODUCTION
PHIL BALSMAN
SINGLE ISSUE DESIGN AND PRODUCTION
JODIE MUIR
SERIES MAIN COVER ARTIST
RACHAEL FULTON
EDITOR
LUCY MILLAR
CEO

With special thanks to Bridget McConnell, Duncan Dornan and Glasgow Life.

Created by Mark Millar and Peter Gross

IMAGE COMICS, INC. • Robert Kirkman: Chief Operating Officer • Erik Larsen: Chief Financial Officer • Todd McFarlane: President • Marc Silvestri: Chief Executive Officer • Jim Valentino: Vice President • Eric Stephenson: Publisher / Chief Creative Officer • Jeff Boison: Director of Publishing Planning & Book Trade Sales • Chris Ross: Director of Digital Services • Jeff Stang: Director of Direct Market Sales • Kat Salazar: Director of PR & Marketing • Drew Gill: Cover Editor • Heather Doornink: Production Director • Nicole Lapalme: Controller • IMAGECOMICS.COM

AMERICAN JESUS, VOL. 2. First printing. April 2020. Published by Image Comics, Inc. Office of publication: 2701 NW Vaughn St., Suite 780, Portland, OR 97210. Printed in the USA. For information regarding the CPSIA on this printed material call: 203-595-3636. For international rights, contact: lucy@netflixmw.com. ISBN: 978-1-5343-1512-9.

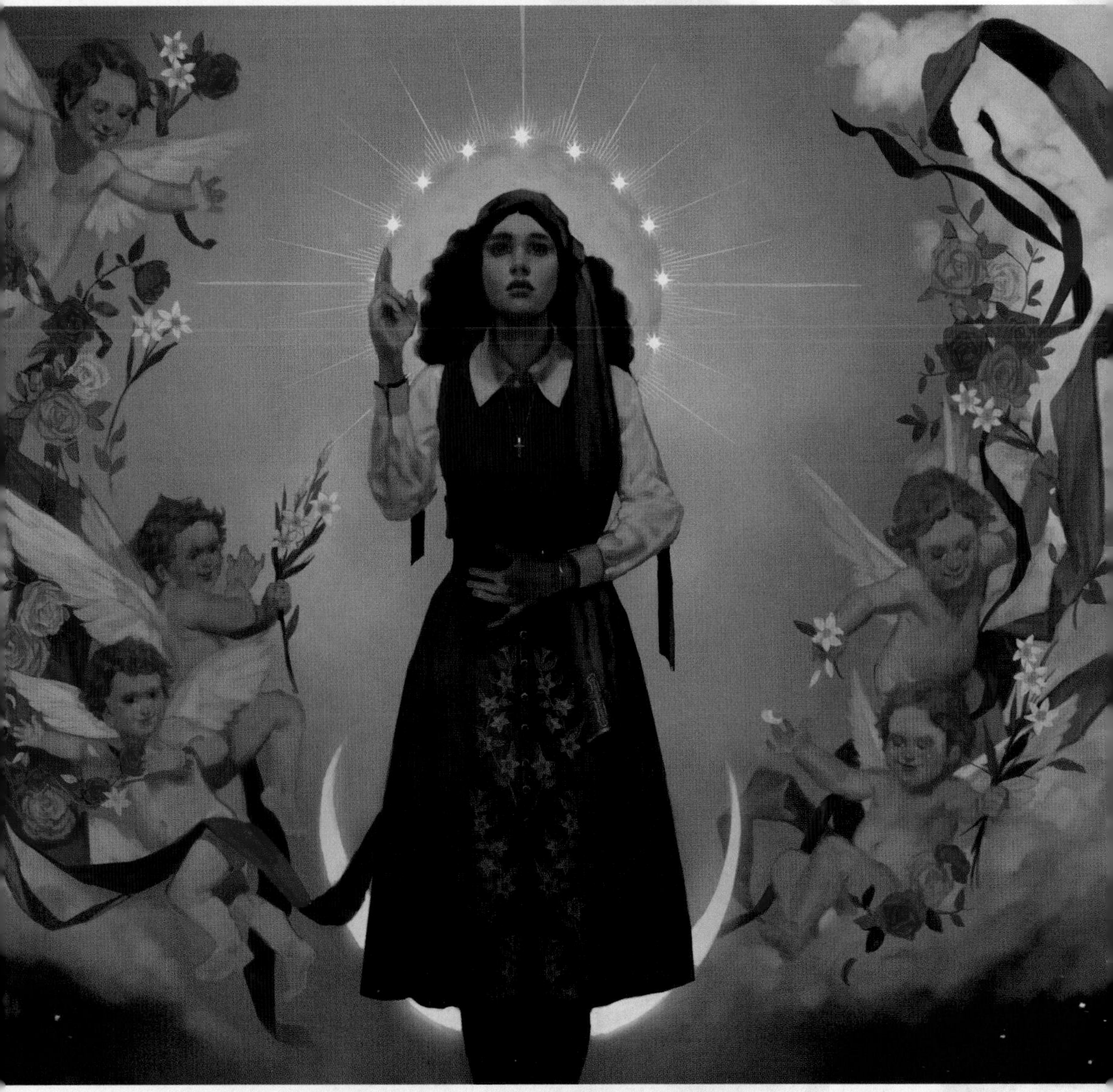

CHAPTER 1

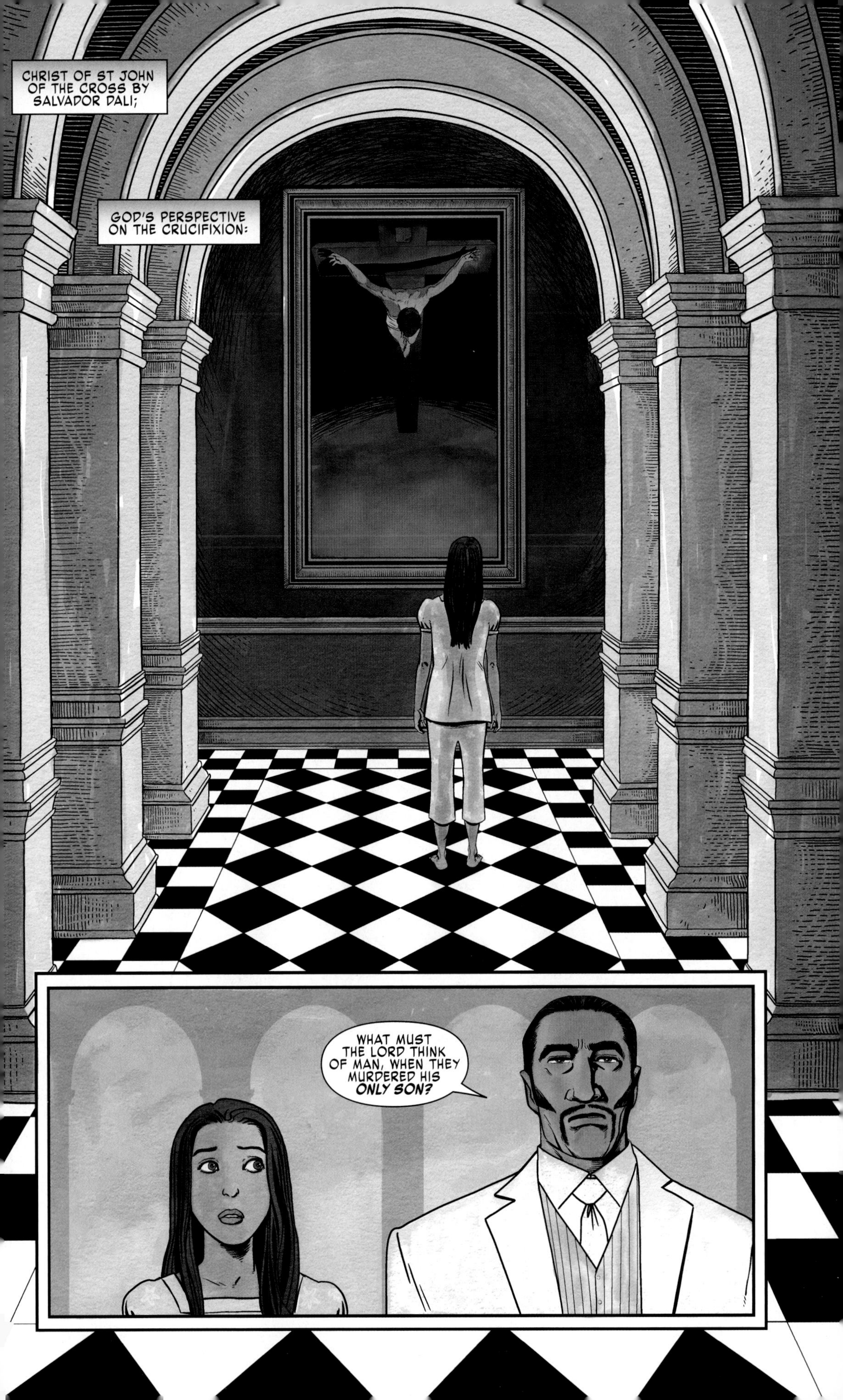
CHRIST OF ST JOHN OF THE CROSS BY SALVADOR DALI;
GOD'S PERSPECTIVE ON THE CRUCIFIXION:
WHAT MUST THE LORD THINK OF MAN, WHEN THEY MURDERED HIS *ONLY SON?*

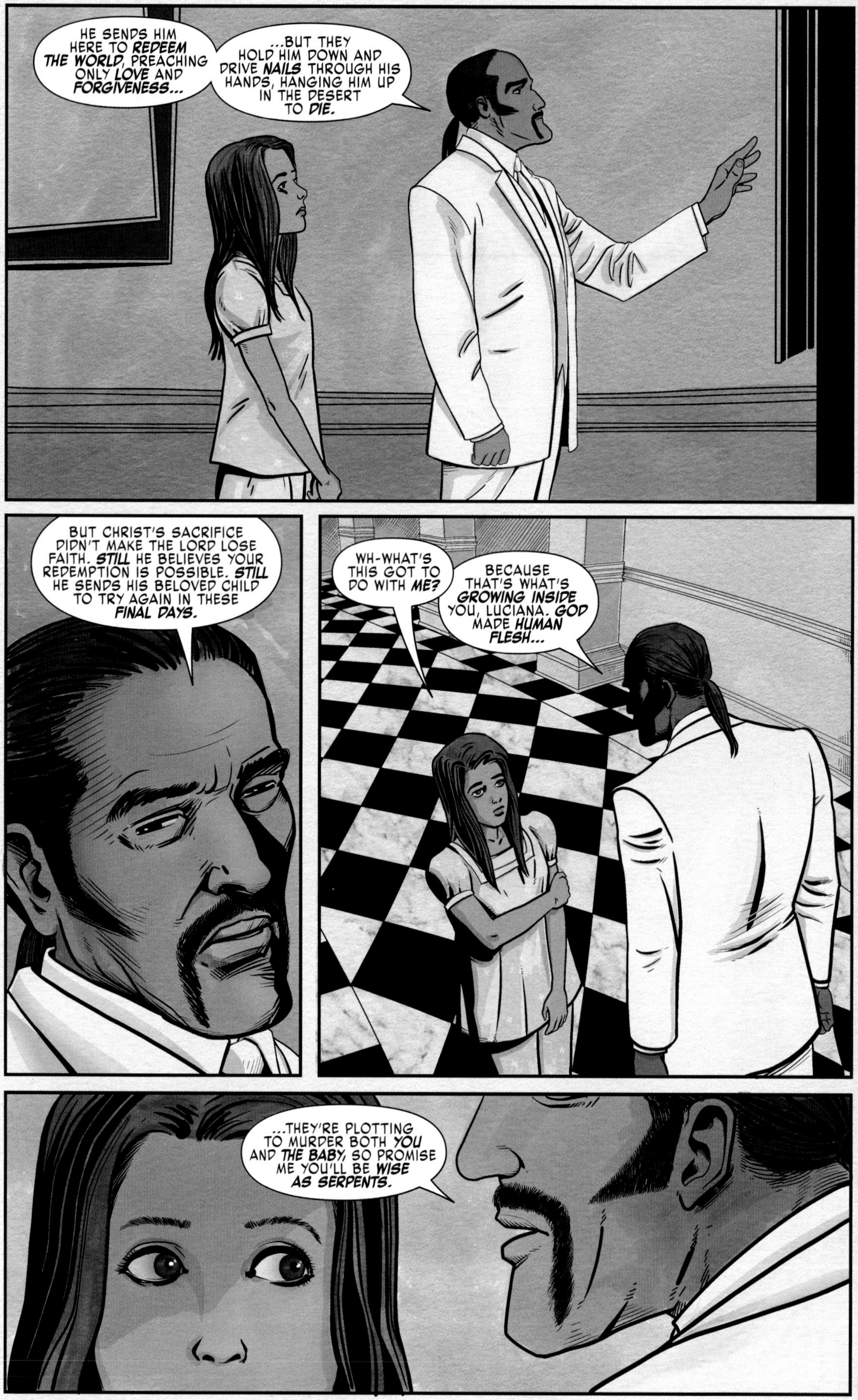
HE SENDS HIM HERE TO REDEEM THE WORLD, PREACHING ONLY LOVE AND FORGIVENESS...
...BUT THEY HOLD HIM DOWN AND DRIVE NAILS THROUGH HIS HANDS, HANGING HIM UP IN THE DESERT TO DIE.
BUT CHRIST'S SACRIFICE DIDN'T MAKE THE LORD LOSE FAITH. STILL HE BELIEVES YOUR REDEMPTION IS POSSIBLE. STILL HE SENDS HIS BELOVED CHILD TO TRY AGAIN IN THESE FINAL DAYS.
WH-WHAT'S THIS GOT TO DO WITH ME?
BECAUSE THAT'S WHAT'S GROWING INSIDE YOU, LUCIANA. GOD MADE HUMAN FLESH...
...THEY'RE PLOTTING TO MURDER BOTH YOU AND THE BABY, SO PROMISE ME YOU'LL BE WISE AS SERPENTS.

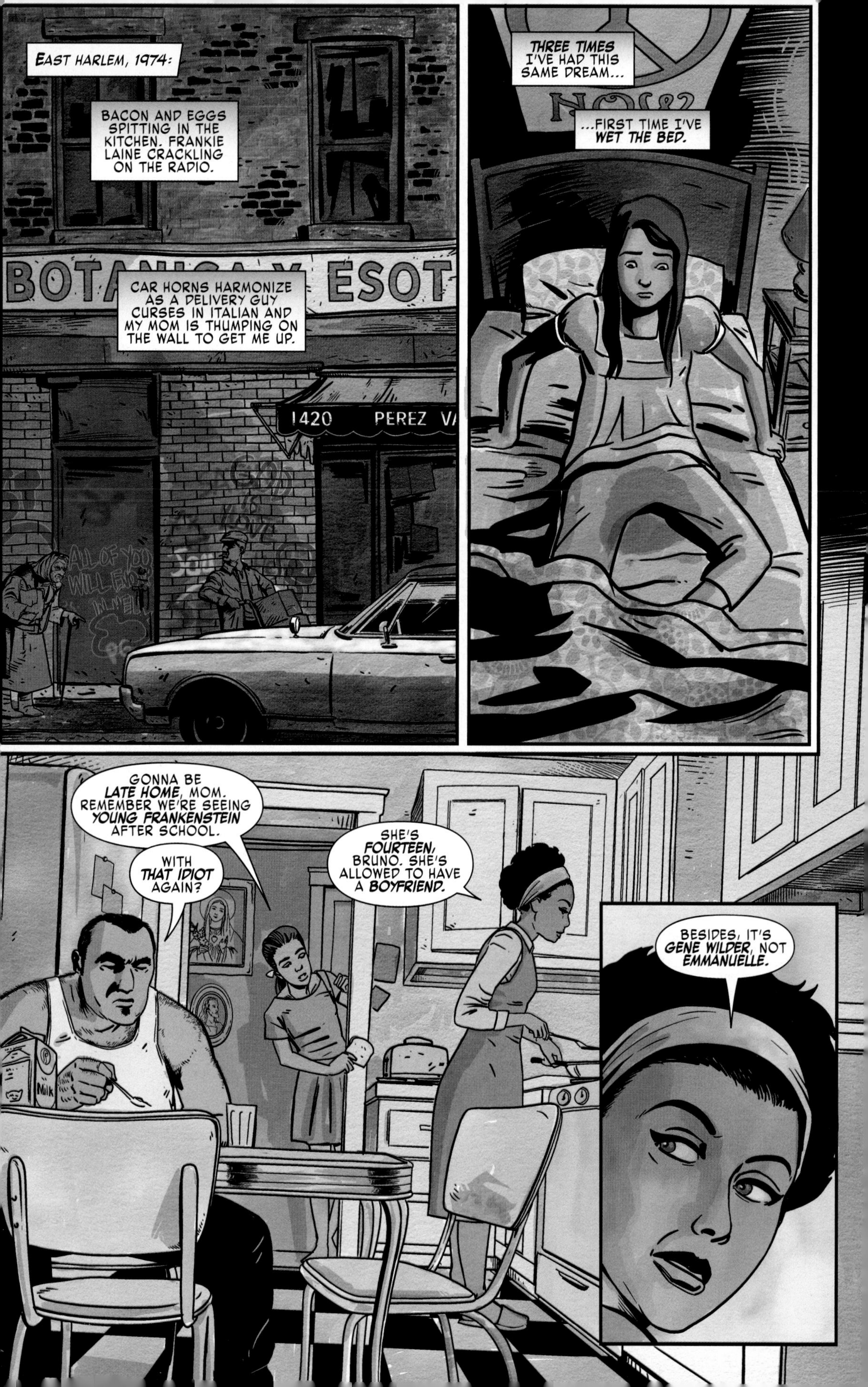
EAST HARLEM, 1974:
BACON AND EGGS SPITTING IN THE KITCHEN. FRANKIE LAINE CRACKLING ON THE RADIO.
BOTANICA Y ESOT
CAR HORNS HARMONIZE AS A DELIVERY GUY CURSES IN ITALIAN AND MY MOM IS THUMPING ON THE WALL TO GET ME UP.
1420 PEREZ VA
ALL OF YOU WILL EN IN HELL
THREE TIMES I'VE HAD THIS SAME DREAM...
...FIRST TIME I'VE WET THE BED.
GONNA BE LATE HOME, MOM. REMEMBER WE'RE SEEING YOUNG FRANKENSTEIN AFTER SCHOOL.
WITH THAT IDIOT AGAIN?
SHE'S FOURTEEN, BRUNO. SHE'S ALLOWED TO HAVE A BOYFRIEND.
MILK
BESIDES, IT'S GENE WILDER, NOT EMMANUELLE.

WHAT DOES IT MEAN IF YOU DREAM YOU'RE *PREGNANT* WITH THE *BABY JESUS,* JENNA? DOES THAT MEAN *GOOD LUCK?*

SOUNDS TO ME LIKE *CATHOLIC GUILT...*

HAVE *YOU* AND *EDDIE* BEEN--

DON'T BE *STUPID.*

MEL BROOKS YOUNG FRANKENSTEIN

DO YOU WANT TO GO SEE *HERBIE* NEXT FRIDAY? IT'S ONLY *PLAYING* FOR ONE MORE WEEK AND I REALLY LIKED *THE LOVE BUG.*

DEFINITELY.

1ST DIED UR SINS

GOD IS ALIVE!

JESUS IS CALLING THE YOUNG! JOIN THE PENTECOSTAL MARINE AND WORK FOR THE LORD

TIME IS OUT COME! TO JESUS NOW!

El sabot de calidad de las Américas

IN TIMES LIKE THESE CHRIST! IS WHAT YOU NEED

SUCH A WEIRD IDEA FOR A *MOVIE,* HUH? A CAR WITH A BRAIN THAT THINKS FOR *ITSELF.* FREDDIE IN SCHOOL SAYS IT'S *HITLER'S GHOST.*

I DON'T *GET* IT.

STAURANT

Famous PIZZA

SHOE REPAIR

FOR RENT

REINCARNATED AS A *GERMAN VOLKSWAGEN.* TRYING TO MAKE UP FOR ALL THE *BAD THINGS* HE DID.

WASN'T HITLER *FIFTY-THREE* WHEN HE DIED *TOO?* MAYBE THAT'S WHAT THE NUMBER ON THE *HOOD'S* ALL ABOUT.

YOU'RE *NUTS.* YOU KNOW THAT?

KS CASHE

S CAMBIAMOS

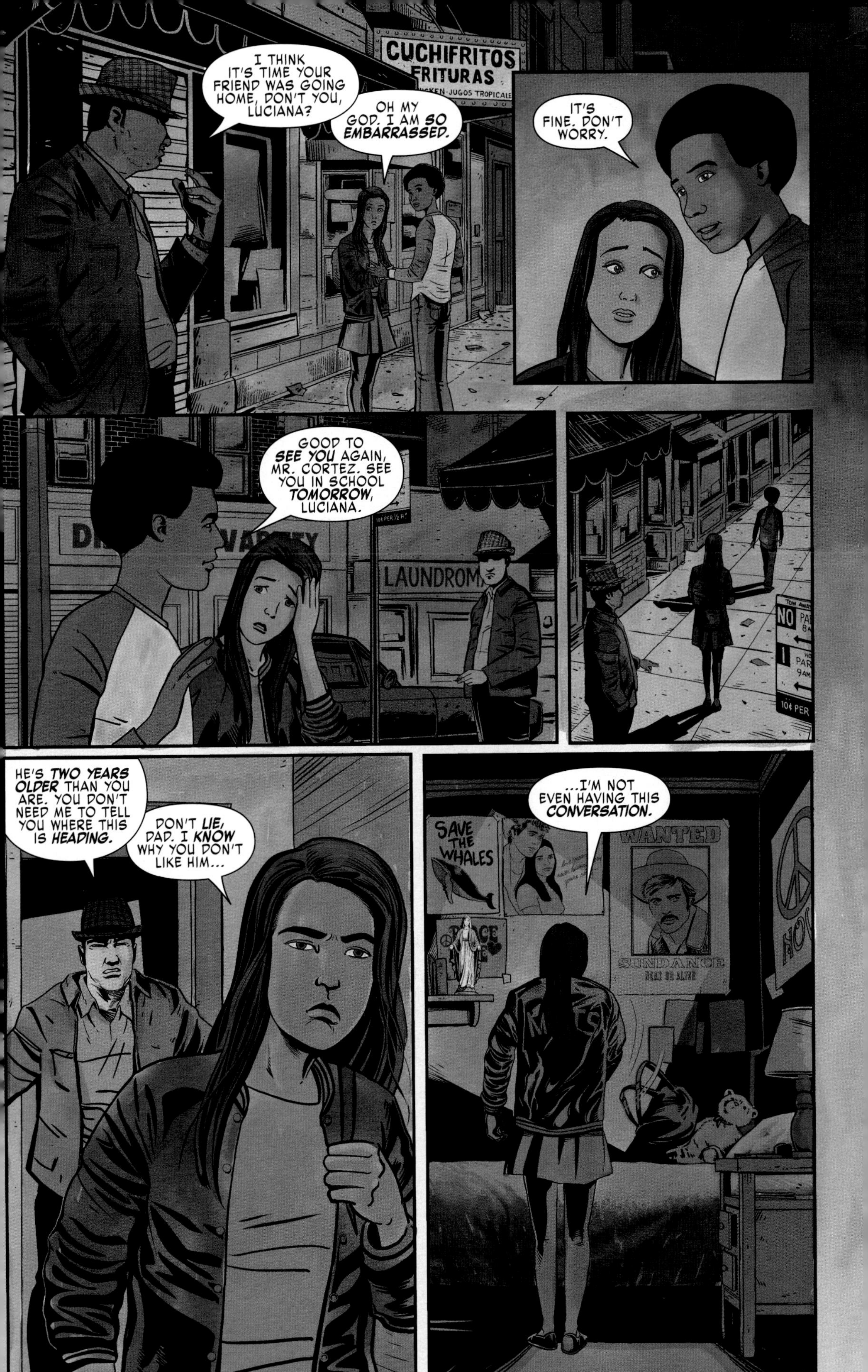
CUCHIFRITOS
FRITURAS
I THINK IT'S TIME YOUR FRIEND WAS GOING HOME, DON'T YOU, LUCIANA?
OH MY GOD. I AM SO EMBARRASSED.
IT'S FINE. DON'T WORRY.
GOOD TO SEE YOU AGAIN, MR. CORTEZ. SEE YOU IN SCHOOL TOMORROW, LUCIANA.
LAUNDROM
HE'S TWO YEARS OLDER THAN YOU ARE. YOU DON'T NEED ME TO TELL YOU WHERE THIS IS HEADING.
DON'T LIE, DAD. I KNOW WHY YOU DON'T LIKE HIM...
...I'M NOT EVEN HAVING THIS CONVERSATION.
SAVE THE WHALES
WANTED
SUNDANCE

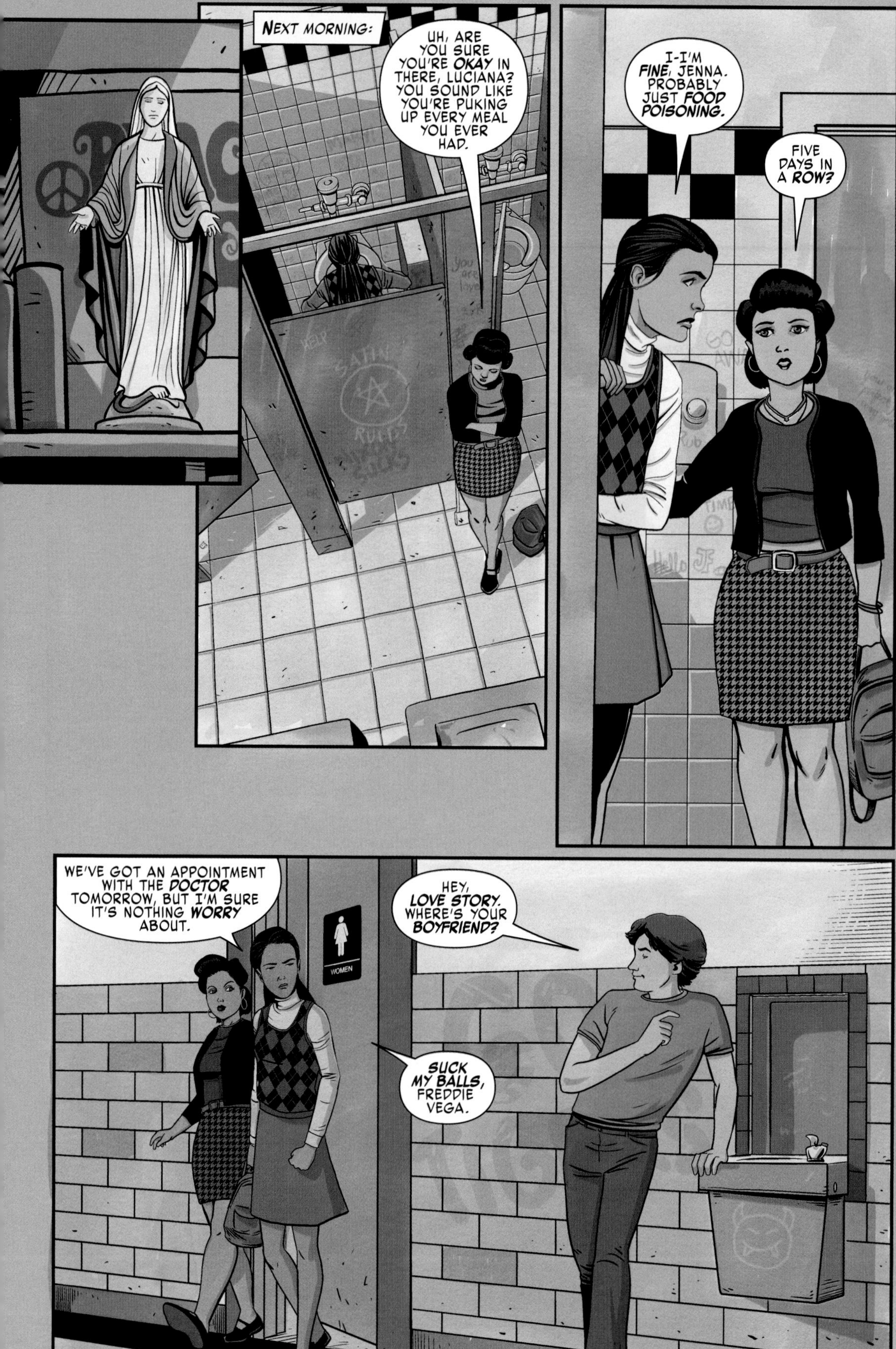
NEXT MORNING:
UH, ARE YOU SURE YOU'RE OKAY IN THERE, LUCIANA? YOU SOUND LIKE YOU'RE PUKING UP EVERY MEAL YOU EVER HAD.
I-I'M FINE, JENNA. PROBABLY JUST FOOD POISONING.
FIVE DAYS IN A ROW?
WE'VE GOT AN APPOINTMENT WITH THE DOCTOR TOMORROW, BUT I'M SURE IT'S NOTHING WORRY ABOUT.
WOMEN
HEY, LOVE STORY. WHERE'S YOUR BOYFRIEND?
SUCK MY BALLS, FREDDIE VEGA.

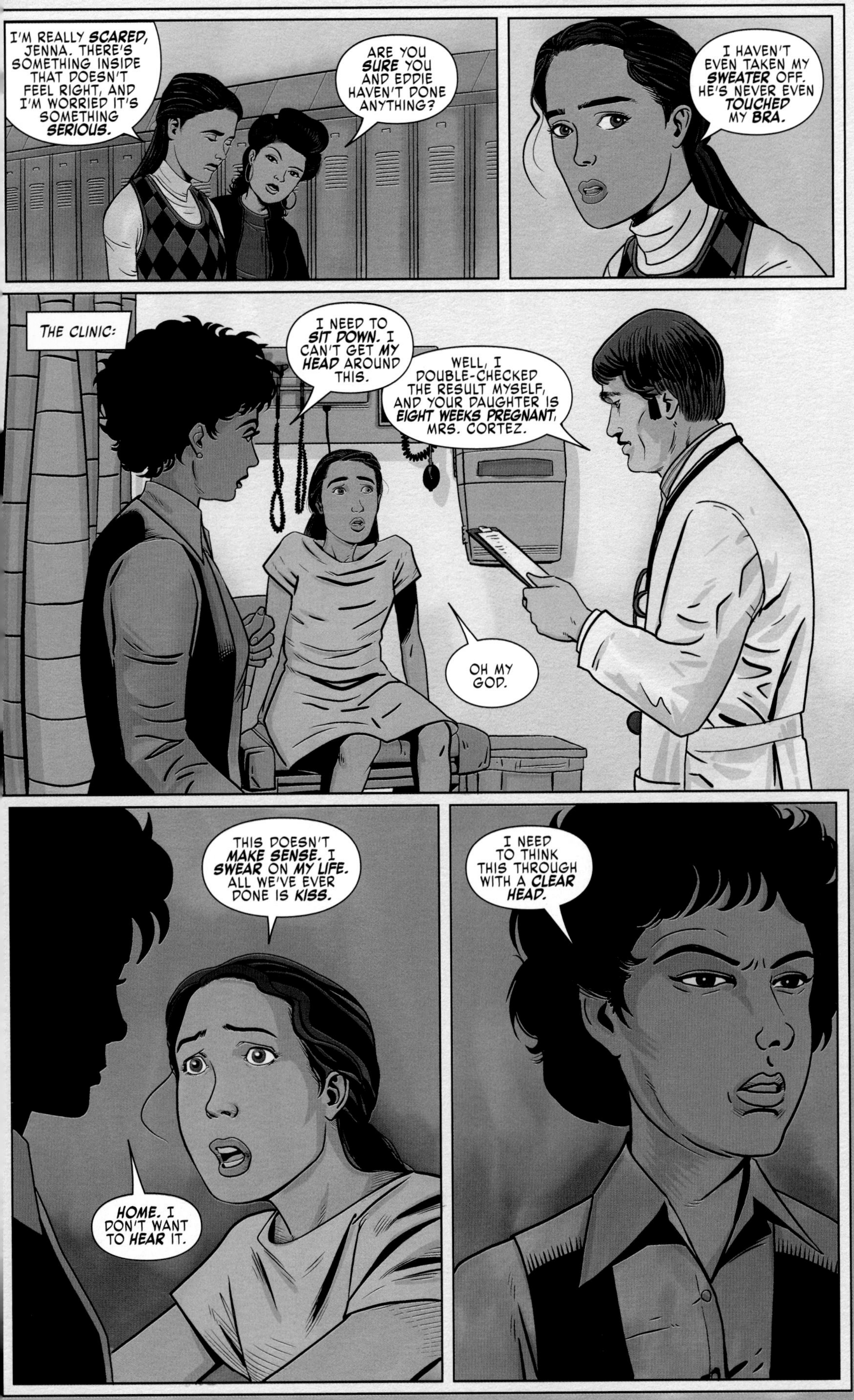
I'M REALLY SCARED, JENNA. THERE'S SOMETHING INSIDE THAT DOESN'T FEEL RIGHT, AND I'M WORRIED IT'S SOMETHING SERIOUS.
ARE YOU SURE YOU AND EDDIE HAVEN'T DONE ANYTHING?
I HAVEN'T EVEN TAKEN MY SWEATER OFF. HE'S NEVER EVEN TOUCHED MY BRA.
THE CLINIC:
WELL, I DOUBLE-CHECKED THE RESULT MYSELF, AND YOUR DAUGHTER IS EIGHT WEEKS PREGNANT, MRS. CORTEZ.
I NEED TO SIT DOWN. I CAN'T GET MY HEAD AROUND THIS.
OH MY GOD.
THIS DOESN'T MAKE SENSE. I SWEAR ON MY LIFE. ALL WE'VE EVER DONE IS KISS.
HOME. I DON'T WANT TO HEAR IT.
I NEED TO THINK THIS THROUGH WITH A CLEAR HEAD.

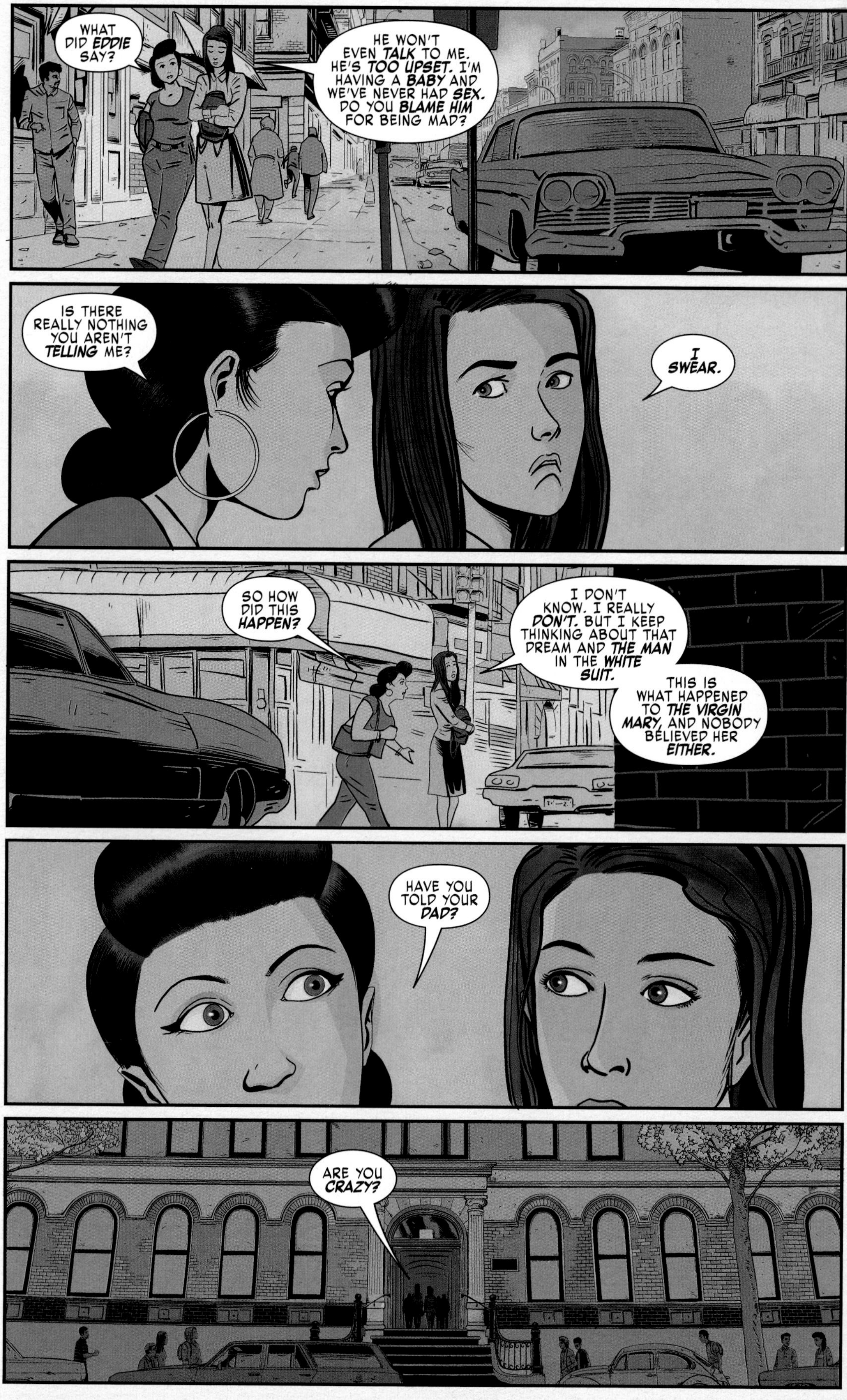
WHAT DID EDDIE SAY?
HE WON'T EVEN TALK TO ME. HE'S TOO UPSET. I'M HAVING A BABY AND WE'VE NEVER HAD SEX. DO YOU BLAME HIM FOR BEING MAD?
IS THERE REALLY NOTHING YOU AREN'T TELLING ME?
I SWEAR.
SO HOW DID THIS HAPPEN?
I DON'T KNOW. I REALLY DON'T. BUT I KEEP THINKING ABOUT THAT DREAM AND THE MAN IN THE WHITE SUIT.
THIS IS WHAT HAPPENED TO THE VIRGIN MARY, AND NOBODY BELIEVED HER EITHER.
HAVE YOU TOLD YOUR DAD?
ARE YOU CRAZY?

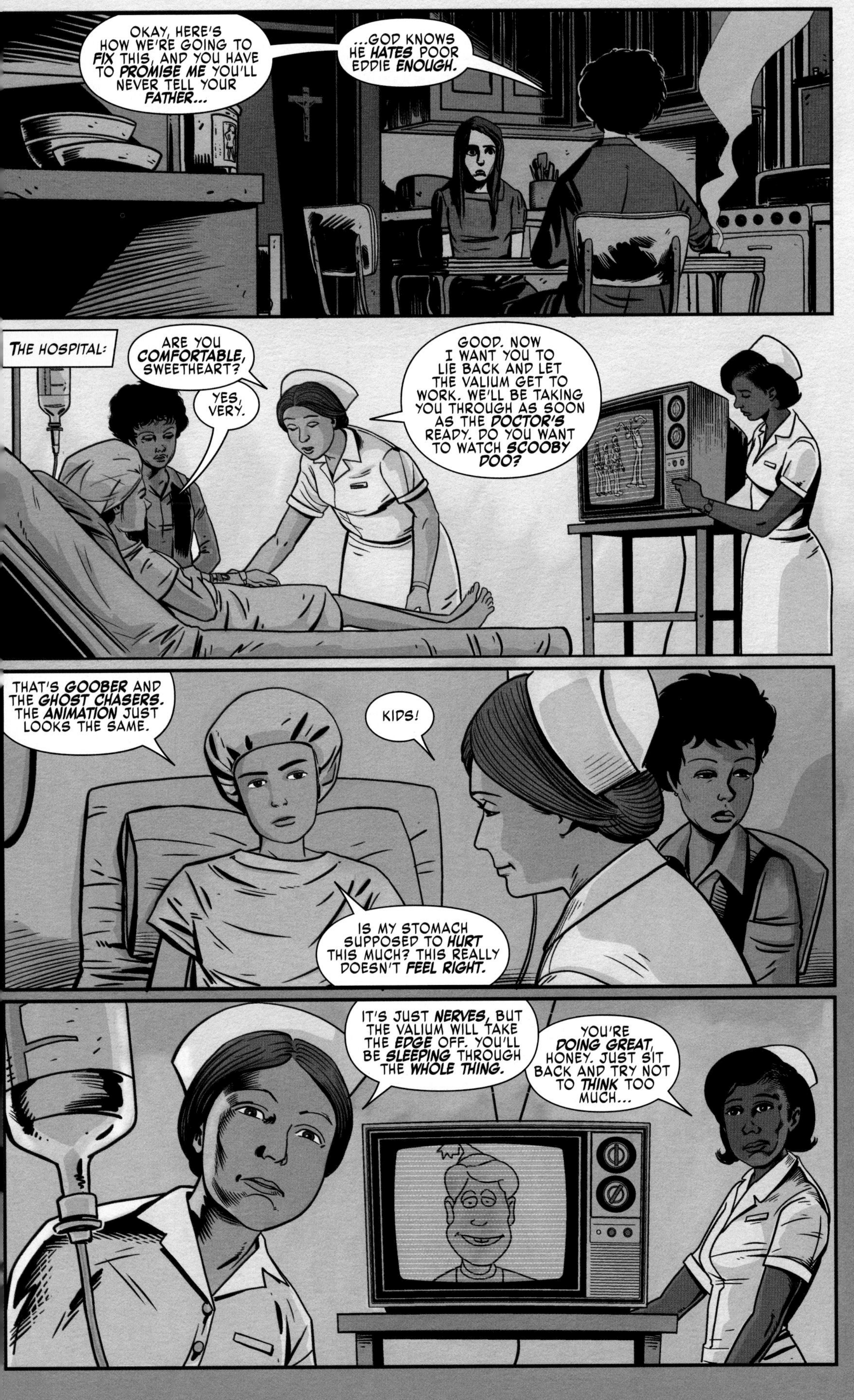

OKAY, HERE'S HOW WE'RE GOING TO FIX THIS, AND YOU HAVE TO PROMISE ME YOU'LL NEVER TELL YOUR FATHER...
...GOD KNOWS HE HATES POOR EDDIE ENOUGH.
THE HOSPITAL:
ARE YOU COMFORTABLE, SWEETHEART?
YES, VERY.
GOOD. NOW I WANT YOU TO LIE BACK AND LET THE VALIUM GET TO WORK. WE'LL BE TAKING YOU THROUGH AS SOON AS THE DOCTOR'S READY. DO YOU WANT TO WATCH SCOOBY DOO?
THAT'S GOOBER AND THE GHOST CHASERS. THE ANIMATION JUST LOOKS THE SAME.
KIDS!
IS MY STOMACH SUPPOSED TO HURT THIS MUCH? THIS REALLY DOESN'T FEEL RIGHT.
IT'S JUST NERVES, BUT THE VALIUM WILL TAKE THE EDGE OFF. YOU'LL BE SLEEPING THROUGH THE WHOLE THING.
YOU'RE DOING GREAT, HONEY. JUST SIT BACK AND TRY NOT TO THINK TOO MUCH...

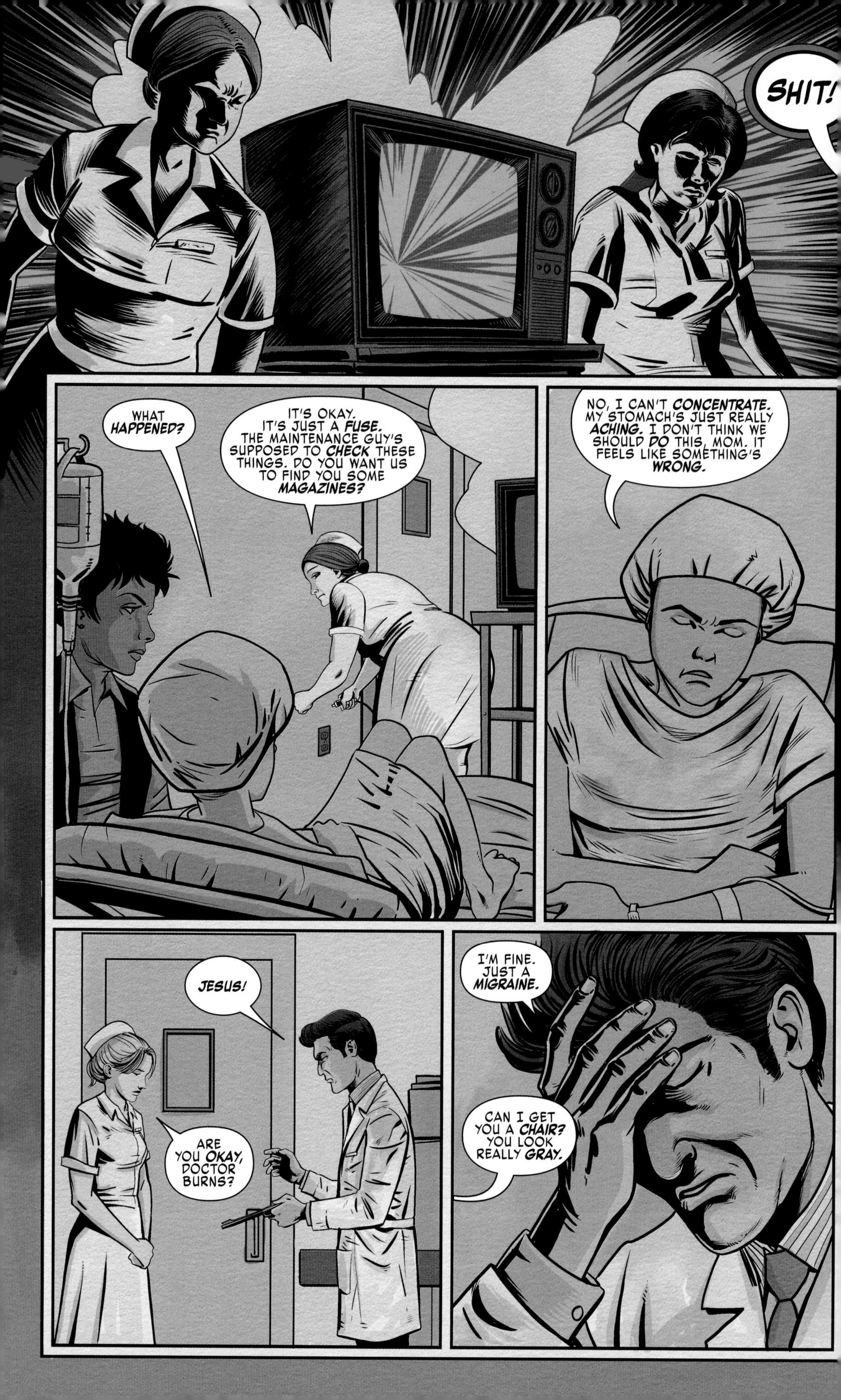
SHIT!
WHAT HAPPENED?
IT'S OKAY. IT'S JUST A FUSE. THE MAINTENANCE GUY'S SUPPOSED TO CHECK THESE THINGS. DO YOU WANT US TO FIND YOU SOME MAGAZINES?
NO, I CAN'T CONCENTRATE. MY STOMACH'S JUST REALLY ACHING. I DON'T THINK WE SHOULD DO THIS, MOM. IT FEELS LIKE SOMETHING'S WRONG.
JESUS!
ARE YOU OKAY, DOCTOR BURNS?
I'M FINE. JUST A MIGRAINE.
CAN I GET YOU A CHAIR? YOU LOOK REALLY GRAY.

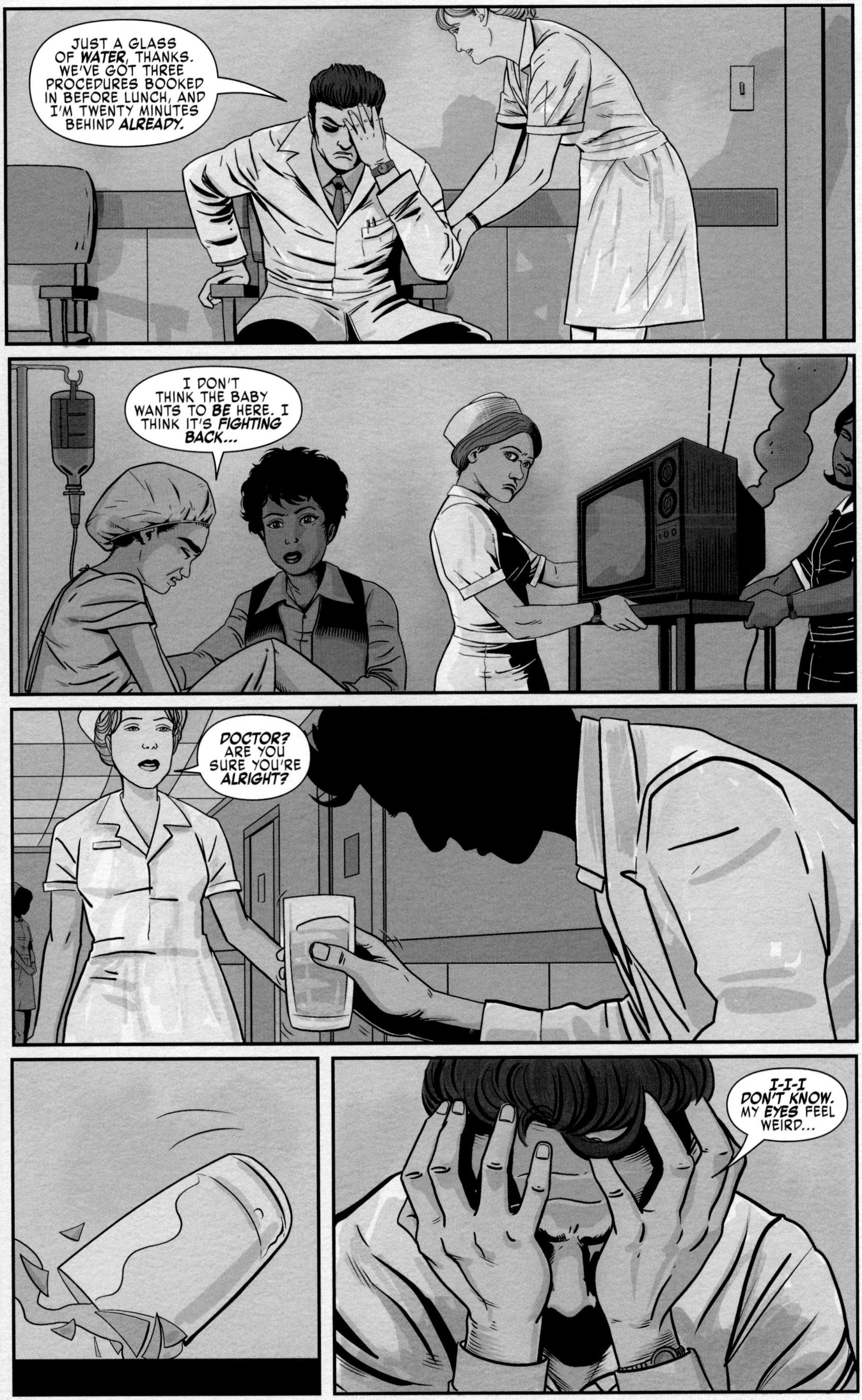
JUST A GLASS OF WATER, THANKS. WE'VE GOT THREE PROCEDURES BOOKED IN BEFORE LUNCH, AND I'M TWENTY MINUTES BEHIND ALREADY.
I DON'T THINK THE BABY WANTS TO BE HERE. I THINK IT'S FIGHTING BACK...
DOCTOR? ARE YOU SURE YOU'RE ALRIGHT?
I-I-I DON'T KNOW. MY EYES FEEL WEIRD...

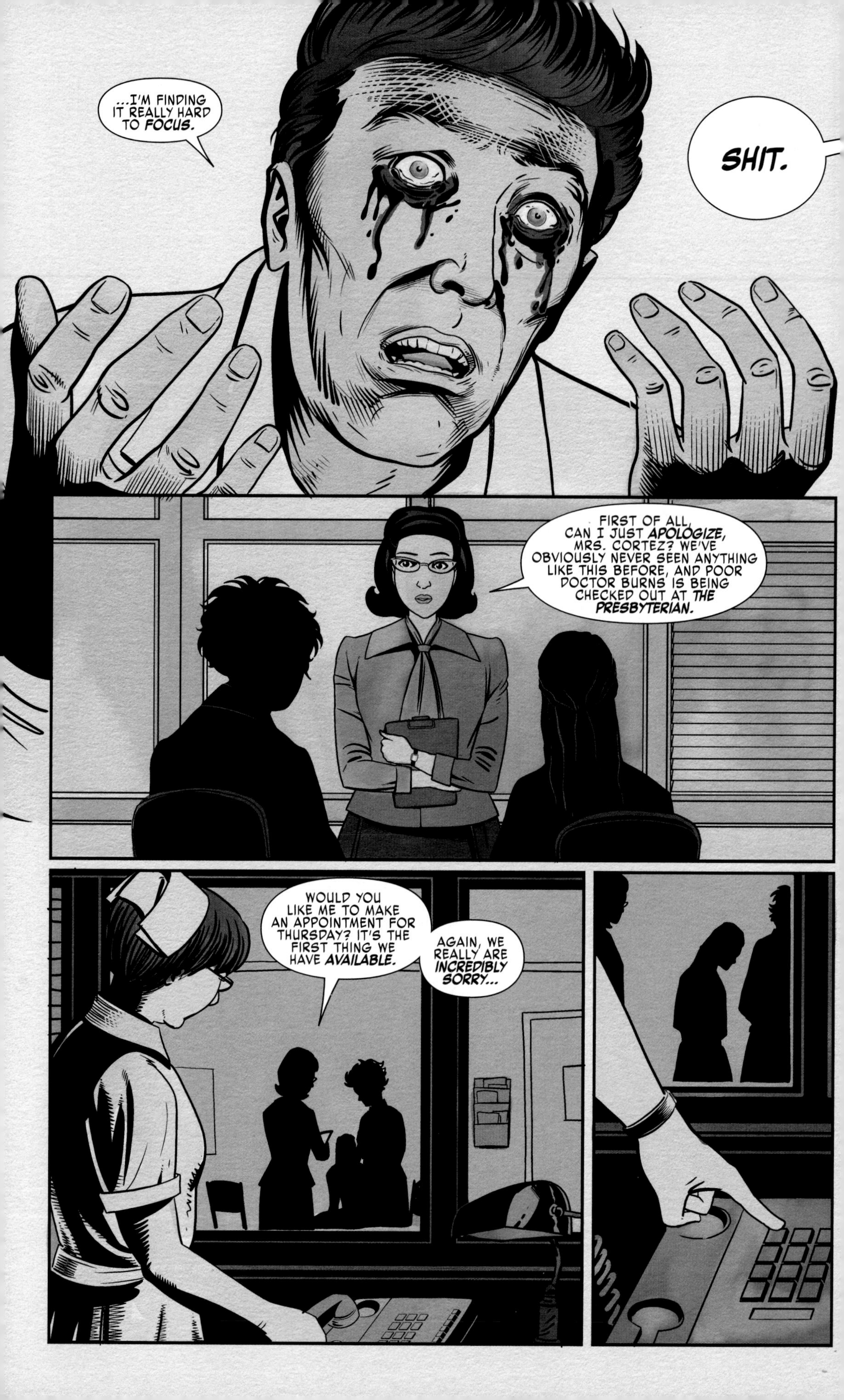
...I'M FINDING IT REALLY HARD TO FOCUS.
SHIT.
FIRST OF ALL, CAN I JUST APOLOGIZE, MRS. CORTEZ? WE'VE OBVIOUSLY NEVER SEEN ANYTHING LIKE THIS BEFORE, AND POOR DOCTOR BURNS IS BEING CHECKED OUT AT THE PRESBYTERIAN.
WOULD YOU LIKE ME TO MAKE AN APPOINTMENT FOR THURSDAY? IT'S THE FIRST THING WE HAVE AVAILABLE.
AGAIN, WE REALLY ARE INCREDIBLY SORRY...

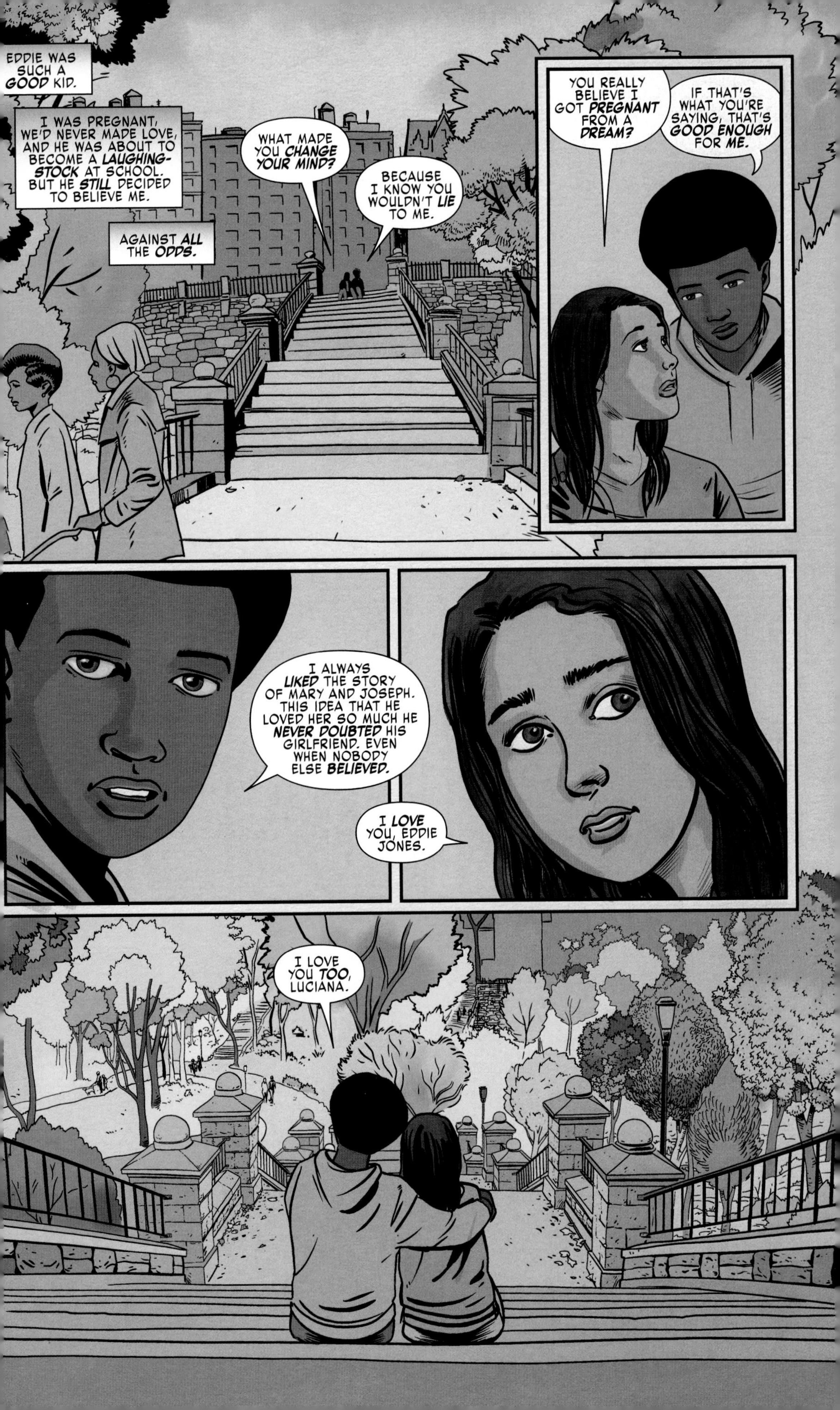

EDDIE WAS SUCH A GOOD KID.
I WAS PREGNANT, WE'D NEVER MADE LOVE, AND HE WAS ABOUT TO BECOME A LAUGHING-STOCK AT SCHOOL. BUT HE STILL DECIDED TO BELIEVE ME.
AGAINST ALL THE ODDS.
WHAT MADE YOU CHANGE YOUR MIND?
BECAUSE I KNOW YOU WOULDN'T LIE TO ME.
YOU REALLY BELIEVE I GOT PREGNANT FROM A DREAM?
IF THAT'S WHAT YOU'RE SAYING, THAT'S GOOD ENOUGH FOR ME.
I ALWAYS LIKED THE STORY OF MARY AND JOSEPH. THIS IDEA THAT HE LOVED HER SO MUCH HE NEVER DOUBTED HIS GIRLFRIEND. EVEN WHEN NOBODY ELSE BELIEVED.
I LOVE YOU, EDDIE JONES.
I LOVE YOU TOO, LUCIANA.

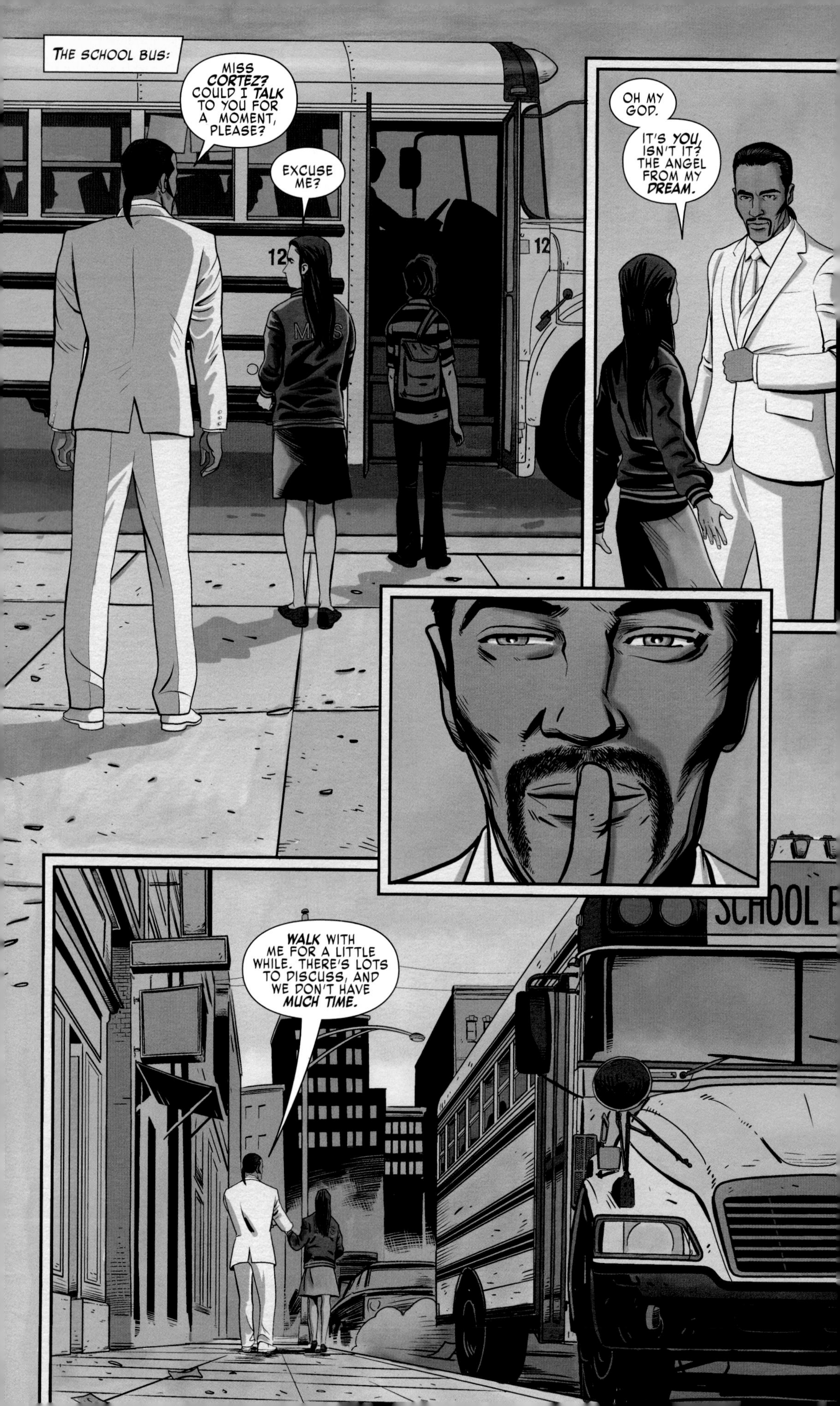
THE SCHOOL BUS:
MISS CORTEZ? COULD I TALK TO YOU FOR A MOMENT, PLEASE?
EXCUSE ME?
12
12
OH MY GOD.
IT'S YOU, ISN'T IT? THE ANGEL FROM MY DREAM.
SCHOOL B
WALK WITH ME FOR A LITTLE WHILE. THERE'S LOTS TO DISCUSS, AND WE DON'T HAVE MUCH TIME.

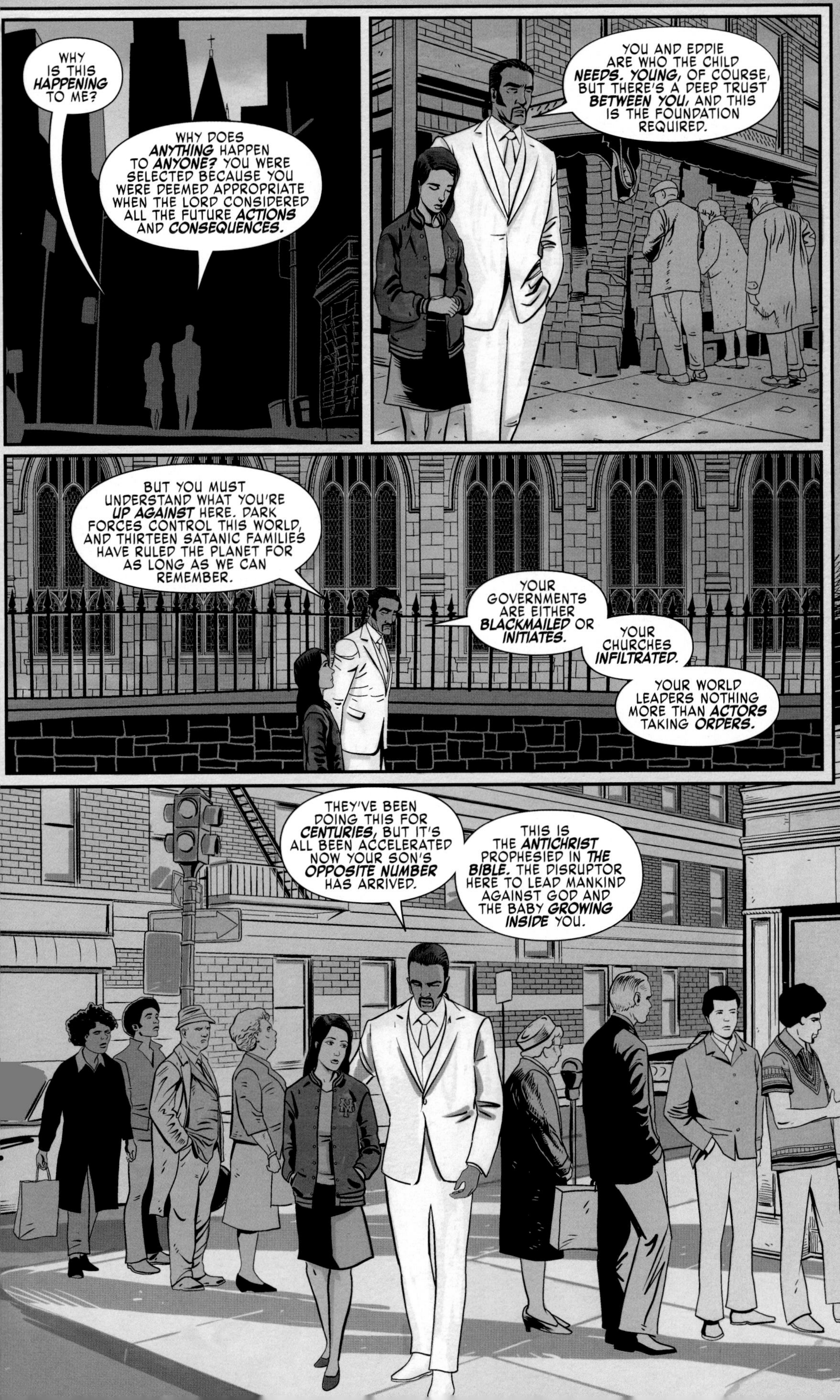

WHY IS THIS HAPPENING TO ME?
WHY DOES ANYTHING HAPPEN TO ANYONE? YOU WERE SELECTED BECAUSE YOU WERE DEEMED APPROPRIATE WHEN THE LORD CONSIDERED ALL THE FUTURE ACTIONS AND CONSEQUENCES.
YOU AND EDDIE ARE WHO THE CHILD NEEDS. YOUNG, OF COURSE, BUT THERE'S A DEEP TRUST BETWEEN YOU, AND THIS IS THE FOUNDATION REQUIRED.
BUT YOU MUST UNDERSTAND WHAT YOU'RE UP AGAINST HERE. DARK FORCES CONTROL THIS WORLD, AND THIRTEEN SATANIC FAMILIES HAVE RULED THE PLANET FOR AS LONG AS WE CAN REMEMBER.
YOUR GOVERNMENTS ARE EITHER BLACKMAILED OR INITIATES.
YOUR CHURCHES INFILTRATED.
YOUR WORLD LEADERS NOTHING MORE THAN ACTORS TAKING ORDERS.
THEY'VE BEEN DOING THIS FOR CENTURIES, BUT IT'S ALL BEEN ACCELERATED NOW YOUR SON'S OPPOSITE NUMBER HAS ARRIVED.
THIS IS THE ANTICHRIST PROPHESIED IN THE BIBLE. THE DISRUPTOR HERE TO LEAD MANKIND AGAINST GOD AND THE BABY GROWING INSIDE YOU.

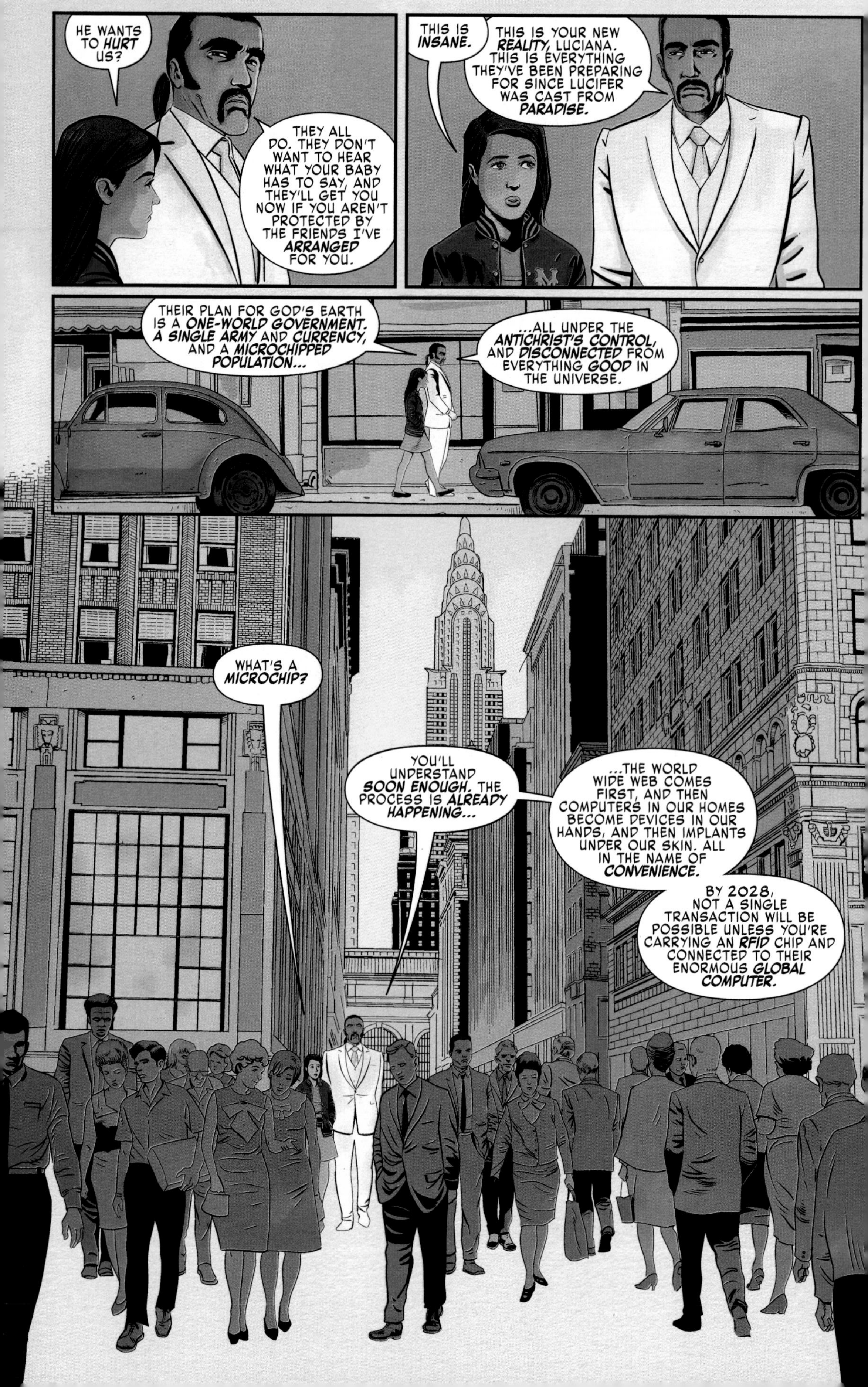

HE WANTS TO HURT US?
THEY ALL DO. THEY DON'T WANT TO HEAR WHAT YOUR BABY HAS TO SAY, AND THEY'LL GET YOU NOW IF YOU AREN'T PROTECTED BY THE FRIENDS I'VE ARRANGED FOR YOU.
THIS IS INSANE.
THIS IS YOUR NEW REALITY, LUCIANA. THIS IS EVERYTHING THEY'VE BEEN PREPARING FOR SINCE LUCIFER WAS CAST FROM PARADISE.
THEIR PLAN FOR GOD'S EARTH IS A ONE-WORLD GOVERNMENT. A SINGLE ARMY AND CURRENCY, AND A MICROCHIPPED POPULATION...
...ALL UNDER THE ANTICHRIST'S CONTROL, AND DISCONNECTED FROM EVERYTHING GOOD IN THE UNIVERSE.
WHAT'S A MICROCHIP?
YOU'LL UNDERSTAND SOON ENOUGH. THE PROCESS IS ALREADY HAPPENING...
...THE WORLD WIDE WEB COMES FIRST, AND THEN COMPUTERS IN OUR HOMES BECOME DEVICES IN OUR HANDS, AND THEN IMPLANTS UNDER OUR SKIN. ALL IN THE NAME OF CONVENIENCE.
BY 2028, NOT A SINGLE TRANSACTION WILL BE POSSIBLE UNLESS YOU'RE CARRYING AN RFID CHIP AND CONNECTED TO THEIR ENORMOUS GLOBAL COMPUTER.

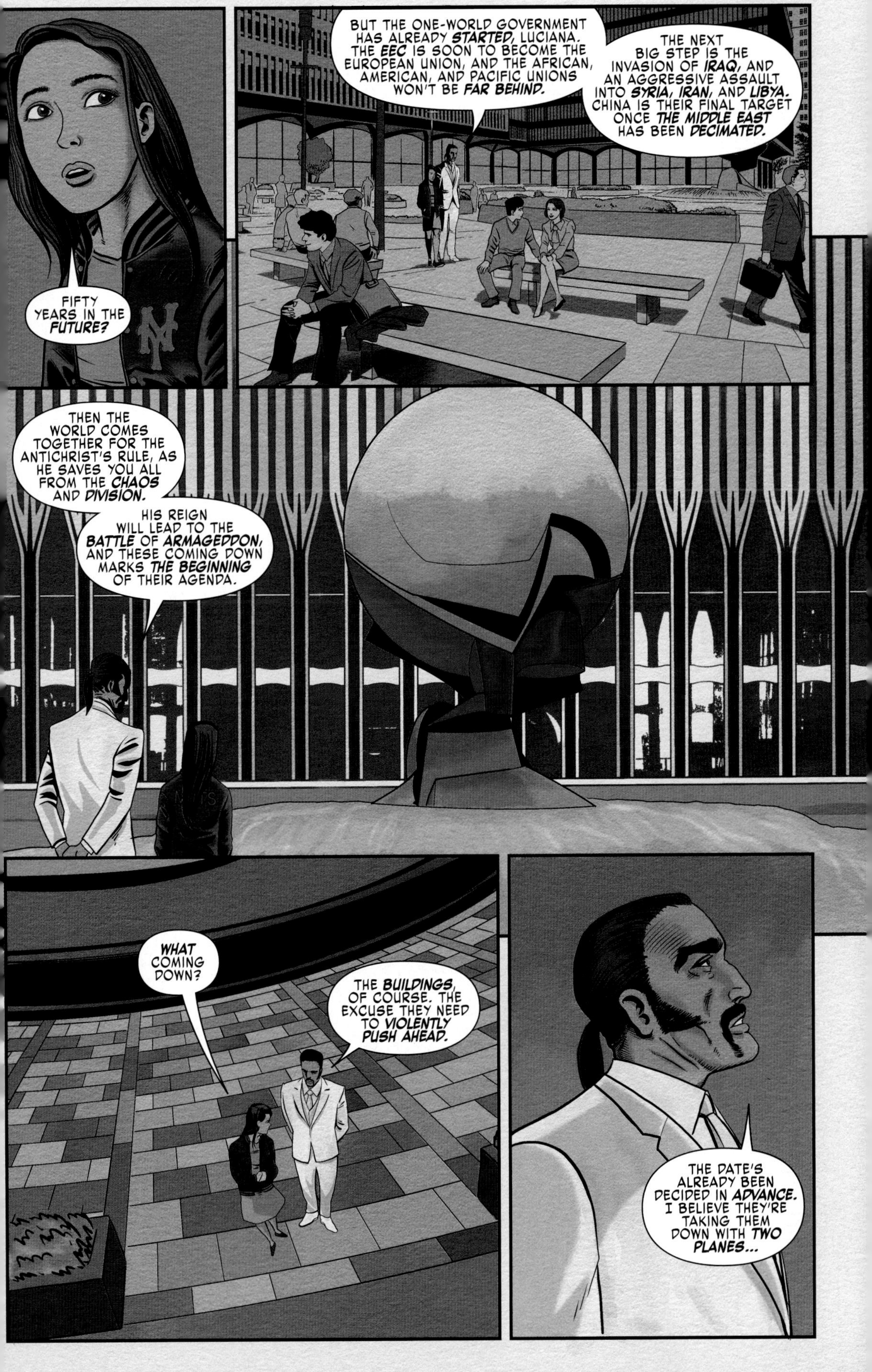
FIFTY YEARS IN THE FUTURE?
BUT THE ONE-WORLD GOVERNMENT HAS ALREADY STARTED, LUCIANA. THE EEC IS SOON TO BECOME THE EUROPEAN UNION, AND THE AFRICAN, AMERICAN, AND PACIFIC UNIONS WON'T BE FAR BEHIND.
THE NEXT BIG STEP IS THE INVASION OF IRAQ, AND AN AGGRESSIVE ASSAULT INTO SYRIA, IRAN, AND LIBYA. CHINA IS THEIR FINAL TARGET ONCE THE MIDDLE EAST HAS BEEN DECIMATED.
THEN THE WORLD COMES TOGETHER FOR THE ANTICHRIST'S RULE, AS HE SAVES YOU ALL FROM THE CHAOS AND DIVISION.
HIS REIGN WILL LEAD TO THE BATTLE OF ARMAGEDDON, AND THESE COMING DOWN MARKS THE BEGINNING OF THEIR AGENDA.
WHAT COMING DOWN?
THE BUILDINGS, OF COURSE. THE EXCUSE THEY NEED TO VIOLENTLY PUSH AHEAD.
THE DATE'S ALREADY BEEN DECIDED IN ADVANCE. I BELIEVE THEY'RE TAKING THEM DOWN WITH TWO PLANES...

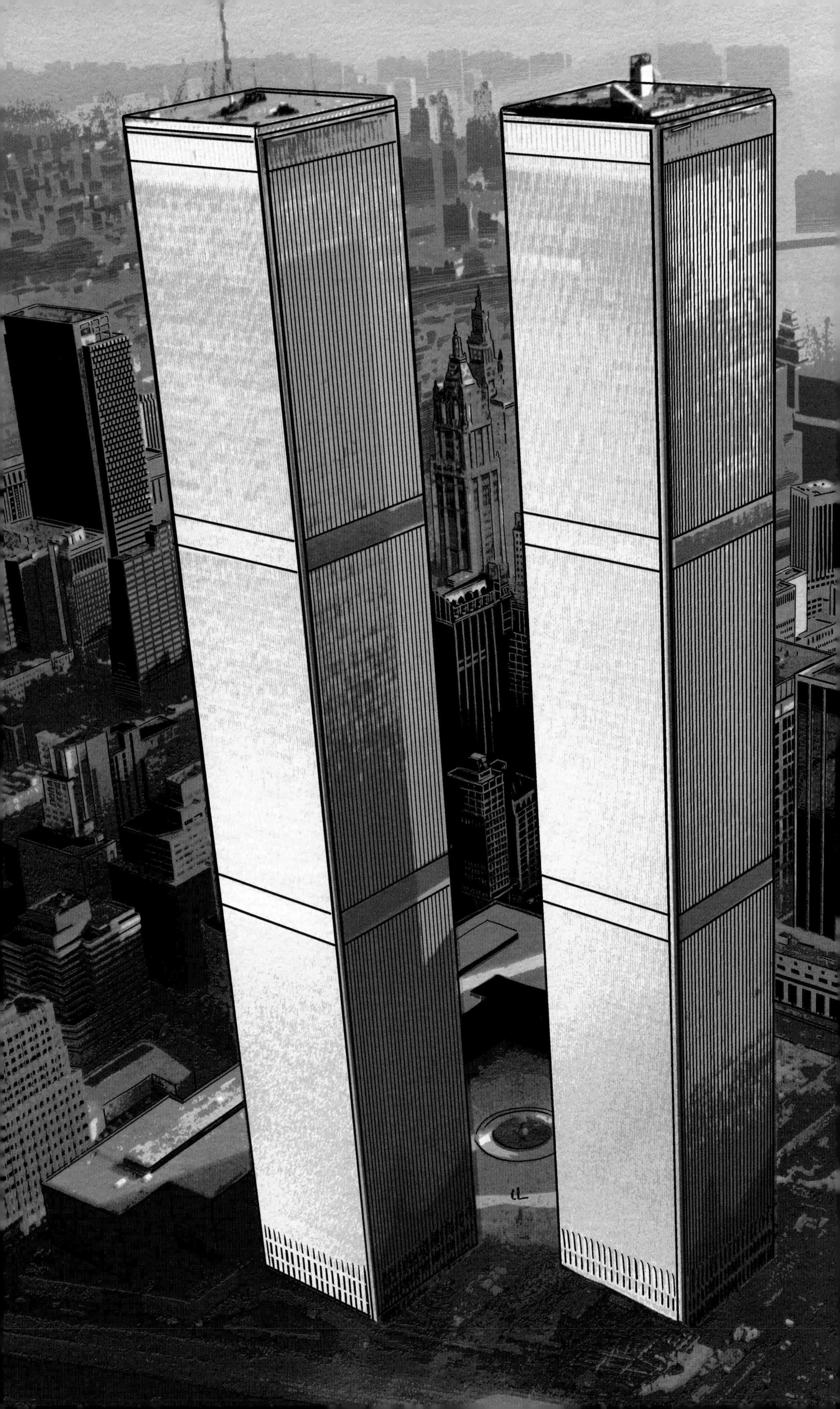

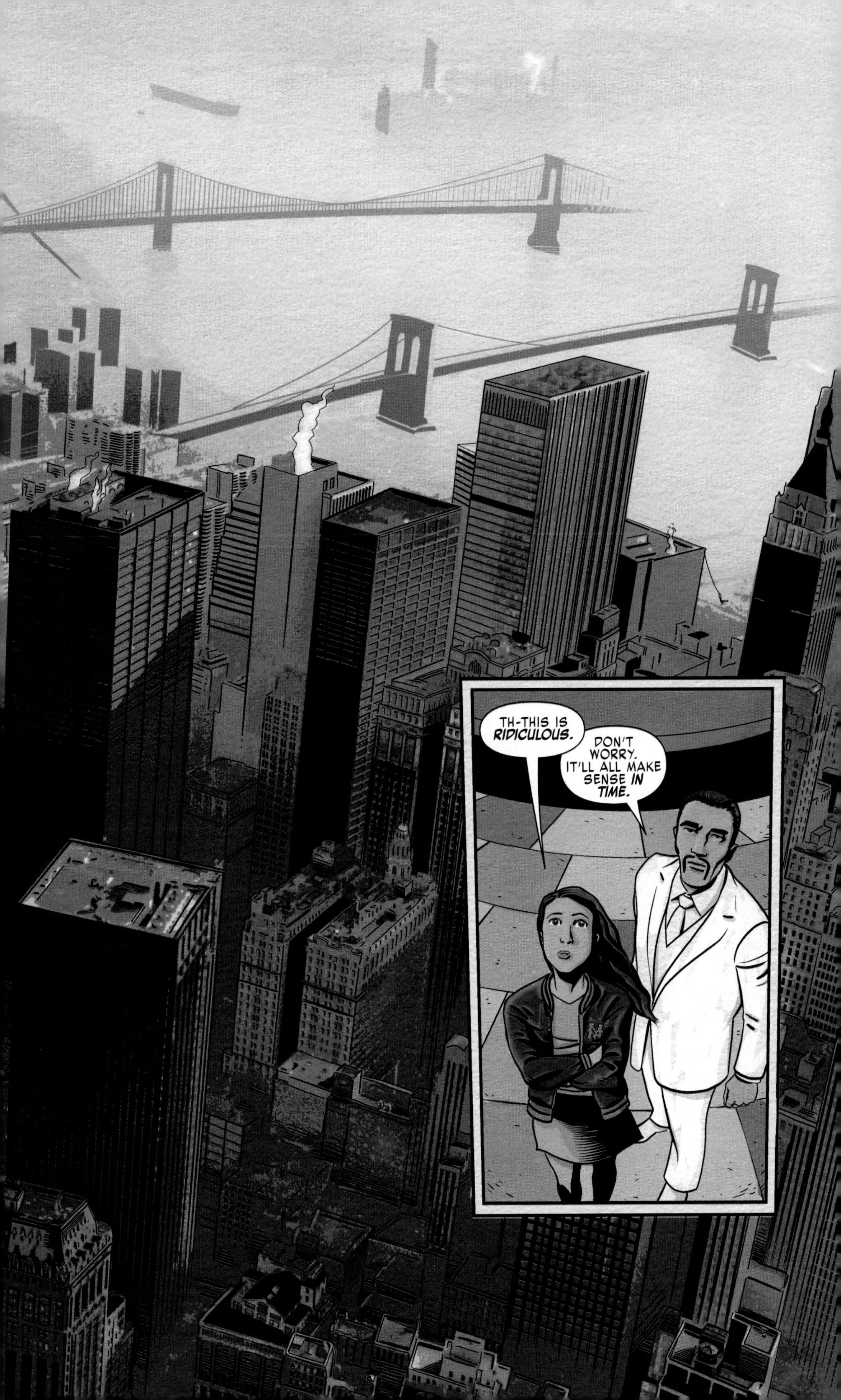
TH-THIS IS RIDICULOUS.
DON'T WORRY. IT'LL ALL MAKE SENSE IN TIME.

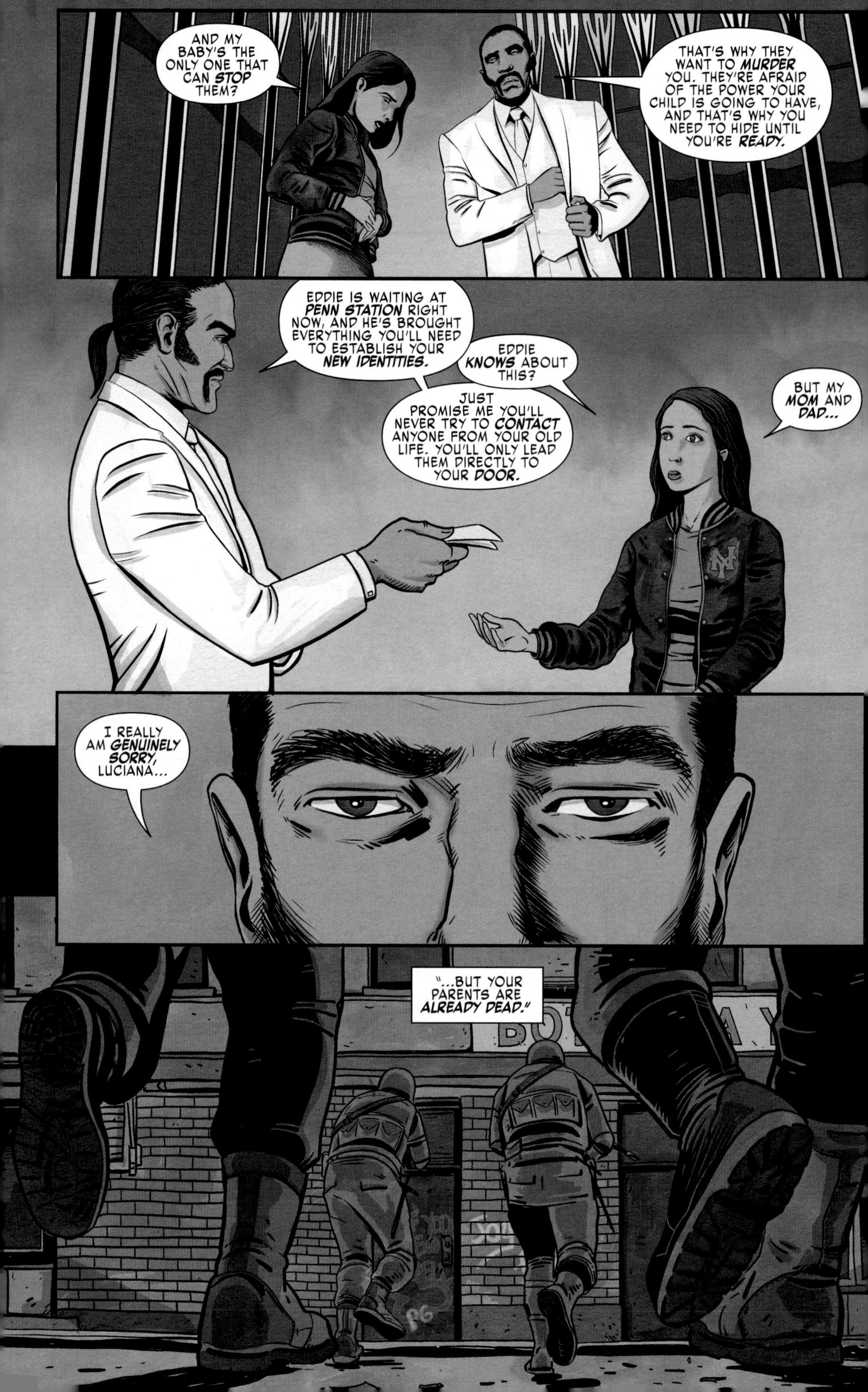
AND MY BABY'S THE ONLY ONE THAT CAN STOP THEM?
THAT'S WHY THEY WANT TO MURDER YOU. THEY'RE AFRAID OF THE POWER YOUR CHILD IS GOING TO HAVE, AND THAT'S WHY YOU NEED TO HIDE UNTIL YOU'RE READY.
EDDIE IS WAITING AT PENN STATION RIGHT NOW, AND HE'S BROUGHT EVERYTHING YOU'LL NEED TO ESTABLISH YOUR NEW IDENTITIES.
EDDIE KNOWS ABOUT THIS?
JUST PROMISE ME YOU'LL NEVER TRY TO CONTACT ANYONE FROM YOUR OLD LIFE. YOU'LL ONLY LEAD THEM DIRECTLY TO YOUR DOOR.
BUT MY MOM AND DAD...
I REALLY AM GENUINELY SORRY, LUCIANA...
"...BUT YOUR PARENTS ARE ALREADY DEAD."

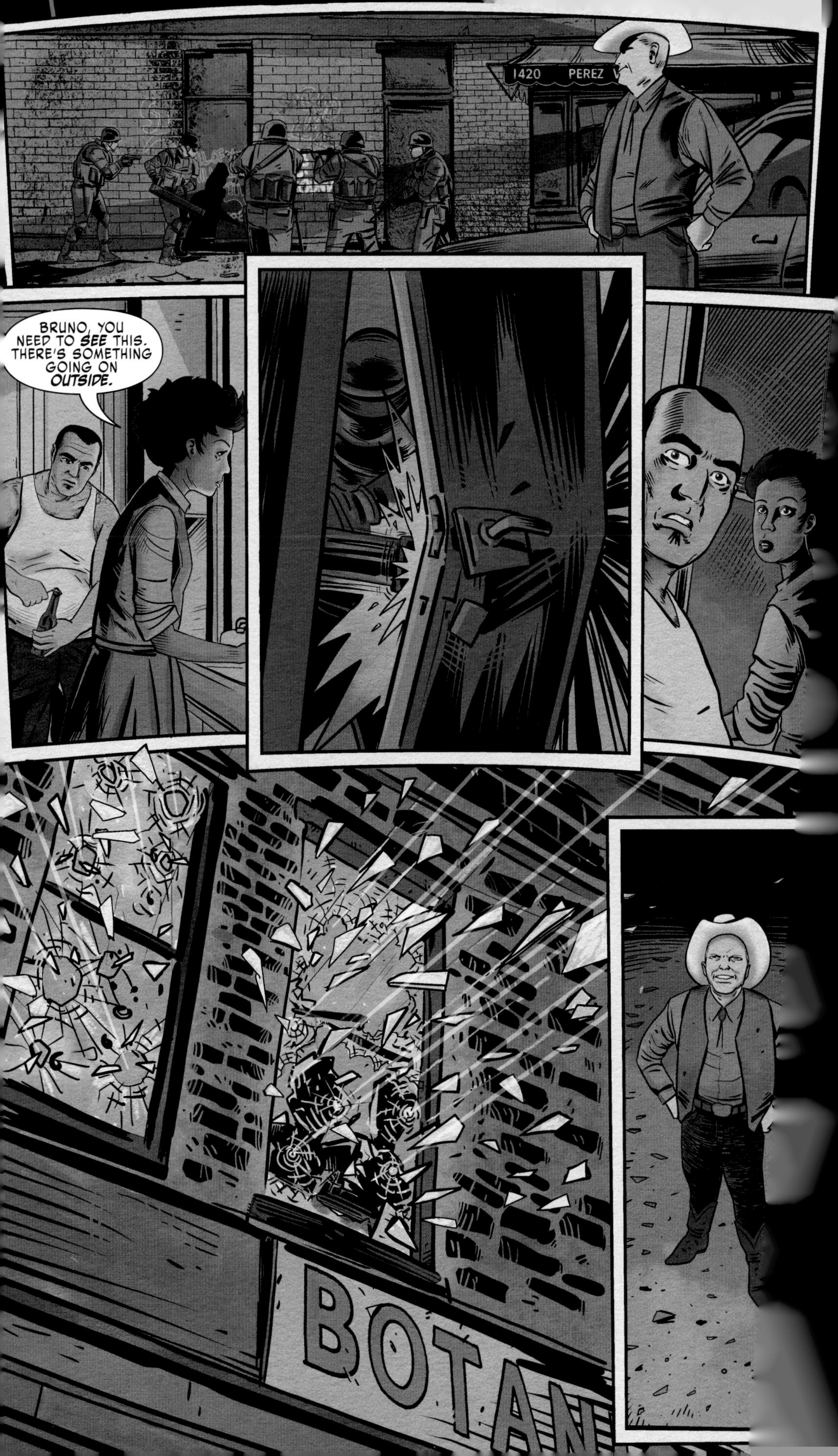
1420 PEREZ
BRUNO, YOU NEED TO SEE THIS. THERE'S SOMETHING GOING ON OUTSIDE.
BOTAN

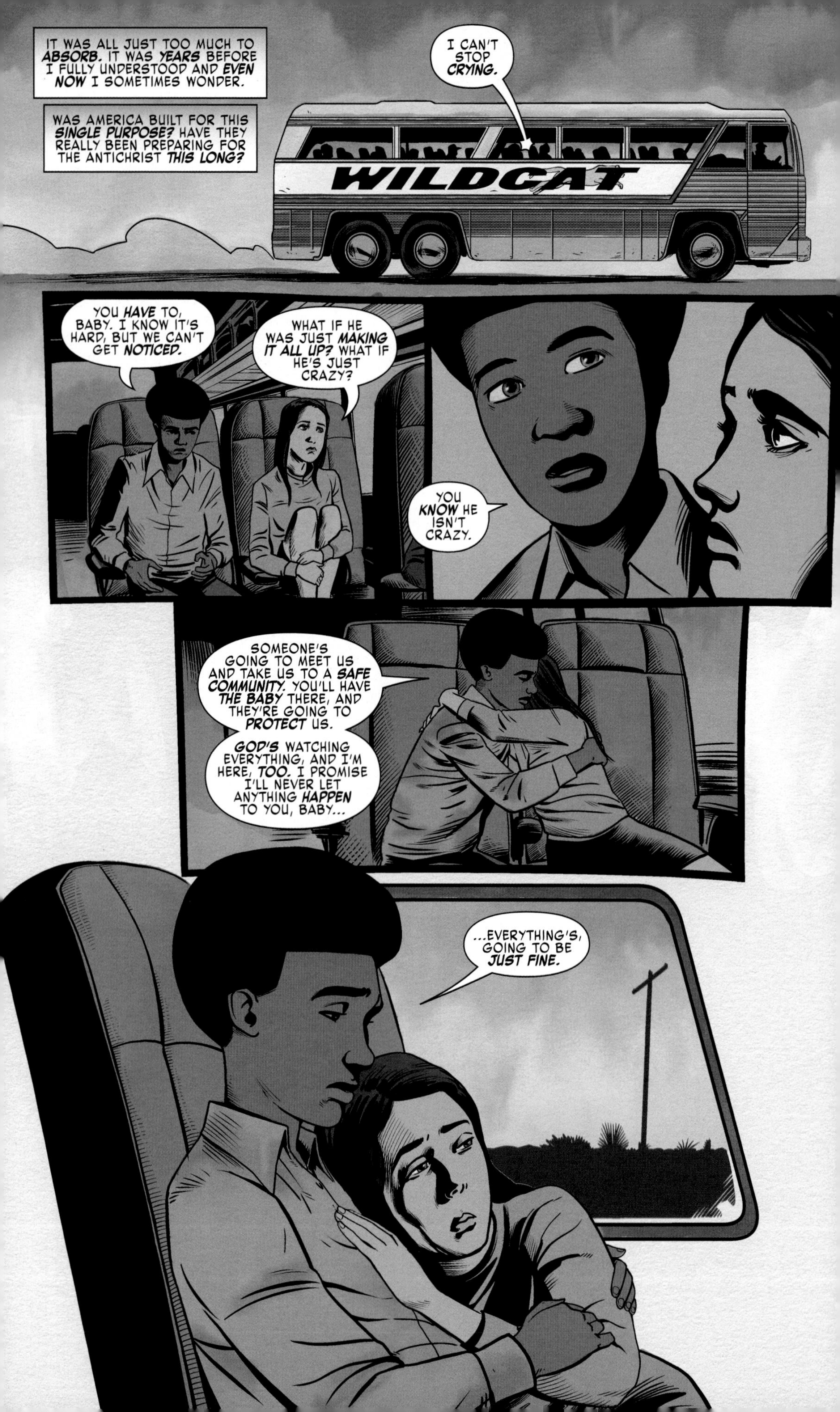
IT WAS ALL JUST TOO MUCH TO ABSORB. IT WAS YEARS BEFORE I FULLY UNDERSTOOD AND EVEN NOW I SOMETIMES WONDER.
WAS AMERICA BUILT FOR THIS SINGLE PURPOSE? HAVE THEY REALLY BEEN PREPARING FOR THE ANTICHRIST THIS LONG?
I CAN'T STOP CRYING.
WILDCAT
YOU HAVE TO, BABY. I KNOW IT'S HARD, BUT WE CAN'T GET NOTICED.
WHAT IF HE WAS JUST MAKING IT ALL UP? WHAT IF HE'S JUST CRAZY?
YOU KNOW HE ISN'T CRAZY.
SOMEONE'S GOING TO MEET US AND TAKE US TO A SAFE COMMUNITY. YOU'LL HAVE THE BABY THERE, AND THEY'RE GOING TO PROTECT US.
GOD'S WATCHING EVERYTHING, AND I'M HERE, TOO. I PROMISE I'LL NEVER LET ANYTHING HAPPEN TO YOU, BABY...
...EVERYTHING'S, GOING TO BE JUST FINE.

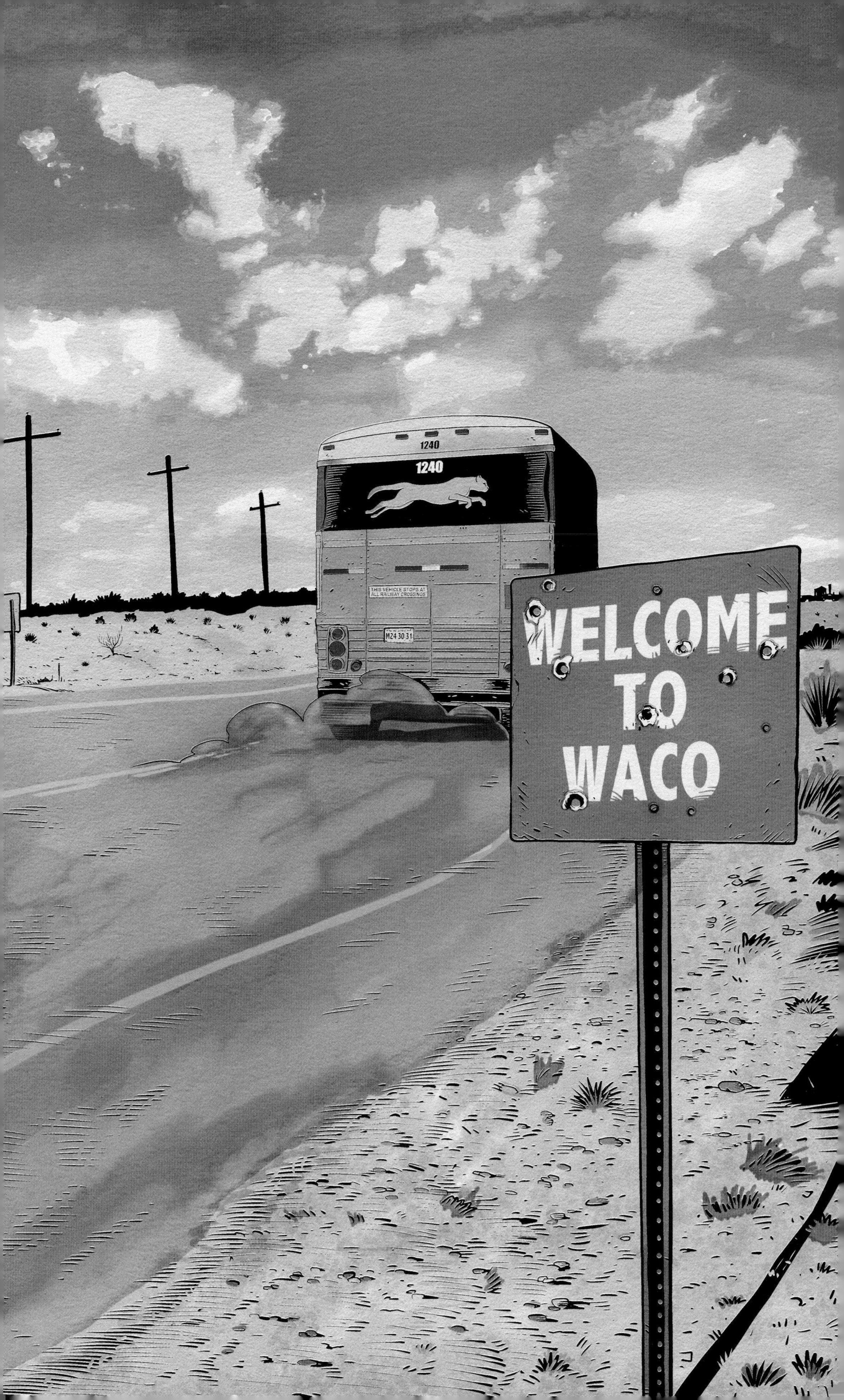
1240
1240
THIS VEHICLE STOPS AT ALL RAILWAY CROSSINGS
M24 30 31
WELCOME TO WACO

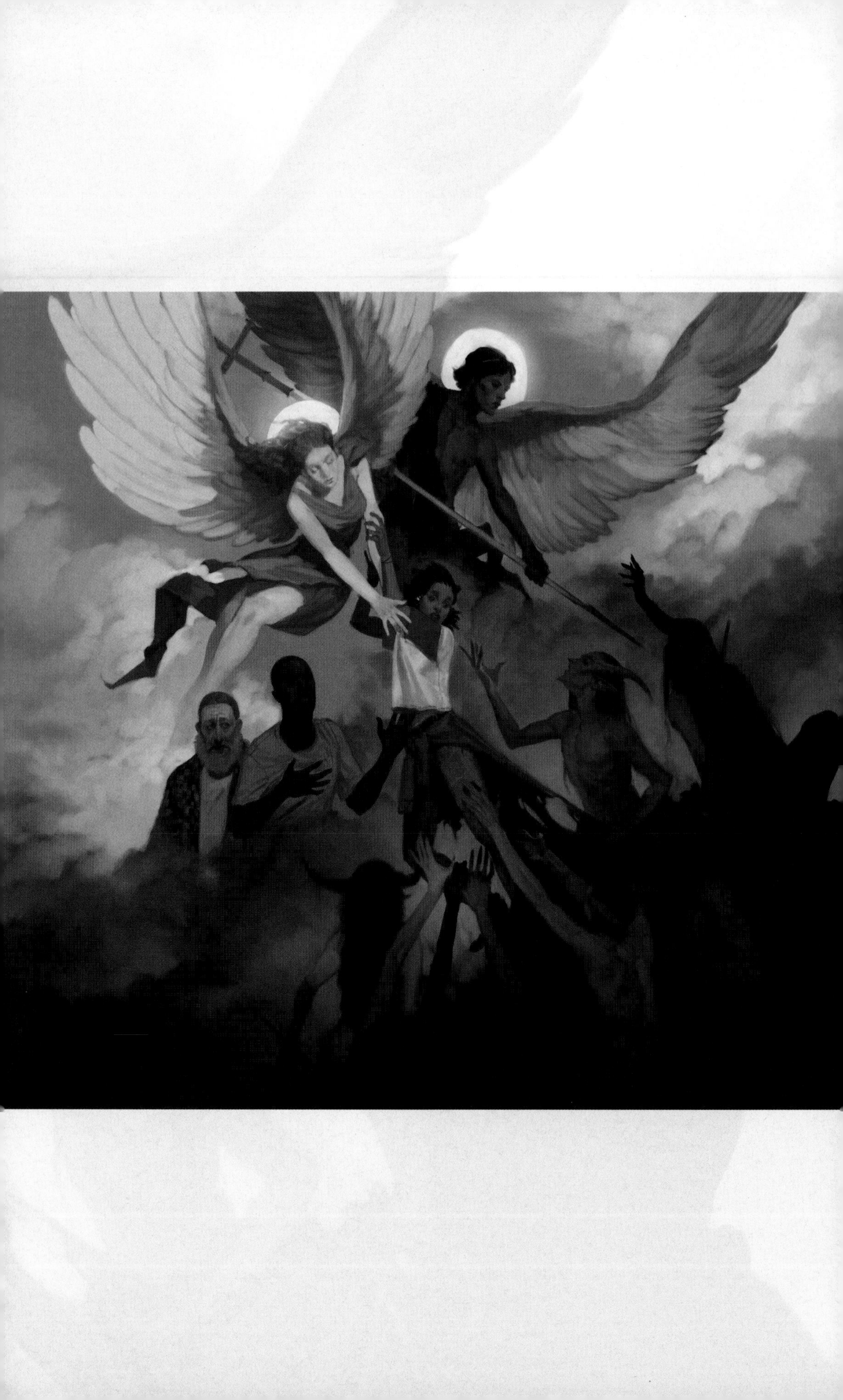

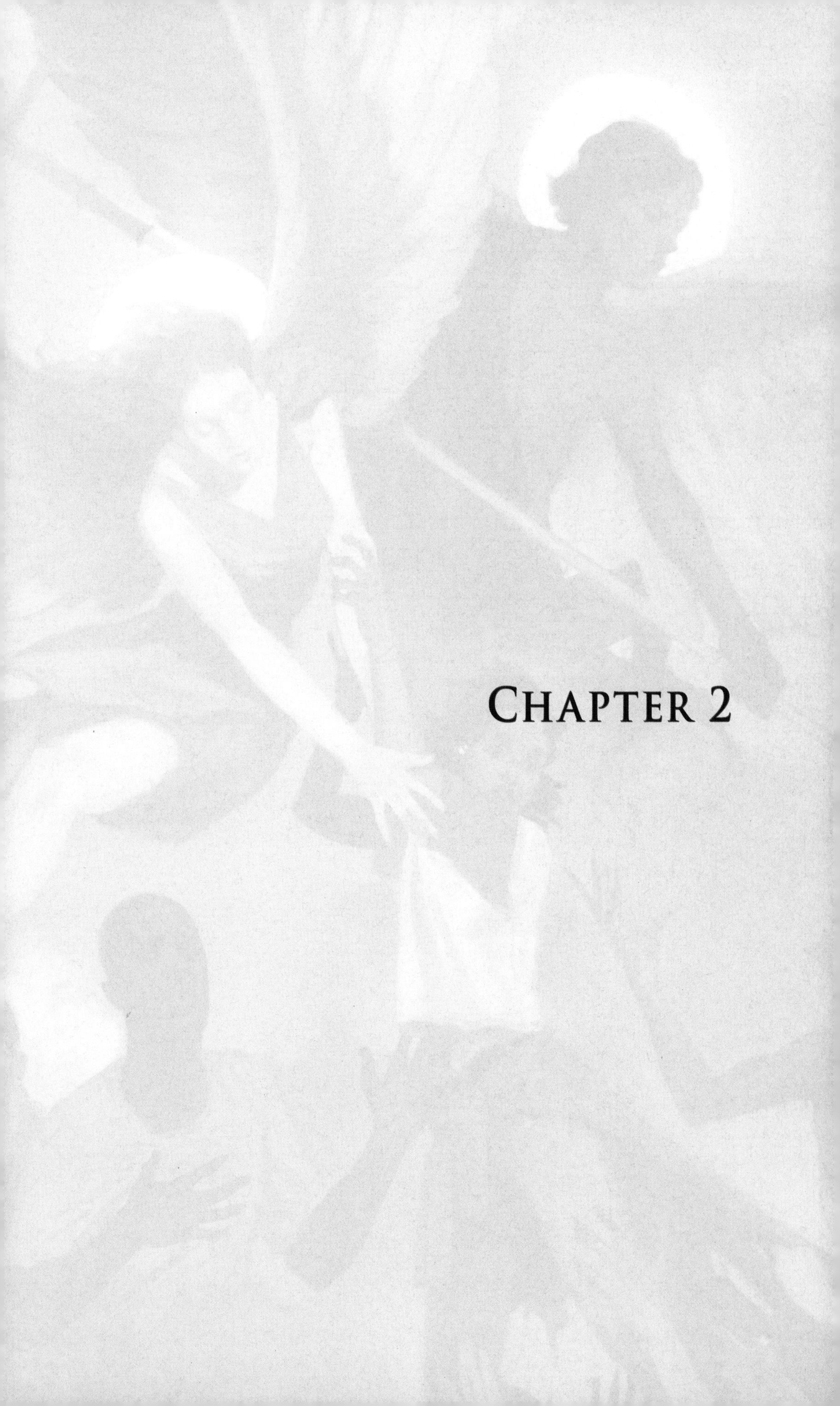

CHAPTER 2

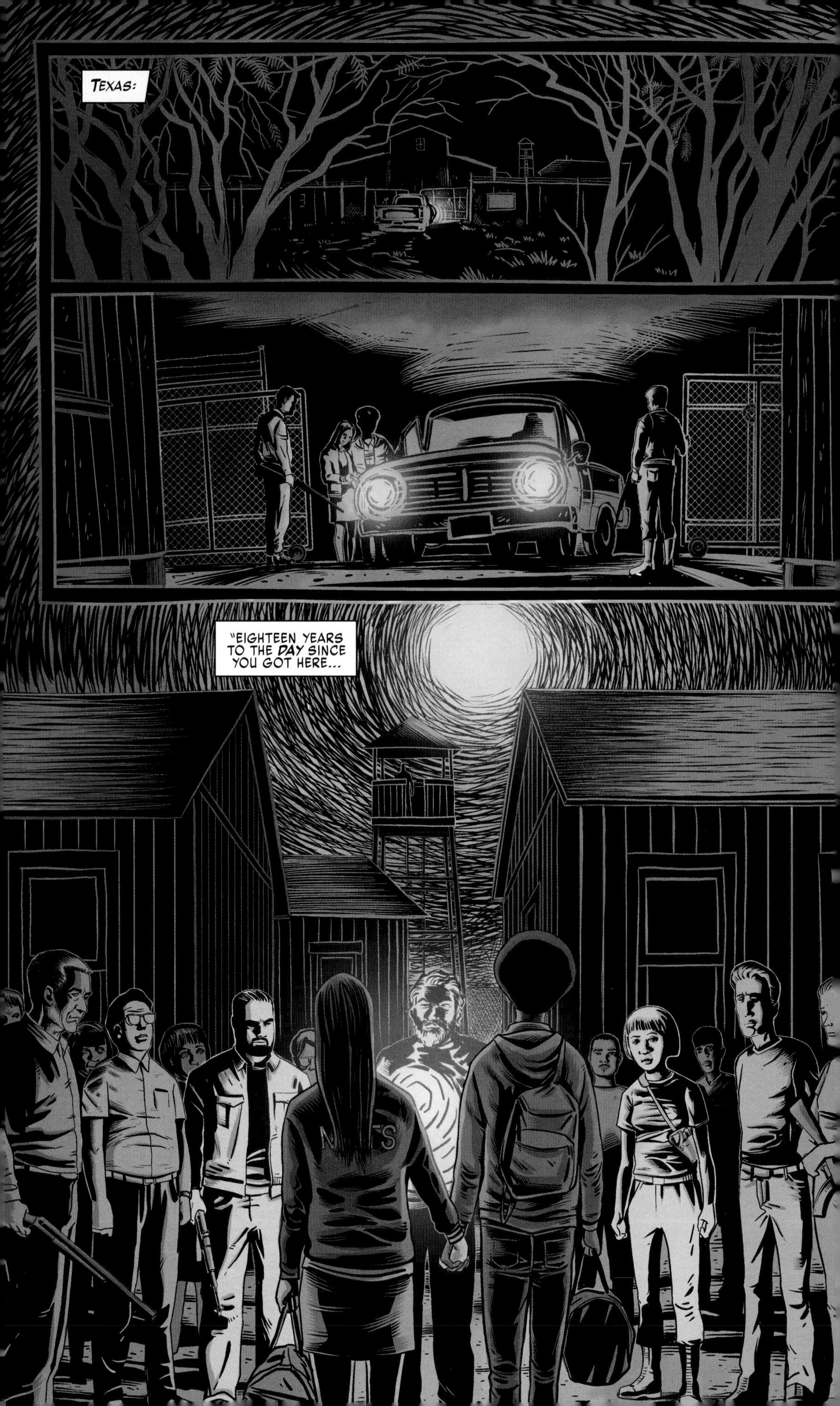
TEXAS:
"EIGHTEEN YEARS TO THE DAY SINCE YOU GOT HERE...

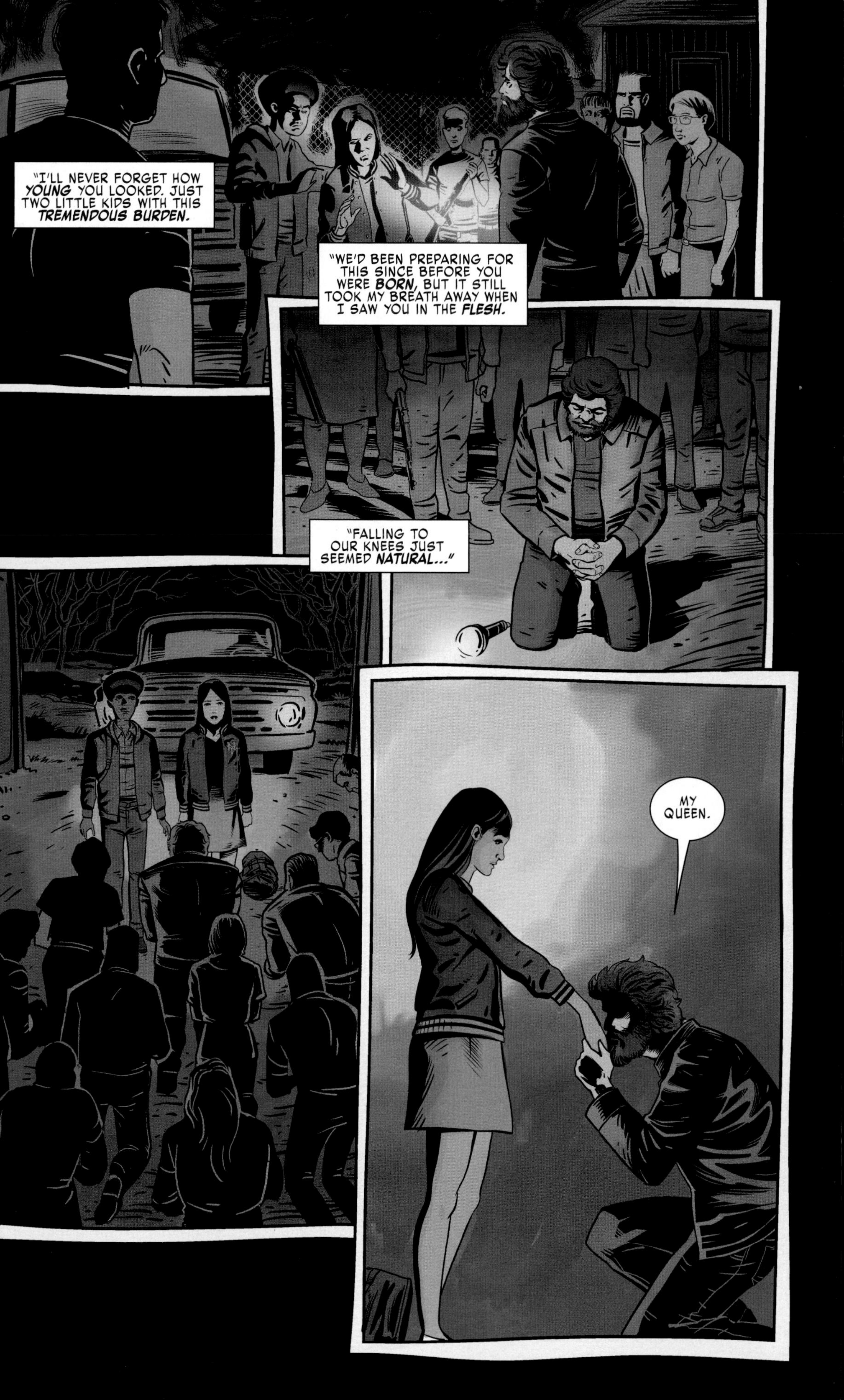
"I'LL NEVER FORGET HOW YOUNG YOU LOOKED. JUST TWO LITTLE KIDS WITH THIS TREMENDOUS BURDEN.
"WE'D BEEN PREPARING FOR THIS SINCE BEFORE YOU WERE BORN, BUT IT STILL TOOK MY BREATH AWAY WHEN I SAW YOU IN THE FLESH.
"FALLING TO OUR KNEES JUST SEEMED NATURAL..."
MY QUEEN.

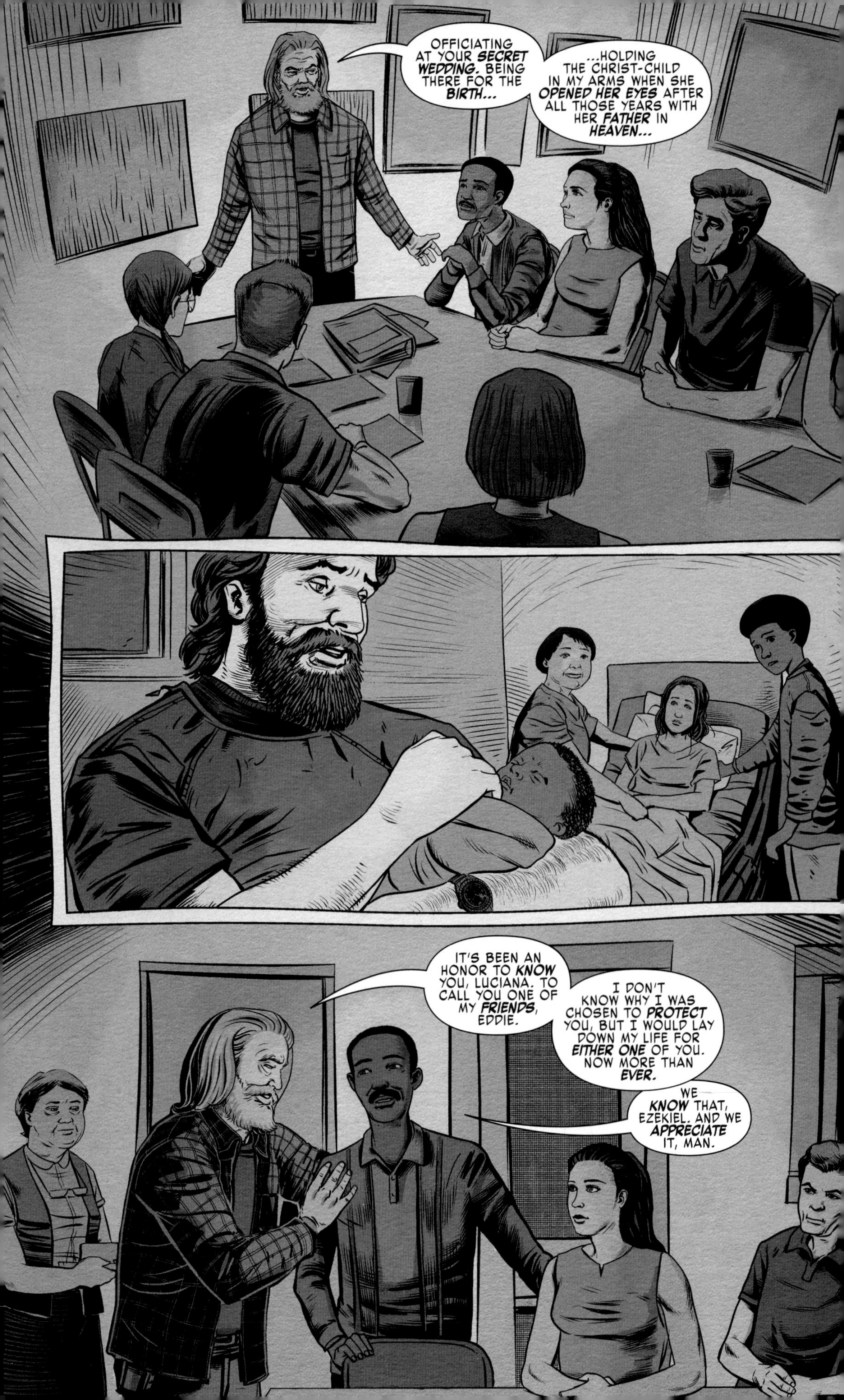
OFFICIATING AT YOUR SECRET WEDDING. BEING THERE FOR THE BIRTH...
...HOLDING THE CHRIST-CHILD IN MY ARMS WHEN SHE OPENED HER EYES AFTER ALL THOSE YEARS WITH HER FATHER IN HEAVEN...
IT'S BEEN AN HONOR TO KNOW YOU, LUCIANA. TO CALL YOU ONE OF MY FRIENDS, EDDIE.
I DON'T KNOW WHY I WAS CHOSEN TO PROTECT YOU, BUT I WOULD LAY DOWN MY LIFE FOR EITHER ONE OF YOU. NOW MORE THAN EVER.
WE KNOW THAT, EZEKIEL. AND WE APPRECIATE IT, MAN.

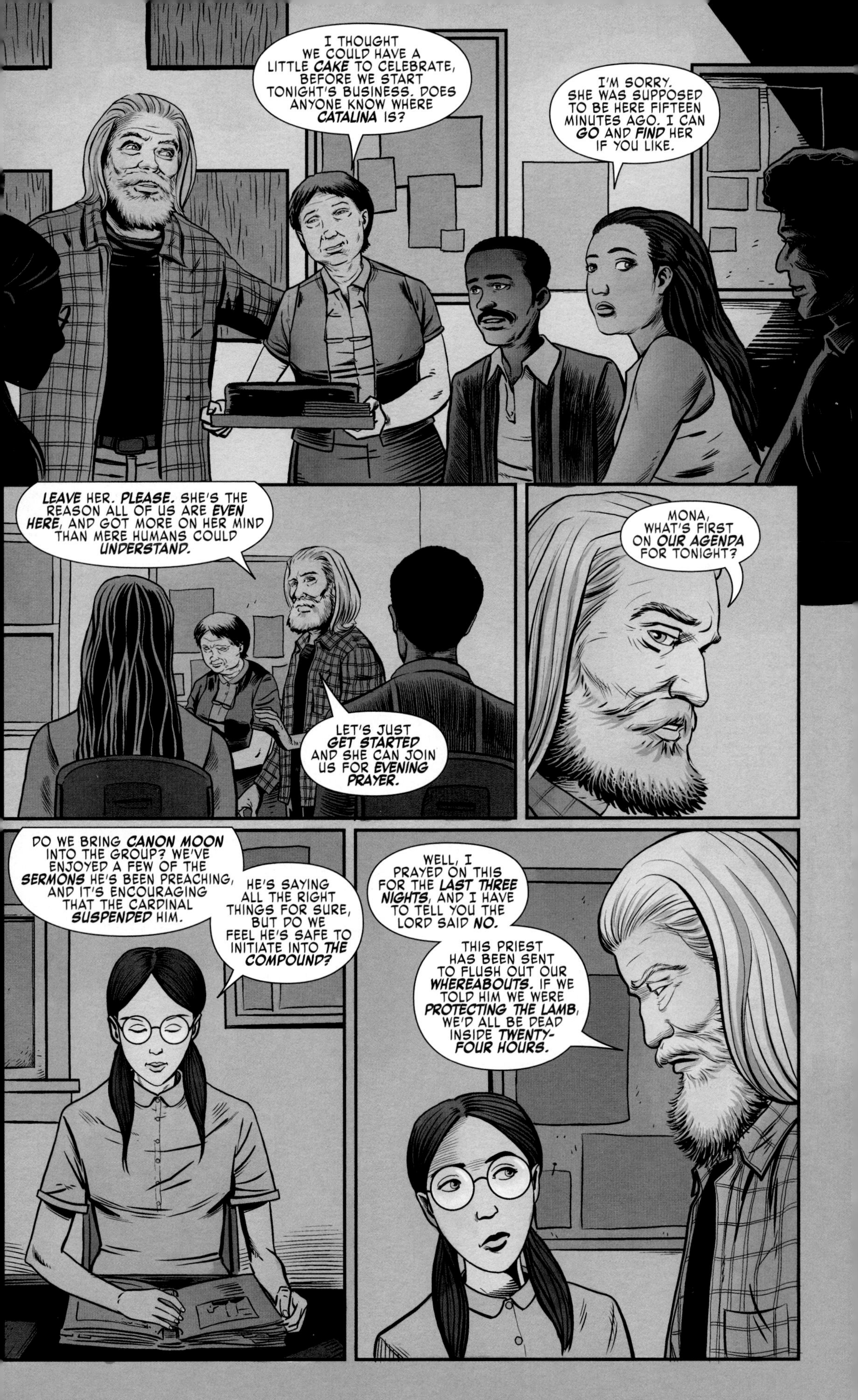
I THOUGHT WE COULD HAVE A LITTLE CAKE TO CELEBRATE, BEFORE WE START TONIGHT'S BUSINESS. DOES ANYONE KNOW WHERE CATALINA IS?
I'M SORRY. SHE WAS SUPPOSED TO BE HERE FIFTEEN MINUTES AGO. I CAN GO AND FIND HER IF YOU LIKE.
LEAVE HER. PLEASE. SHE'S THE REASON ALL OF US ARE EVEN HERE, AND GOT MORE ON HER MIND THAN MERE HUMANS COULD UNDERSTAND.
LET'S JUST GET STARTED AND SHE CAN JOIN US FOR EVENING PRAYER.
MONA, WHAT'S FIRST ON OUR AGENDA FOR TONIGHT?
DO WE BRING CANON MOON INTO THE GROUP? WE'VE ENJOYED A FEW OF THE SERMONS HE'S BEEN PREACHING, AND IT'S ENCOURAGING THAT THE CARDINAL SUSPENDED HIM.
HE'S SAYING ALL THE RIGHT THINGS FOR SURE, BUT DO WE FEEL HE'S SAFE TO INITIATE INTO THE COMPOUND?
WELL, I PRAYED ON THIS FOR THE LAST THREE NIGHTS, AND I HAVE TO TELL YOU THE LORD SAID NO.
THIS PRIEST HAS BEEN SENT TO FLUSH OUT OUR WHEREABOUTS. IF WE TOLD HIM WE WERE PROTECTING THE LAMB, WE'D ALL BE DEAD INSIDE TWENTY-FOUR HOURS.

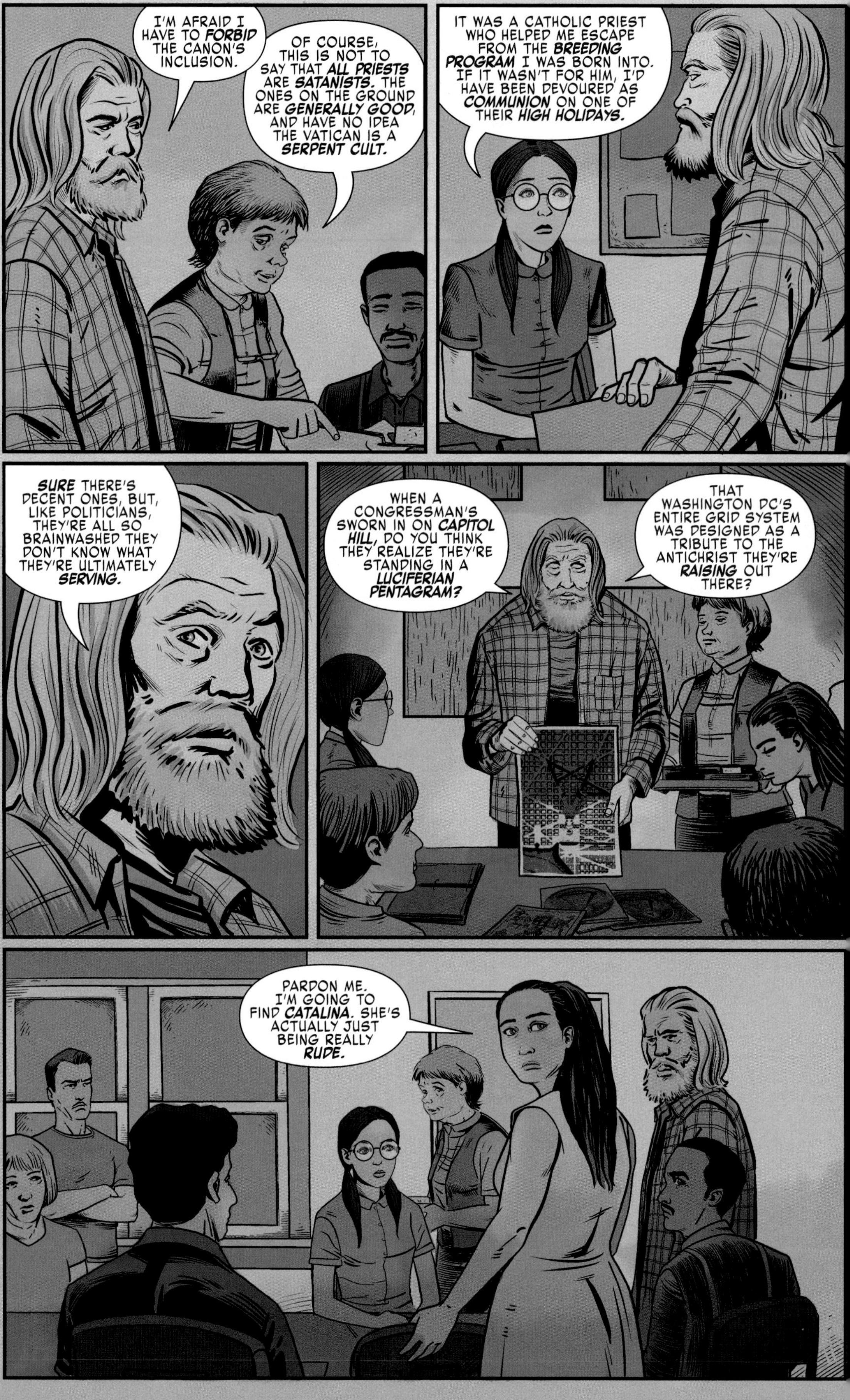
I'M AFRAID I HAVE TO FORBID THE CANON'S INCLUSION.
OF COURSE, THIS IS NOT TO SAY THAT ALL PRIESTS ARE SATANISTS. THE ONES ON THE GROUND ARE GENERALLY GOOD, AND HAVE NO IDEA THE VATICAN IS A SERPENT CULT.
IT WAS A CATHOLIC PRIEST WHO HELPED ME ESCAPE FROM THE BREEDING PROGRAM I WAS BORN INTO. IF IT WASN'T FOR HIM, I'D HAVE BEEN DEVOURED AS COMMUNION ON ONE OF THEIR HIGH HOLIDAYS.
SURE THERE'S DECENT ONES, BUT, LIKE POLITICIANS, THEY'RE ALL SO BRAINWASHED THEY DON'T KNOW WHAT THEY'RE ULTIMATELY SERVING.
WHEN A CONGRESSMAN'S SWORN IN ON CAPITOL HILL, DO YOU THINK THEY REALIZE THEY'RE STANDING IN A LUCIFERIAN PENTAGRAM?
THAT WASHINGTON DC'S ENTIRE GRID SYSTEM WAS DESIGNED AS A TRIBUTE TO THE ANTICHRIST THEY'RE RAISING OUT THERE?
PARDON ME. I'M GOING TO FIND CATALINA. SHE'S ACTUALLY JUST BEING REALLY RUDE.

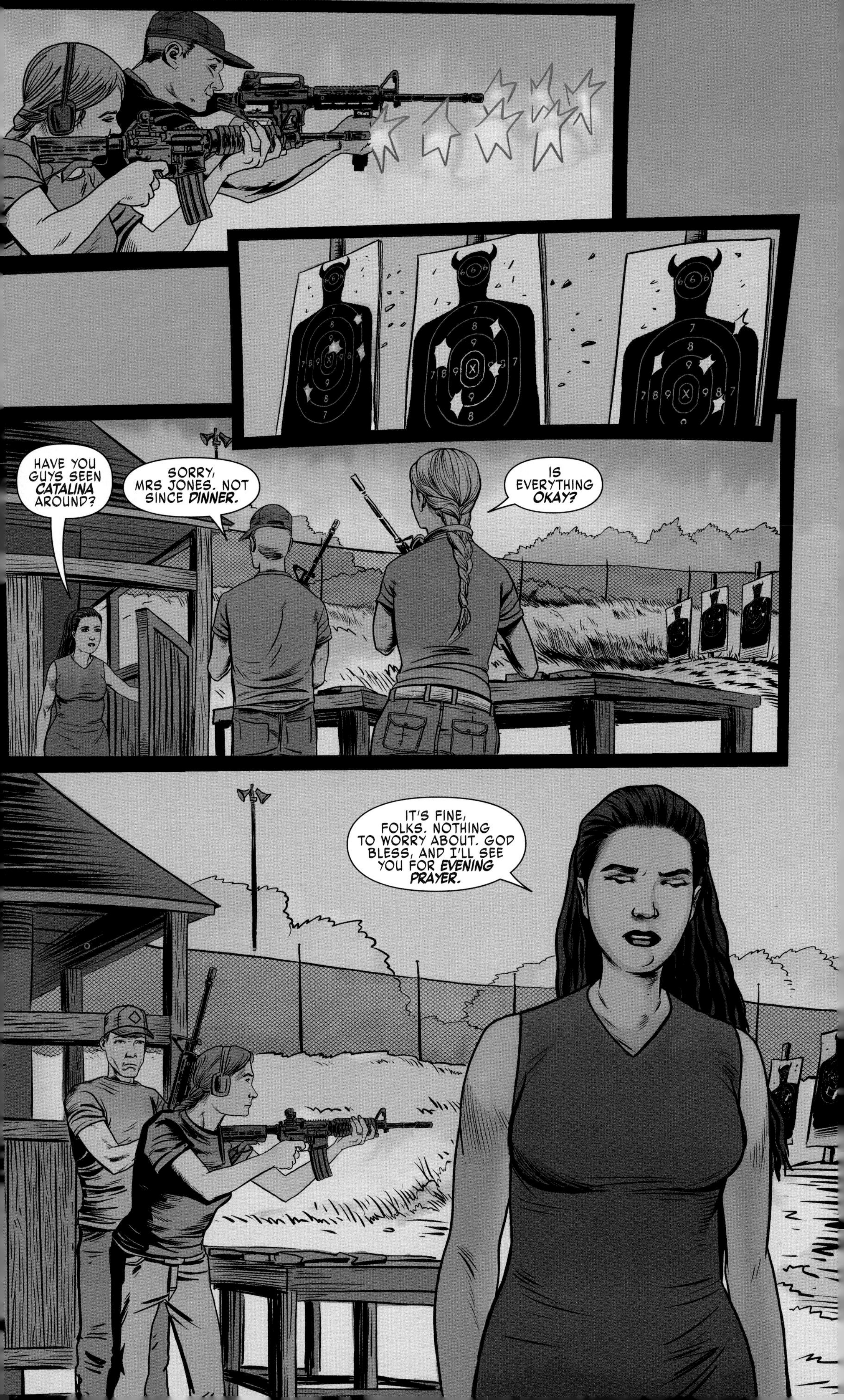
HAVE YOU GUYS SEEN CATALINA AROUND?
SORRY, MRS JONES. NOT SINCE DINNER.
IS EVERYTHING OKAY?
IT'S FINE, FOLKS. NOTHING TO WORRY ABOUT. GOD BLESS, AND I'LL SEE YOU FOR EVENING PRAYER.

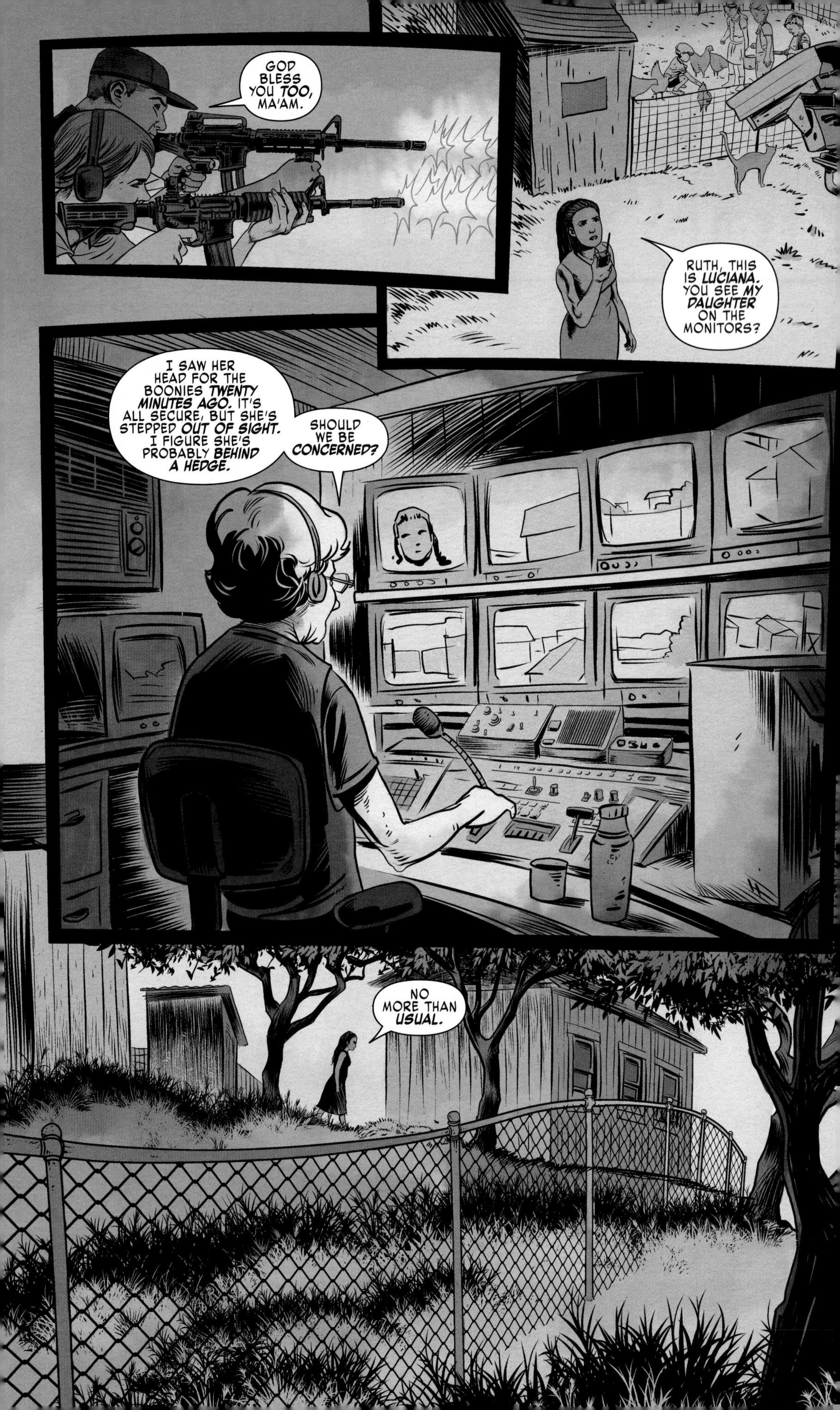
GOD BLESS YOU TOO, MA'AM.
RUTH, THIS IS LUCIANA. YOU SEE MY DAUGHTER ON THE MONITORS?
I SAW HER HEAD FOR THE BOONIES TWENTY MINUTES AGO. IT'S ALL SECURE, BUT SHE'S STEPPED OUT OF SIGHT. I FIGURE SHE'S PROBABLY BEHIND A HEDGE.
SHOULD WE BE CONCERNED?
NO MORE THAN USUAL.

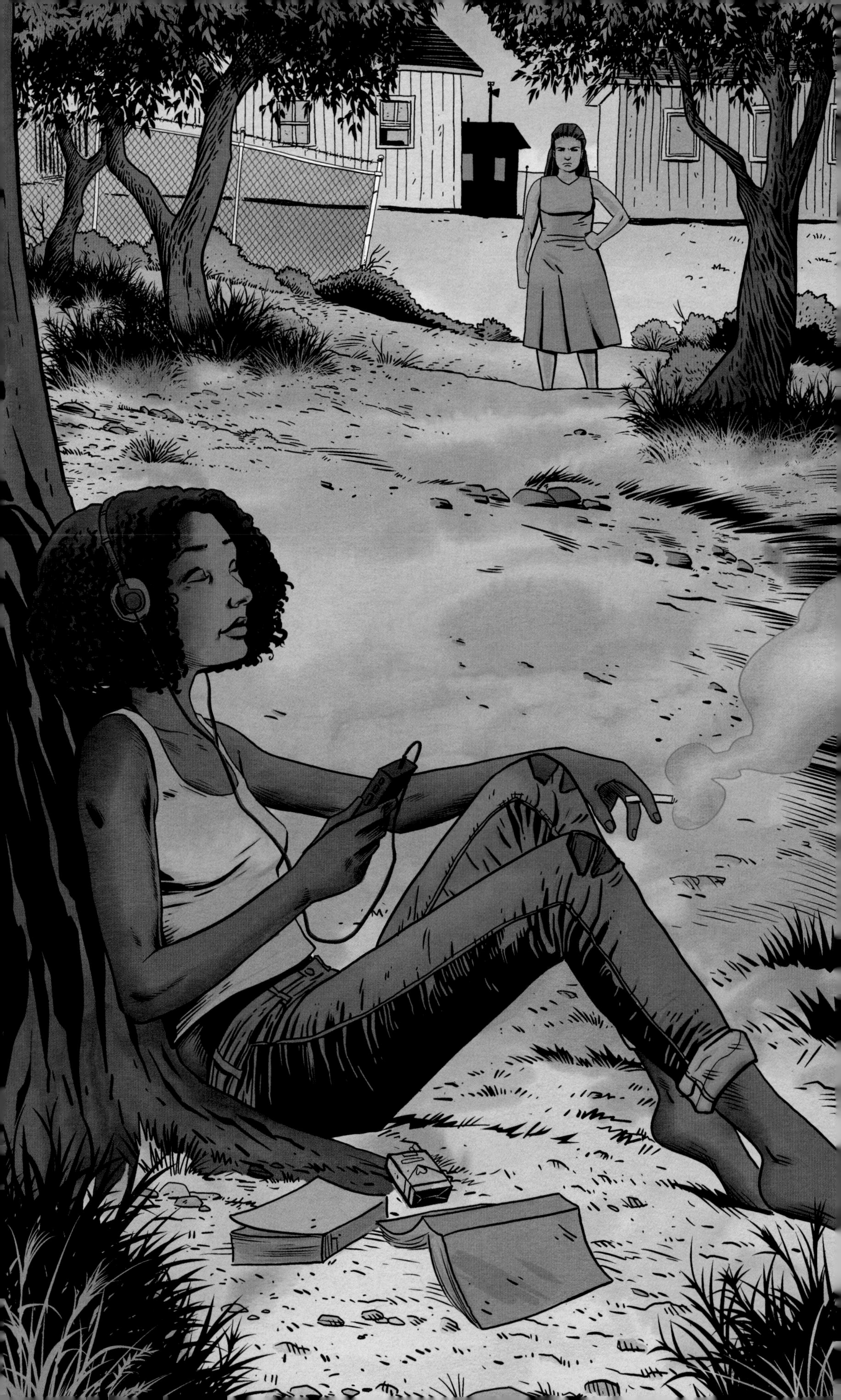

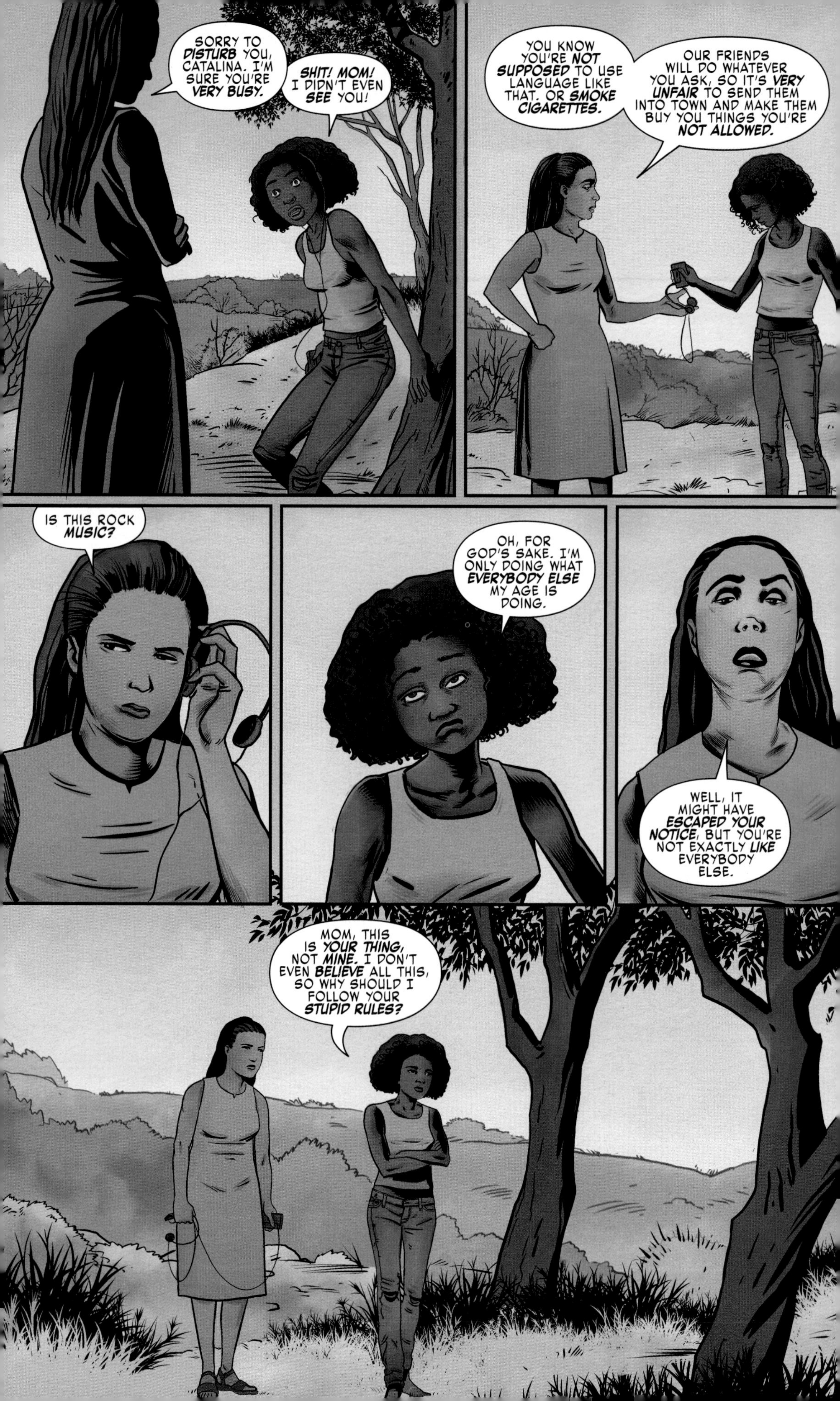
SORRY TO DISTURB YOU, CATALINA. I'M SURE YOU'RE VERY BUSY.
SHIT! MOM! I DIDN'T EVEN SEE YOU!
YOU KNOW YOU'RE NOT SUPPOSED TO USE LANGUAGE LIKE THAT. OR SMOKE CIGARETTES.
OUR FRIENDS WILL DO WHATEVER YOU ASK, SO IT'S VERY UNFAIR TO SEND THEM INTO TOWN AND MAKE THEM BUY YOU THINGS YOU'RE NOT ALLOWED.
IS THIS ROCK MUSIC?
OH, FOR GOD'S SAKE. I'M ONLY DOING WHAT EVERYBODY ELSE MY AGE IS DOING.
WELL, IT MIGHT HAVE ESCAPED YOUR NOTICE, BUT YOU'RE NOT EXACTLY LIKE EVERYBODY ELSE.
MOM, THIS IS YOUR THING, NOT MINE. I DON'T EVEN BELIEVE ALL THIS, SO WHY SHOULD I FOLLOW YOUR STUPID RULES?

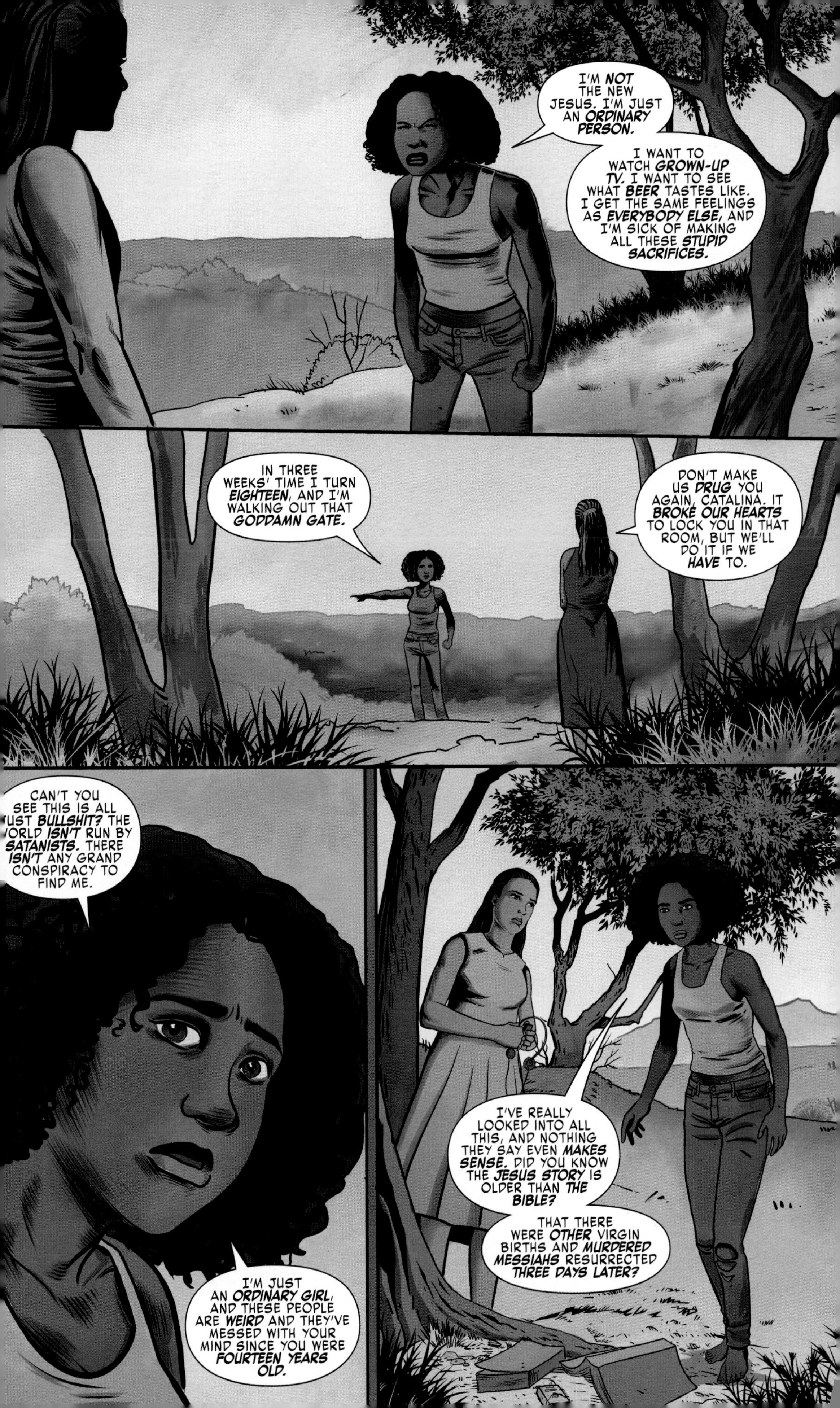

I'M NOT THE NEW JESUS. I'M JUST AN ORDINARY PERSON.
I WANT TO WATCH GROWN-UP TV. I WANT TO SEE WHAT BEER TASTES LIKE. I GET THE SAME FEELINGS AS EVERYBODY ELSE, AND I'M SICK OF MAKING ALL THESE STUPID SACRIFICES.
IN THREE WEEKS' TIME I TURN EIGHTEEN, AND I'M WALKING OUT THAT GODDAMN GATE.
DON'T MAKE US DRUG YOU AGAIN, CATALINA. IT BROKE OUR HEARTS TO LOCK YOU IN THAT ROOM, BUT WE'LL DO IT IF WE HAVE TO.
CAN'T YOU SEE THIS IS ALL JUST BULLSHIT? THE WORLD ISN'T RUN BY SATANISTS. THERE ISN'T ANY GRAND CONSPIRACY TO FIND ME.
I'M JUST AN ORDINARY GIRL, AND THESE PEOPLE ARE WEIRD AND THEY'VE MESSED WITH YOUR MIND SINCE YOU WERE FOURTEEN YEARS OLD.
I'VE REALLY LOOKED INTO ALL THIS, AND NOTHING THEY SAY EVEN MAKES SENSE. DID YOU KNOW THE JESUS STORY IS OLDER THAN THE BIBLE?
THAT THERE WERE OTHER VIRGIN BIRTHS AND MURDERED MESSIAHS RESURRECTED THREE DAYS LATER?

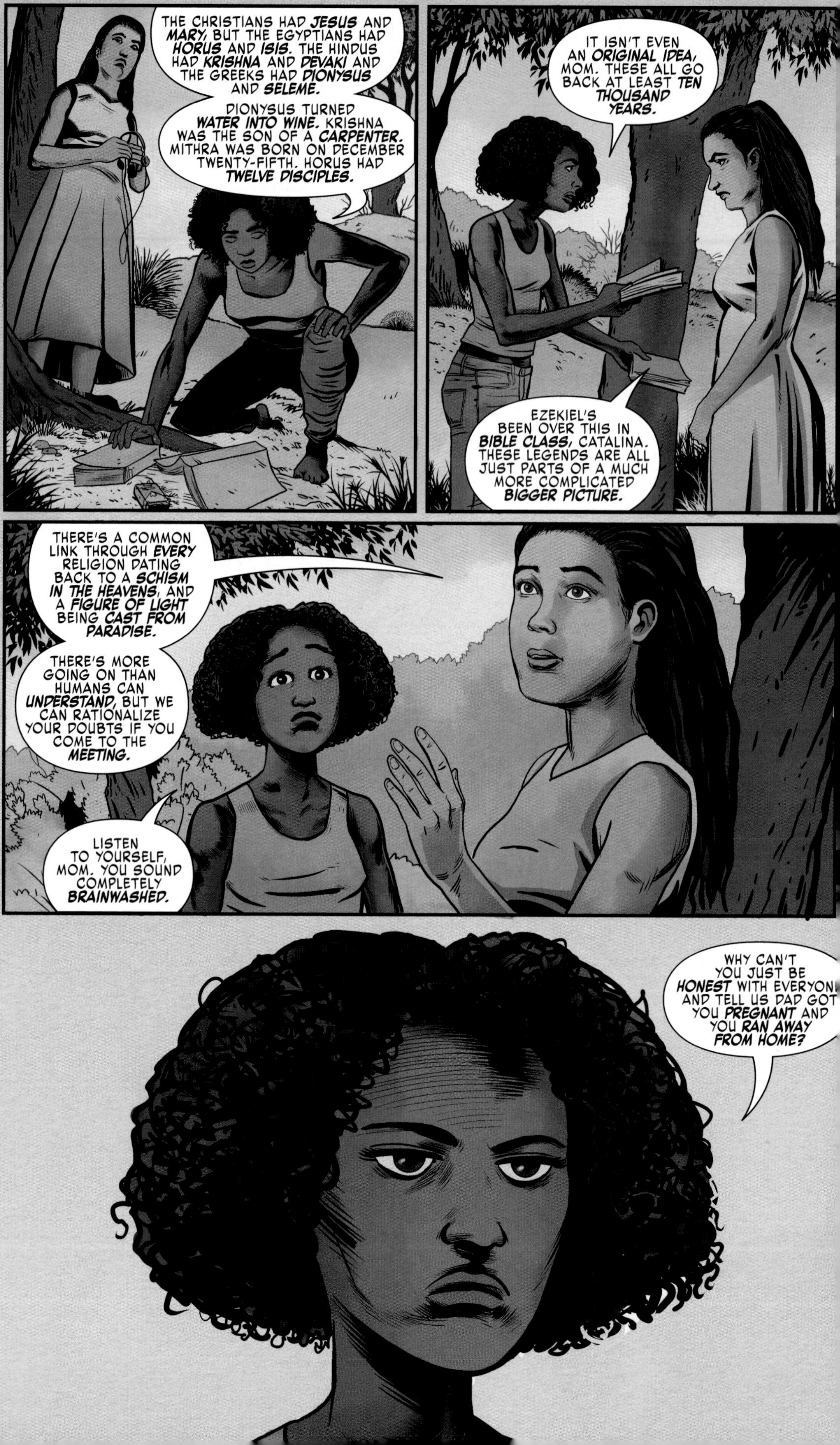
THE CHRISTIANS HAD JESUS AND MARY, BUT THE EGYPTIANS HAD HORUS AND ISIS. THE HINDUS HAD KRISHNA AND DEVAKI AND THE GREEKS HAD DIONYSUS AND SELEME.
DIONYSUS TURNED WATER INTO WINE. KRISHNA WAS THE SON OF A CARPENTER. MITHRA WAS BORN ON DECEMBER TWENTY-FIFTH. HORUS HAD TWELVE DISCIPLES.
IT ISN'T EVEN AN ORIGINAL IDEA, MOM. THESE ALL GO BACK AT LEAST TEN THOUSAND YEARS.
EZEKIEL'S BEEN OVER THIS IN BIBLE CLASS, CATALINA. THESE LEGENDS ARE ALL JUST PARTS OF A MUCH MORE COMPLICATED BIGGER PICTURE.
THERE'S A COMMON LINK THROUGH EVERY RELIGION DATING BACK TO A SCHISM IN THE HEAVENS, AND A FIGURE OF LIGHT BEING CAST FROM PARADISE.
THERE'S MORE GOING ON THAN HUMANS CAN UNDERSTAND, BUT WE CAN RATIONALIZE YOUR DOUBTS IF YOU COME TO THE MEETING.
LISTEN TO YOURSELF, MOM. YOU SOUND COMPLETELY BRAINWASHED.
WHY CAN'T YOU JUST BE HONEST WITH EVERYON AND TELL US DAD GOT YOU PREGNANT AND YOU RAN AWAY FROM HOME?

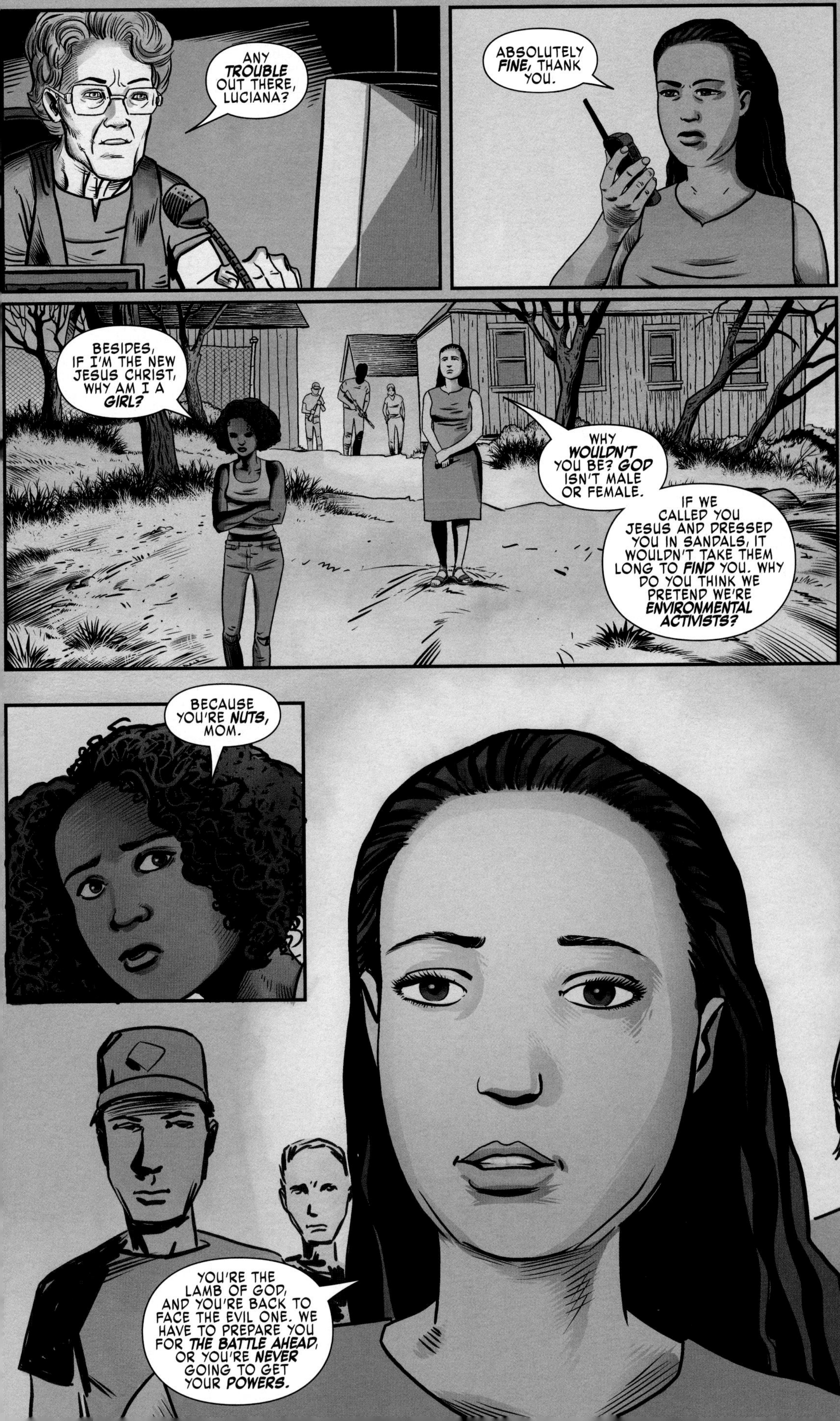
ANY TROUBLE OUT THERE, LUCIANA?
ABSOLUTELY FINE, THANK YOU.
BESIDES, IF I'M THE NEW JESUS CHRIST, WHY AM I A GIRL?
WHY WOULDN'T YOU BE? GOD ISN'T MALE OR FEMALE.
IF WE CALLED YOU JESUS AND DRESSED YOU IN SANDALS, IT WOULDN'T TAKE THEM LONG TO FIND YOU. WHY DO YOU THINK WE PRETEND WE'RE ENVIRONMENTAL ACTIVISTS?
BECAUSE YOU'RE NUTS, MOM.
YOU'RE THE LAMB OF GOD, AND YOU'RE BACK TO FACE THE EVIL ONE. WE HAVE TO PREPARE YOU FOR THE BATTLE AHEAD, OR YOU'RE NEVER GOING TO GET YOUR POWERS.

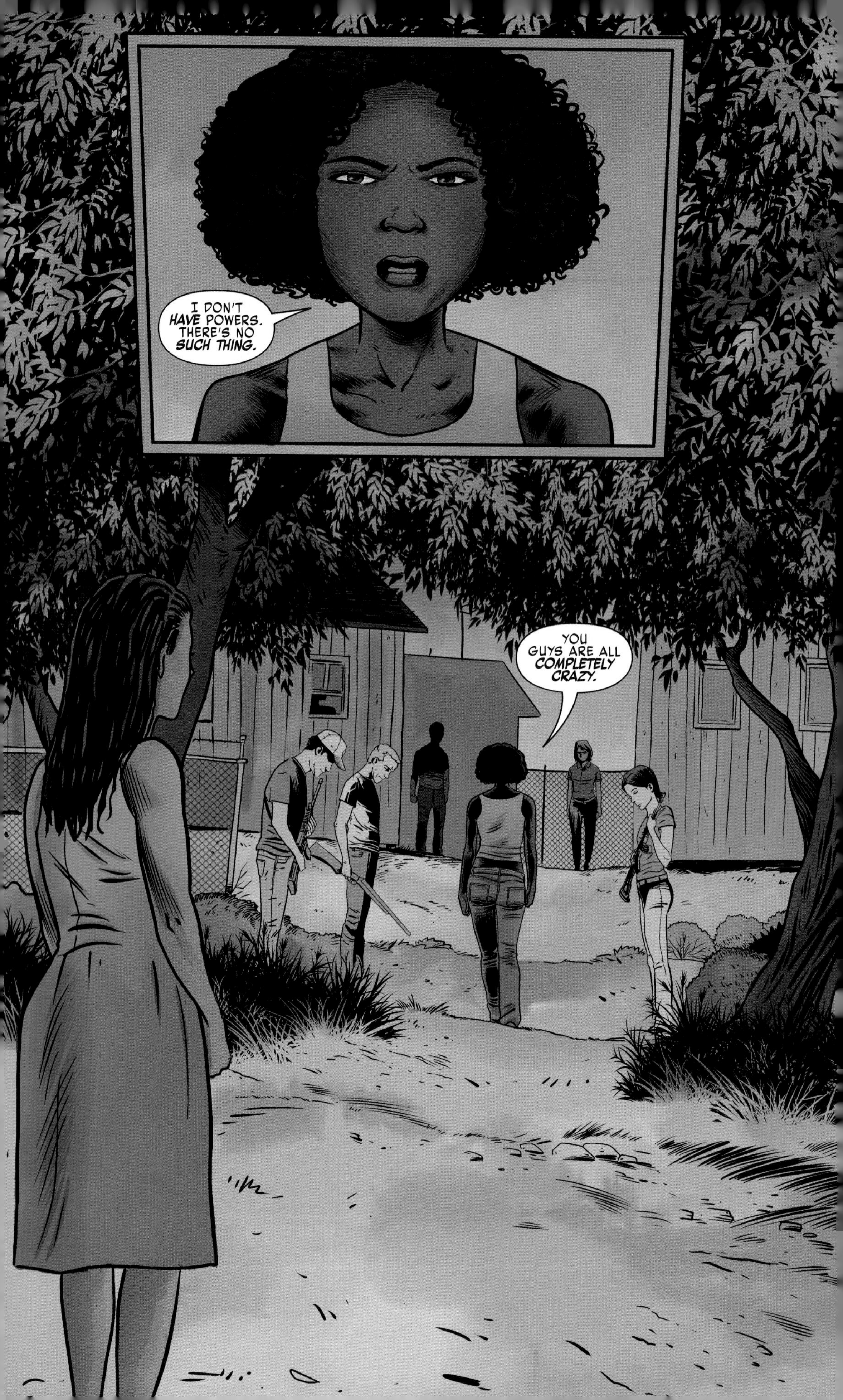
I DON'T HAVE POWERS. THERE'S NO SUCH THING.
YOU GUYS ARE ALL COMPLETELY CRAZY.

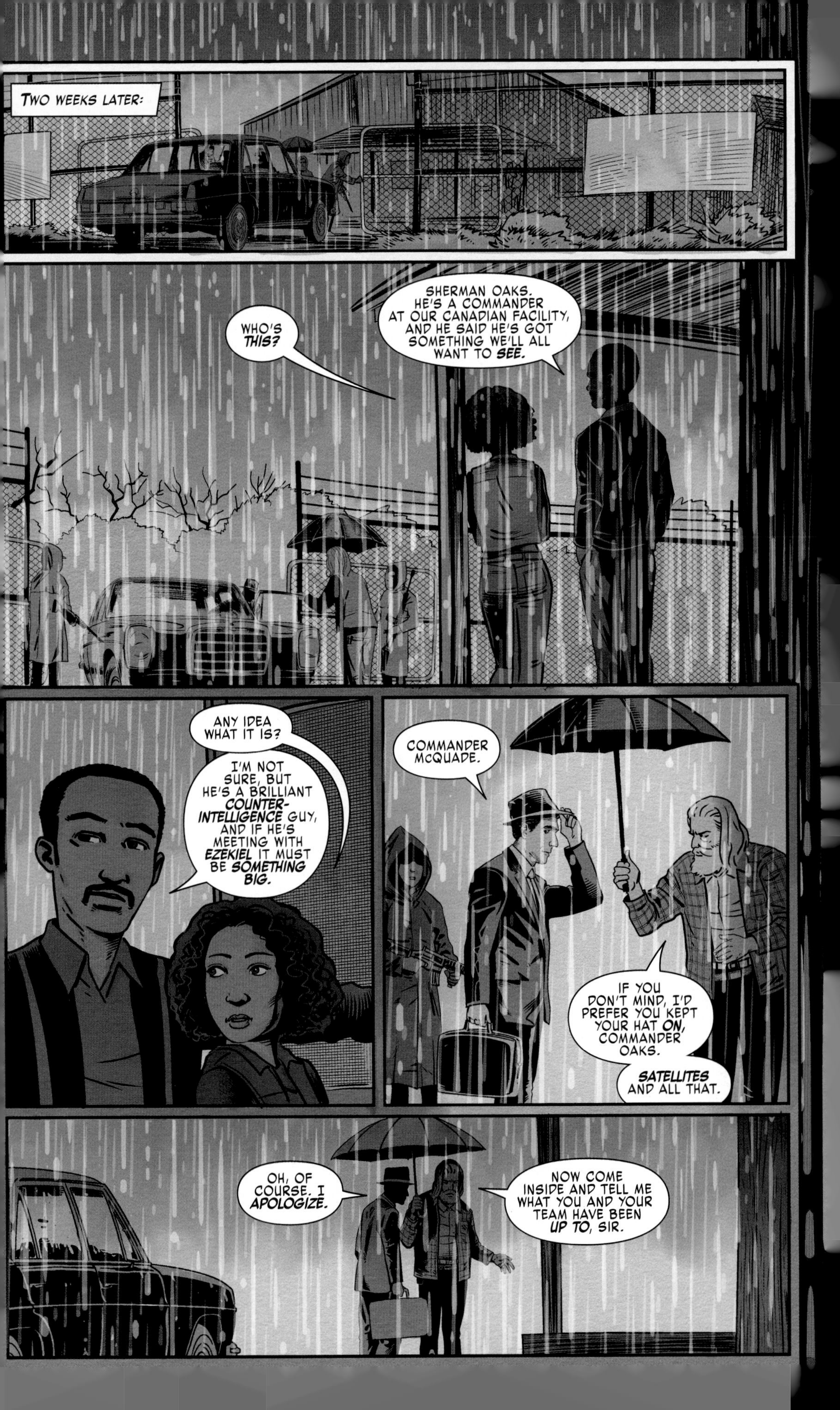
TWO WEEKS LATER:
WHO'S THIS?
SHERMAN OAKS. HE'S A COMMANDER AT OUR CANADIAN FACILITY, AND HE SAID HE'S GOT SOMETHING WE'LL ALL WANT TO SEE.
ANY IDEA WHAT IT IS?
I'M NOT SURE, BUT HE'S A BRILLIANT COUNTER-INTELLIGENCE GUY, AND IF HE'S MEETING WITH EZEKIEL IT MUST BE SOMETHING BIG.
COMMANDER McQUADE.
IF YOU DON'T MIND, I'D PREFER YOU KEPT YOUR HAT ON, COMMANDER OAKS.
SATELLITES AND ALL THAT.
OH, OF COURSE. I APOLOGIZE.
NOW COME INSIDE AND TELL ME WHAT YOU AND YOUR TEAM HAVE BEEN UP TO, SIR.

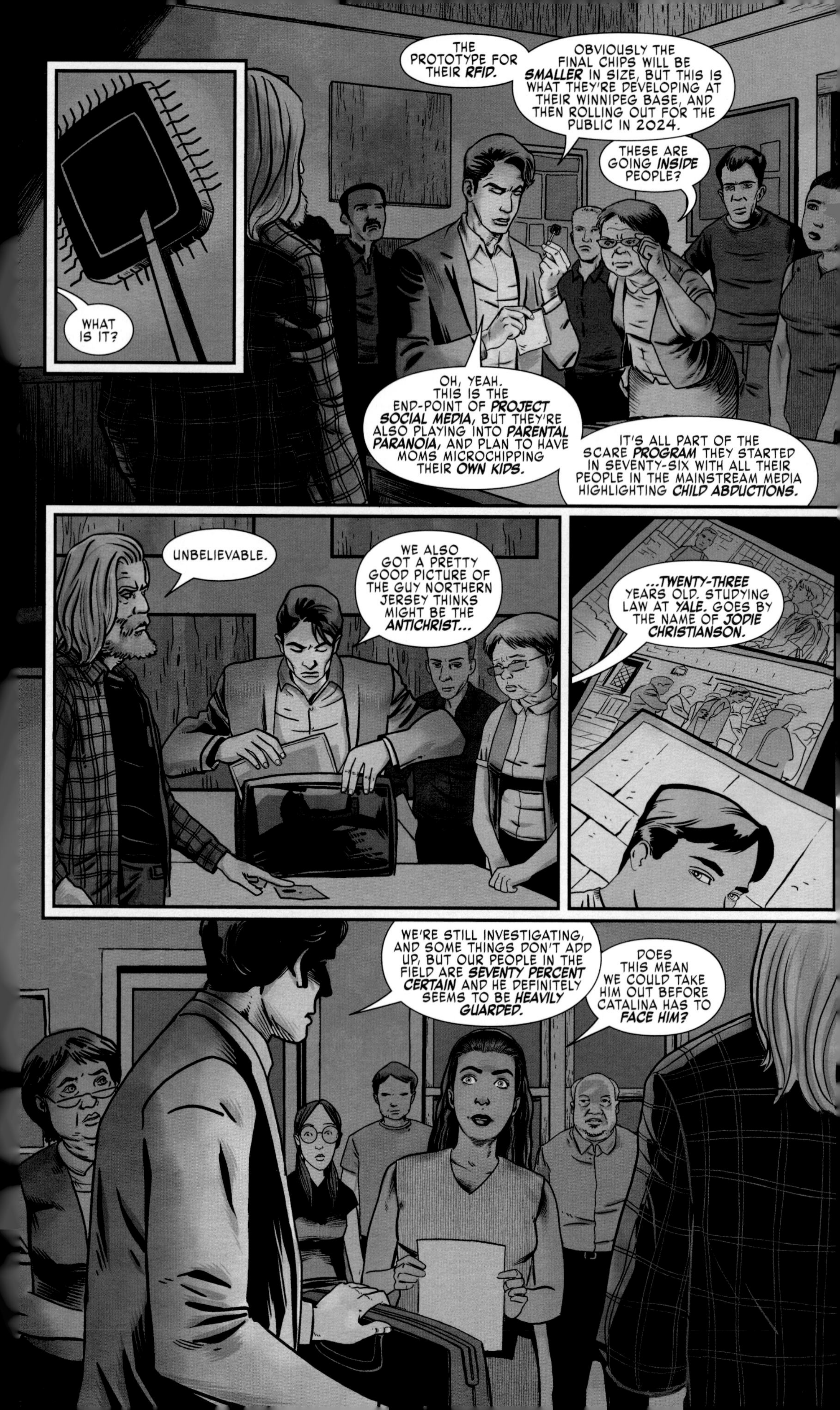

WHAT IS IT?
THE PROTOTYPE FOR THEIR RFID.
OBVIOUSLY THE FINAL CHIPS WILL BE SMALLER IN SIZE, BUT THIS IS WHAT THEY'RE DEVELOPING AT THEIR WINNIPEG BASE, AND THEN ROLLING OUT FOR THE PUBLIC IN 2024.
THESE ARE GOING INSIDE PEOPLE?
OH, YEAH. THIS IS THE END-POINT OF PROJECT SOCIAL MEDIA, BUT THEY'RE ALSO PLAYING INTO PARENTAL PARANOIA, AND PLAN TO HAVE MOMS MICROCHIPPING THEIR OWN KIDS.
IT'S ALL PART OF THE SCARE PROGRAM THEY STARTED IN SEVENTY-SIX WITH ALL THEIR PEOPLE IN THE MAINSTREAM MEDIA HIGHLIGHTING CHILD ABDUCTIONS.
UNBELIEVABLE.
WE ALSO GOT A PRETTY GOOD PICTURE OF THE GUY NORTHERN JERSEY THINKS MIGHT BE THE ANTICHRIST...
...TWENTY-THREE YEARS OLD. STUDYING LAW AT YALE. GOES BY THE NAME OF JODIE CHRISTIANSON.
WE'RE STILL INVESTIGATING, AND SOME THINGS DON'T ADD UP, BUT OUR PEOPLE IN THE FIELD ARE SEVENTY PERCENT CERTAIN AND HE DEFINITELY SEEMS TO BE HEAVILY GUARDED.
DOES THIS MEAN WE COULD TAKE HIM OUT BEFORE CATALINA HAS TO FACE HIM?

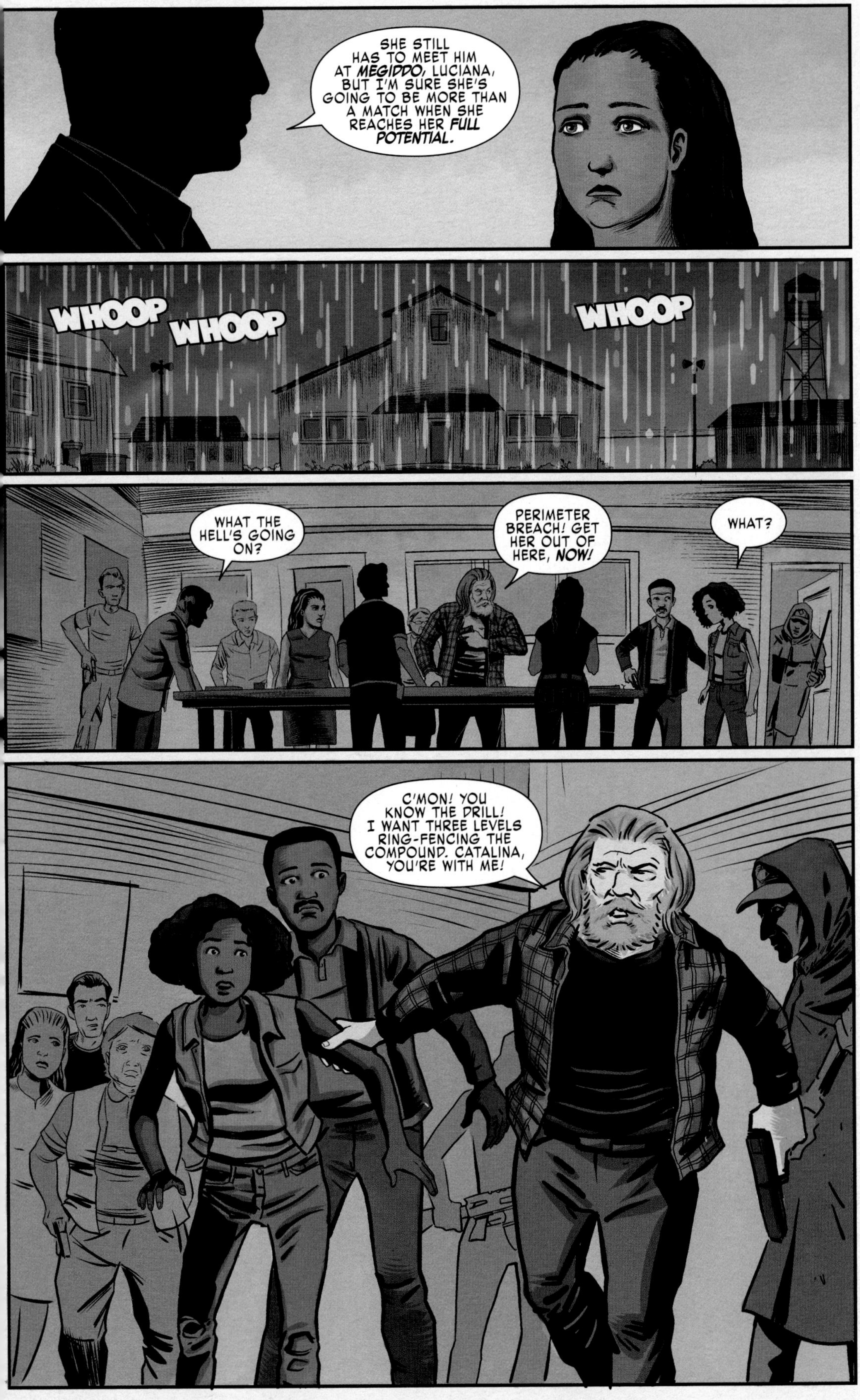
SHE STILL HAS TO MEET HIM AT MEGIDDO, LUCIANA, BUT I'M SURE SHE'S GOING TO BE MORE THAN A MATCH WHEN SHE REACHES HER FULL POTENTIAL.
WHOOP
WHOOP
WHOOP
WHAT THE HELL'S GOING ON?
PERIMETER BREACH! GET HER OUT OF HERE, NOW!
WHAT?
C'MON! YOU KNOW THE DRILL! I WANT THREE LEVELS RING-FENCING THE COMPOUND. CATALINA, YOU'RE WITH ME!

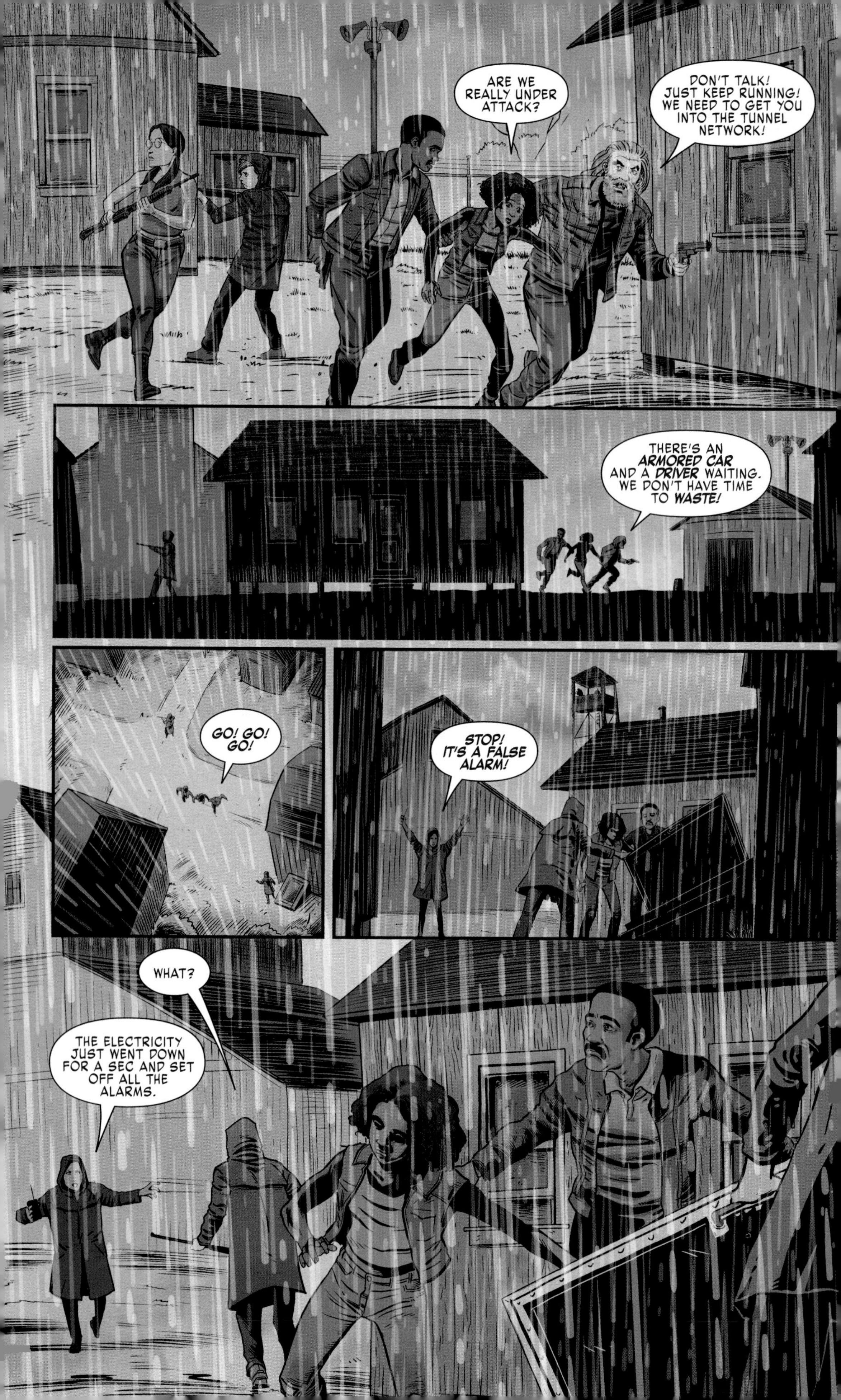
ARE WE REALLY UNDER ATTACK?
DON'T TALK! JUST KEEP RUNNING! WE NEED TO GET YOU INTO THE TUNNEL NETWORK!
THERE'S AN ARMORED CAR AND A DRIVER WAITING. WE DON'T HAVE TIME TO WASTE!
GO! GO! GO!
STOP! IT'S A FALSE ALARM!
WHAT?
THE ELECTRICITY JUST WENT DOWN FOR A SEC AND SET OFF ALL THE ALARMS.

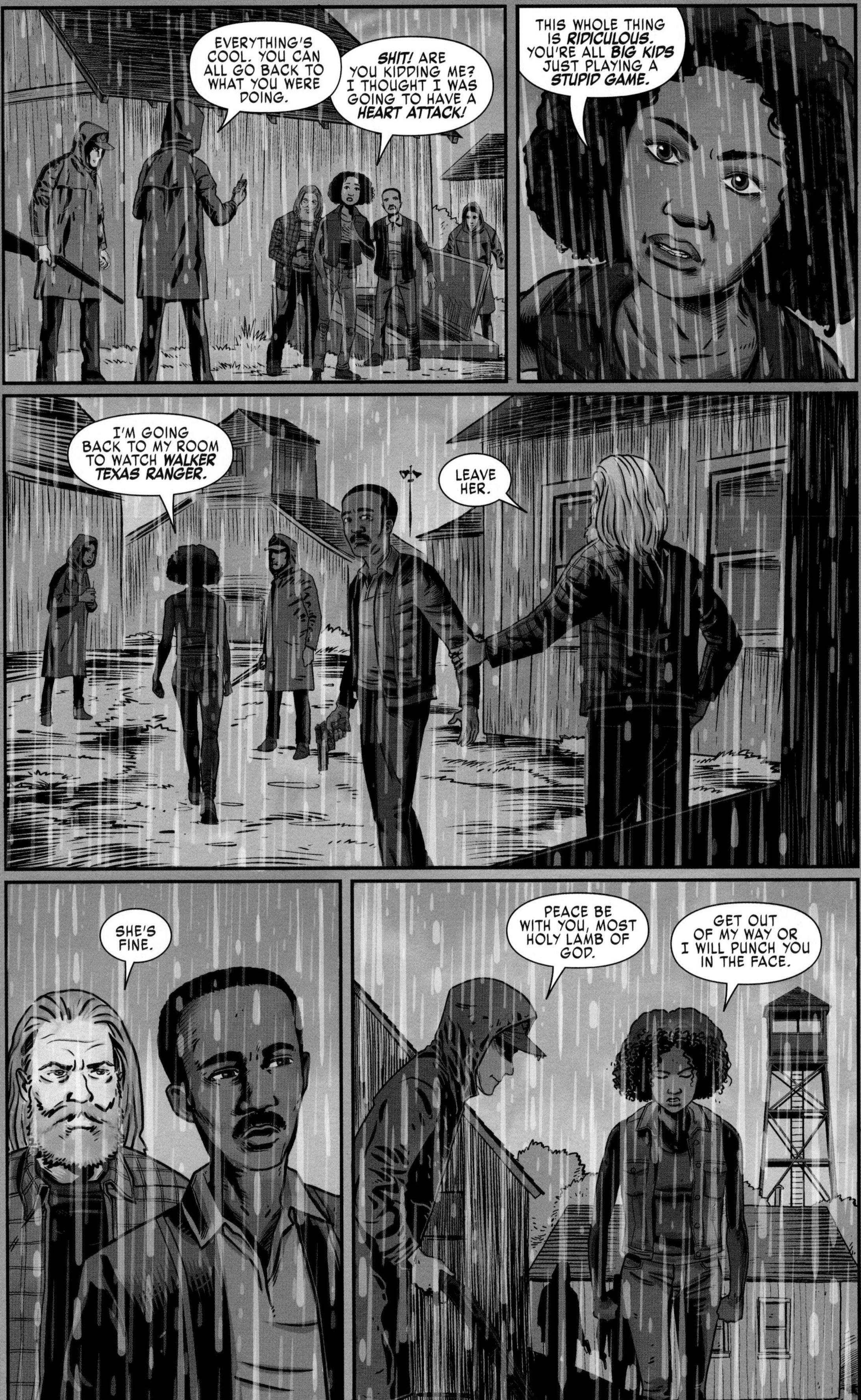
EVERYTHING'S COOL. YOU CAN ALL GO BACK TO WHAT YOU WERE DOING.
SHIT! ARE YOU KIDDING ME? I THOUGHT I WAS GOING TO HAVE A HEART ATTACK!
THIS WHOLE THING IS RIDICULOUS. YOU'RE ALL BIG KIDS JUST PLAYING A STUPID GAME.
I'M GOING BACK TO MY ROOM TO WATCH WALKER TEXAS RANGER.
LEAVE HER.
SHE'S FINE.
PEACE BE WITH YOU, MOST HOLY LAMB OF GOD.
GET OUT OF MY WAY OR I WILL PUNCH YOU IN THE FACE.

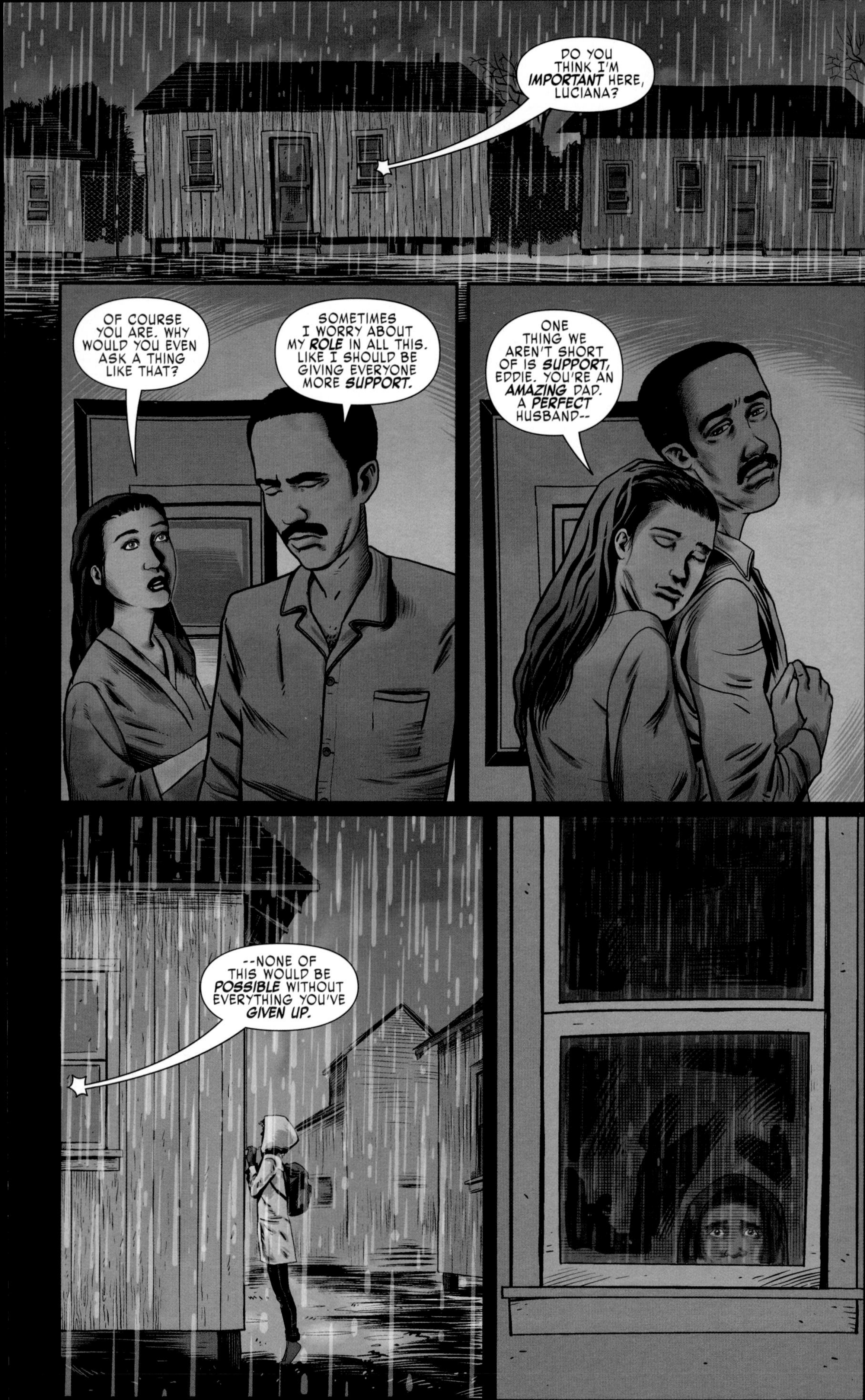
DO YOU THINK I'M IMPORTANT HERE, LUCIANA?
OF COURSE YOU ARE. WHY WOULD YOU EVEN ASK A THING LIKE THAT?
SOMETIMES I WORRY ABOUT MY ROLE IN ALL THIS. LIKE I SHOULD BE GIVING EVERYONE MORE SUPPORT.
ONE THING WE AREN'T SHORT OF IS SUPPORT, EDDIE. YOU'RE AN AMAZING DAD. A PERFECT HUSBAND--
--NONE OF THIS WOULD BE POSSIBLE WITHOUT EVERYTHING YOU'VE GIVEN UP.

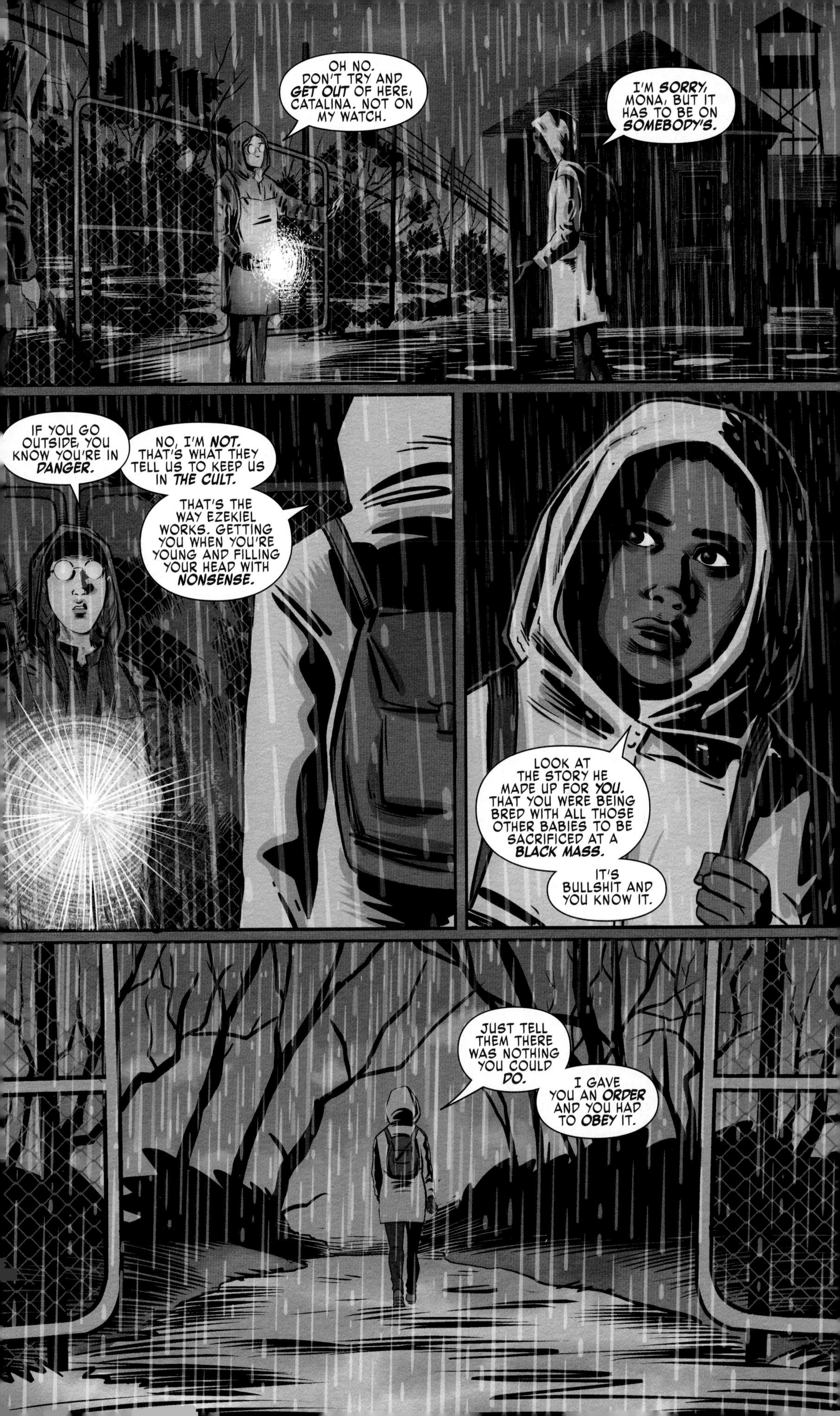
OH NO. DON'T TRY AND **GET OUT** OF HERE, CATALINA. NOT ON MY WATCH.
I'M **SORRY,** MONA, BUT IT HAS TO BE ON **SOMEBODY'S.**
IF YOU GO OUTSIDE, YOU KNOW YOU'RE IN **DANGER.**
NO, I'M **NOT.** THAT'S WHAT THEY TELL US TO KEEP US IN **THE CULT.**
THAT'S THE WAY EZEKIEL WORKS. GETTING YOU WHEN YOU'RE YOUNG AND FILLING YOUR HEAD WITH **NONSENSE.**
LOOK AT THE STORY HE MADE UP FOR **YOU.** THAT YOU WERE BEING BRED WITH ALL THOSE OTHER BABIES TO BE SACRIFICED AT A **BLACK MASS.**
IT'S BULLSHIT AND YOU KNOW IT.
JUST TELL THEM THERE WAS NOTHING YOU COULD **DO.**
I GAVE YOU AN **ORDER** AND YOU HAD TO **OBEY** IT.

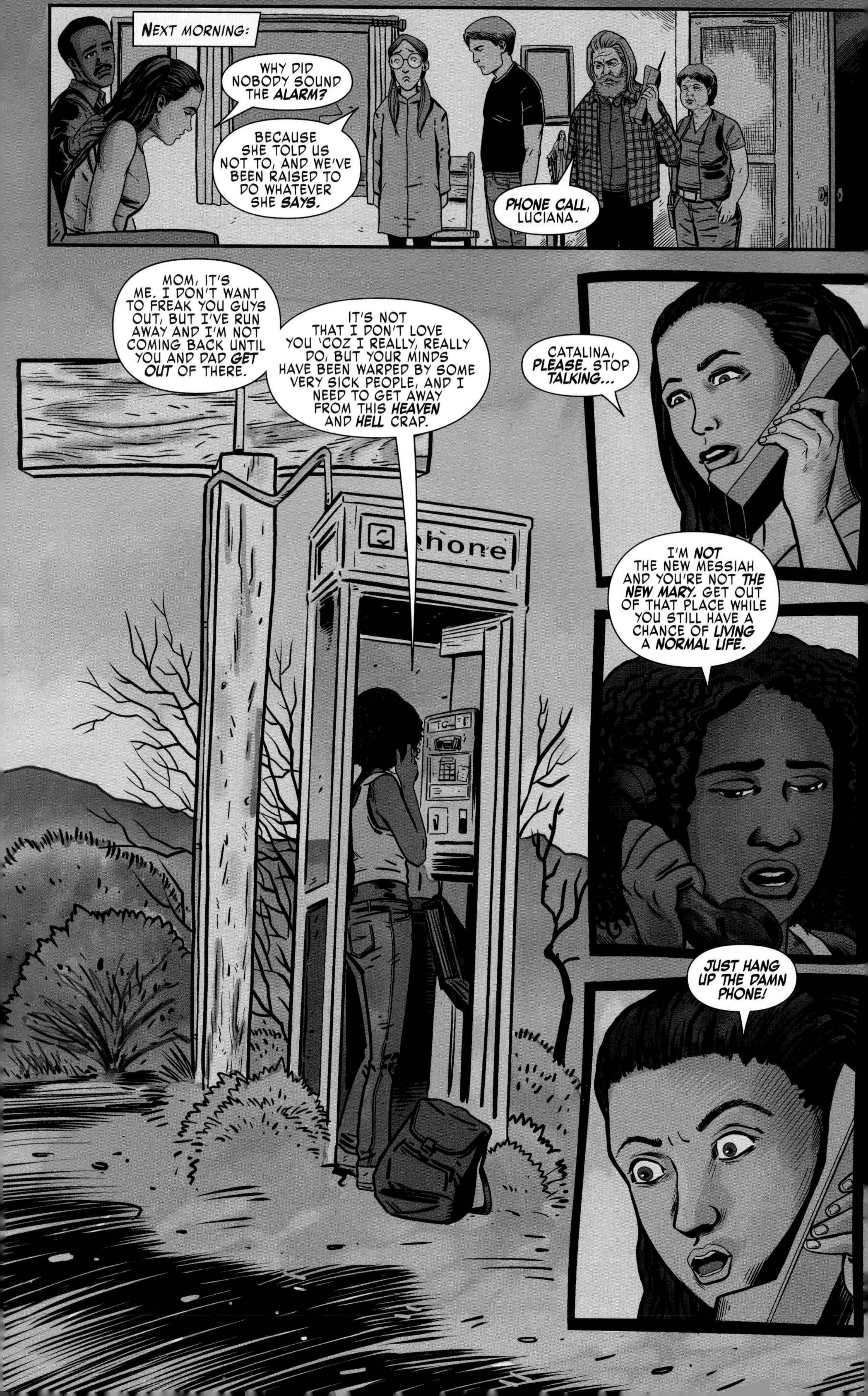
NEXT MORNING:
WHY DID NOBODY SOUND THE ALARM?
BECAUSE SHE TOLD US NOT TO, AND WE'VE BEEN RAISED TO DO WHATEVER SHE SAYS.
PHONE CALL, LUCIANA.
MOM, IT'S ME. I DON'T WANT TO FREAK YOU GUYS OUT, BUT I'VE RUN AWAY AND I'M NOT COMING BACK UNTIL YOU AND DAD GET OUT OF THERE.
IT'S NOT THAT I DON'T LOVE YOU 'COZ I REALLY, REALLY DO, BUT YOUR MINDS HAVE BEEN WARPED BY SOME VERY SICK PEOPLE, AND I NEED TO GET AWAY FROM THIS HEAVEN AND HELL CRAP.
CATALINA, PLEASE. STOP TALKING...
I'M NOT THE NEW MESSIAH AND YOU'RE NOT THE NEW MARY. GET OUT OF THAT PLACE WHILE YOU STILL HAVE A CHANCE OF LIVING A NORMAL LIFE.
JUST HANG UP THE DAMN PHONE!

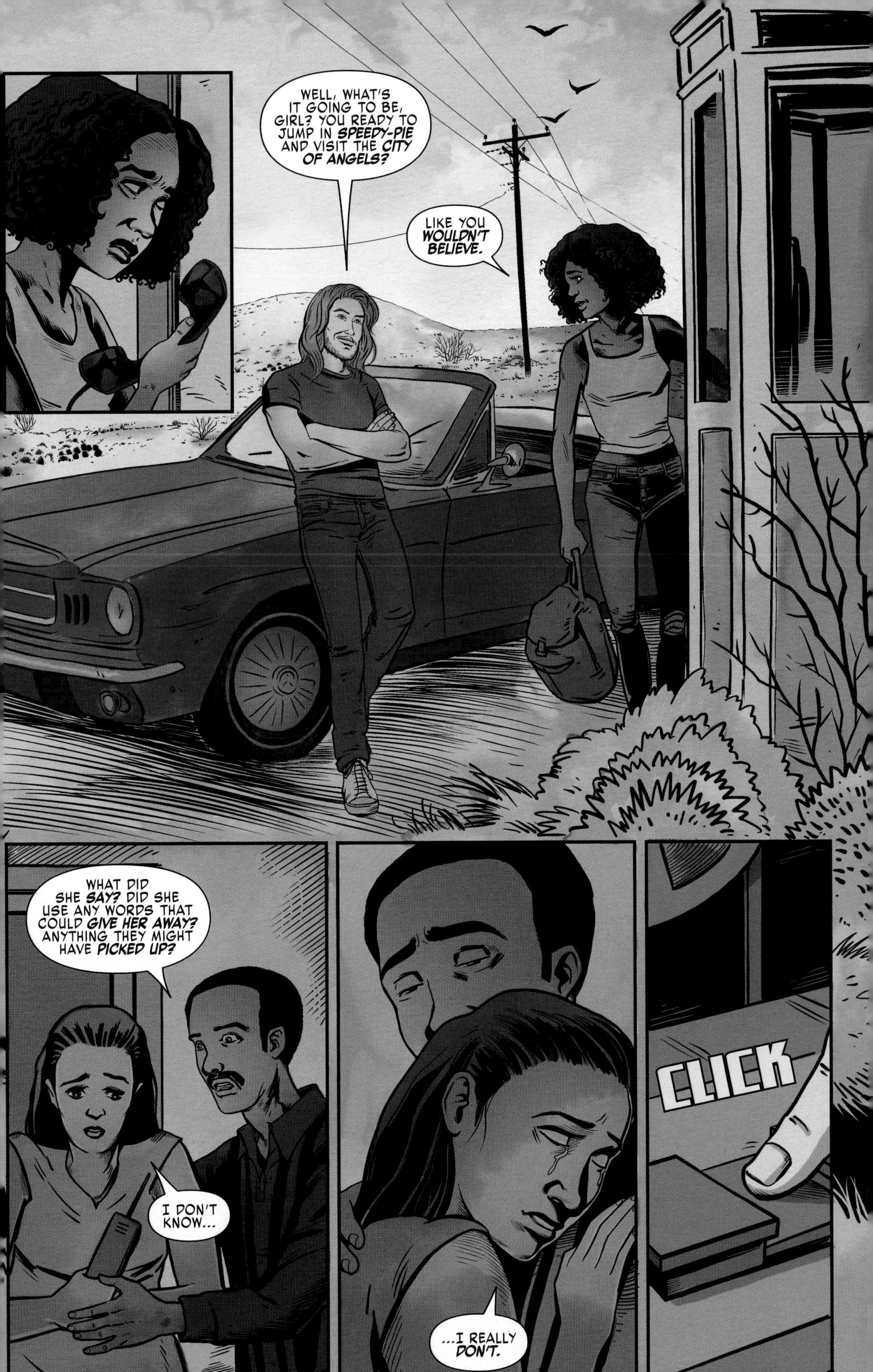
WELL, WHAT'S IT GOING TO BE, GIRL? YOU READY TO JUMP IN SPEEDY-PIE AND VISIT THE CITY OF ANGELS?
LIKE YOU WOULDN'T BELIEVE.
WHAT DID SHE SAY? DID SHE USE ANY WORDS THAT COULD GIVE HER AWAY? ANYTHING THEY MIGHT HAVE PICKED UP?
I DON'T KNOW...
...I REALLY DON'T.
CLICK

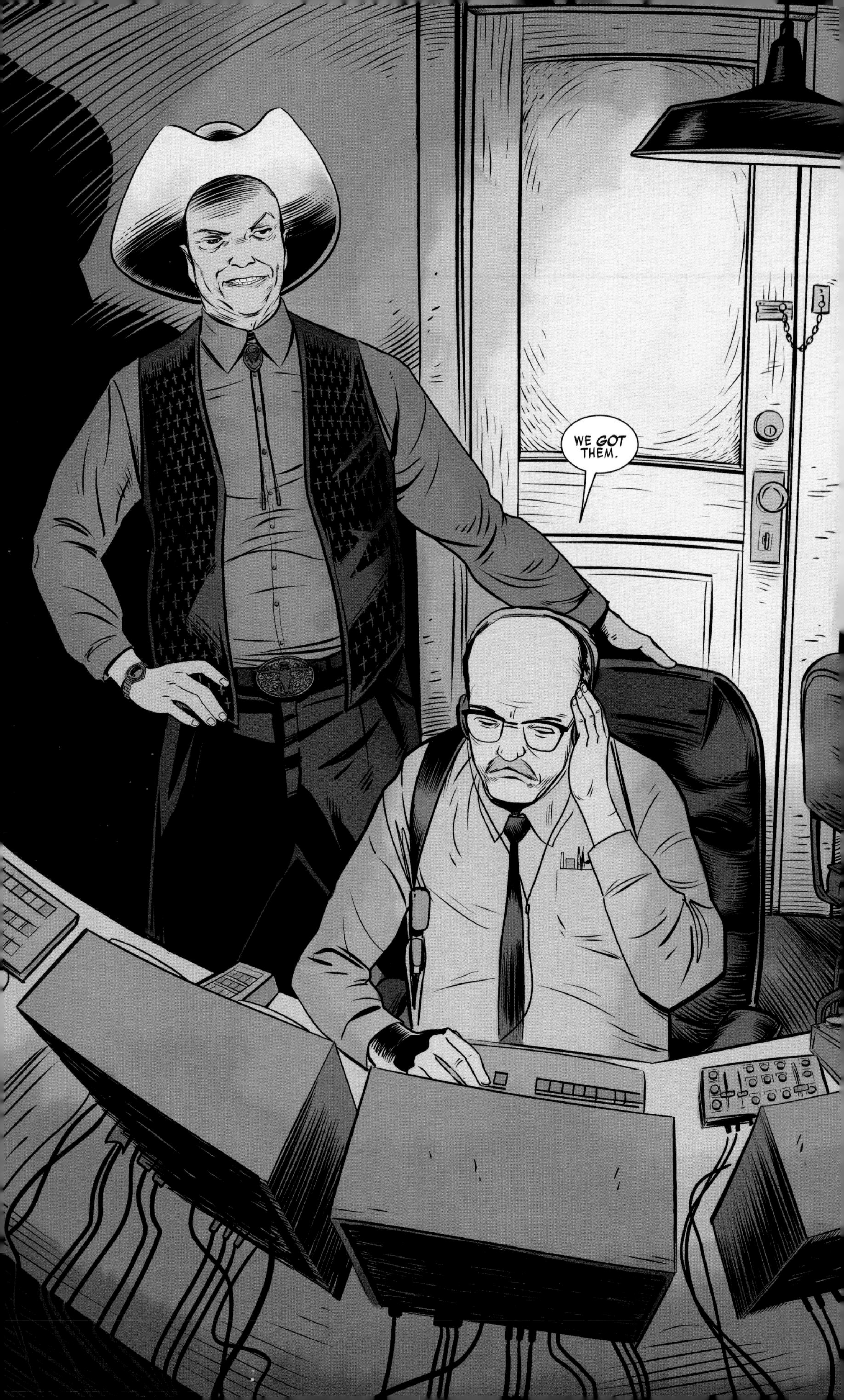
WE GOT THEM.

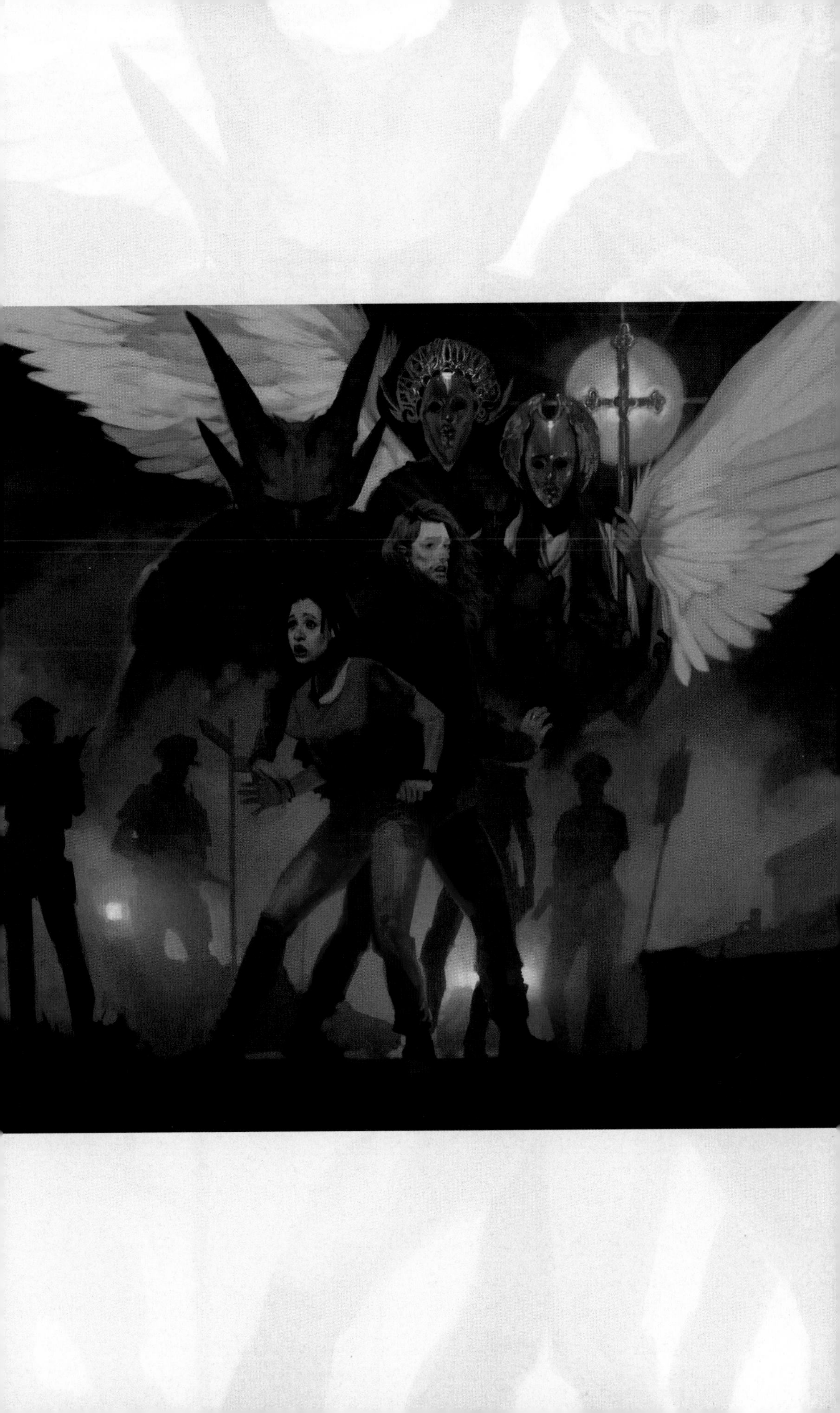

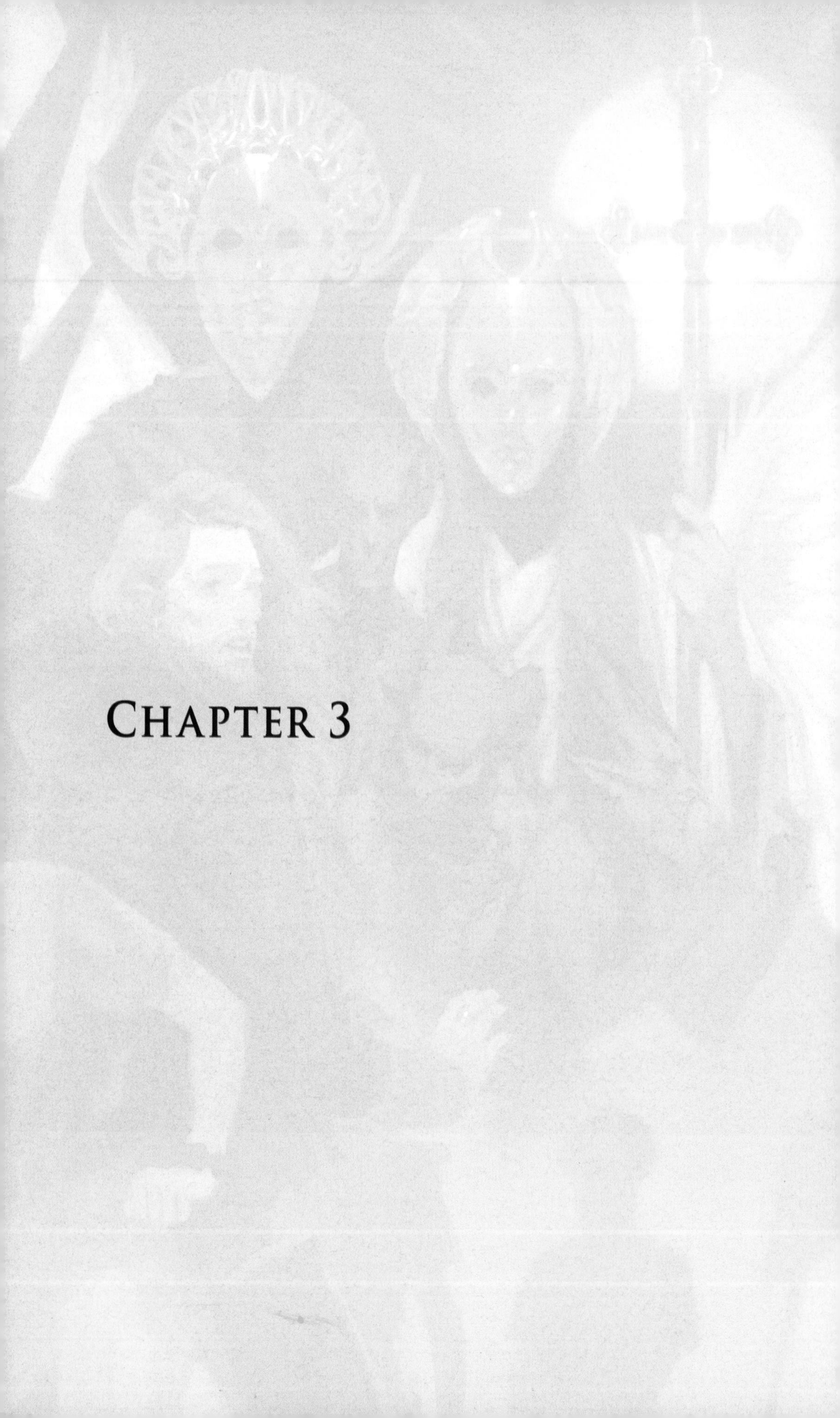

CHAPTER 3

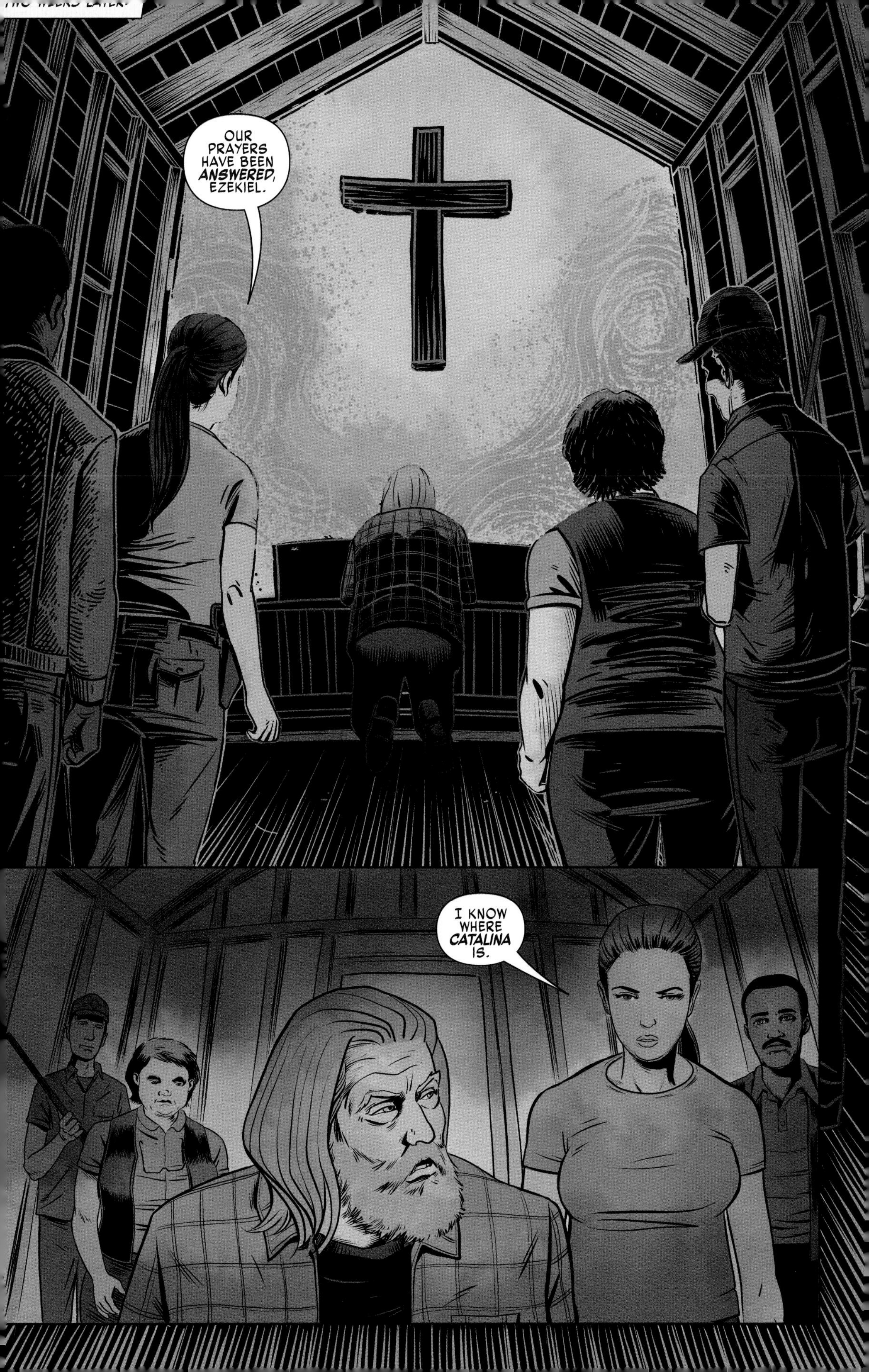
OUR PRAYERS HAVE BEEN ANSWERED, EZEKIEL.
I KNOW WHERE CATALINA IS.

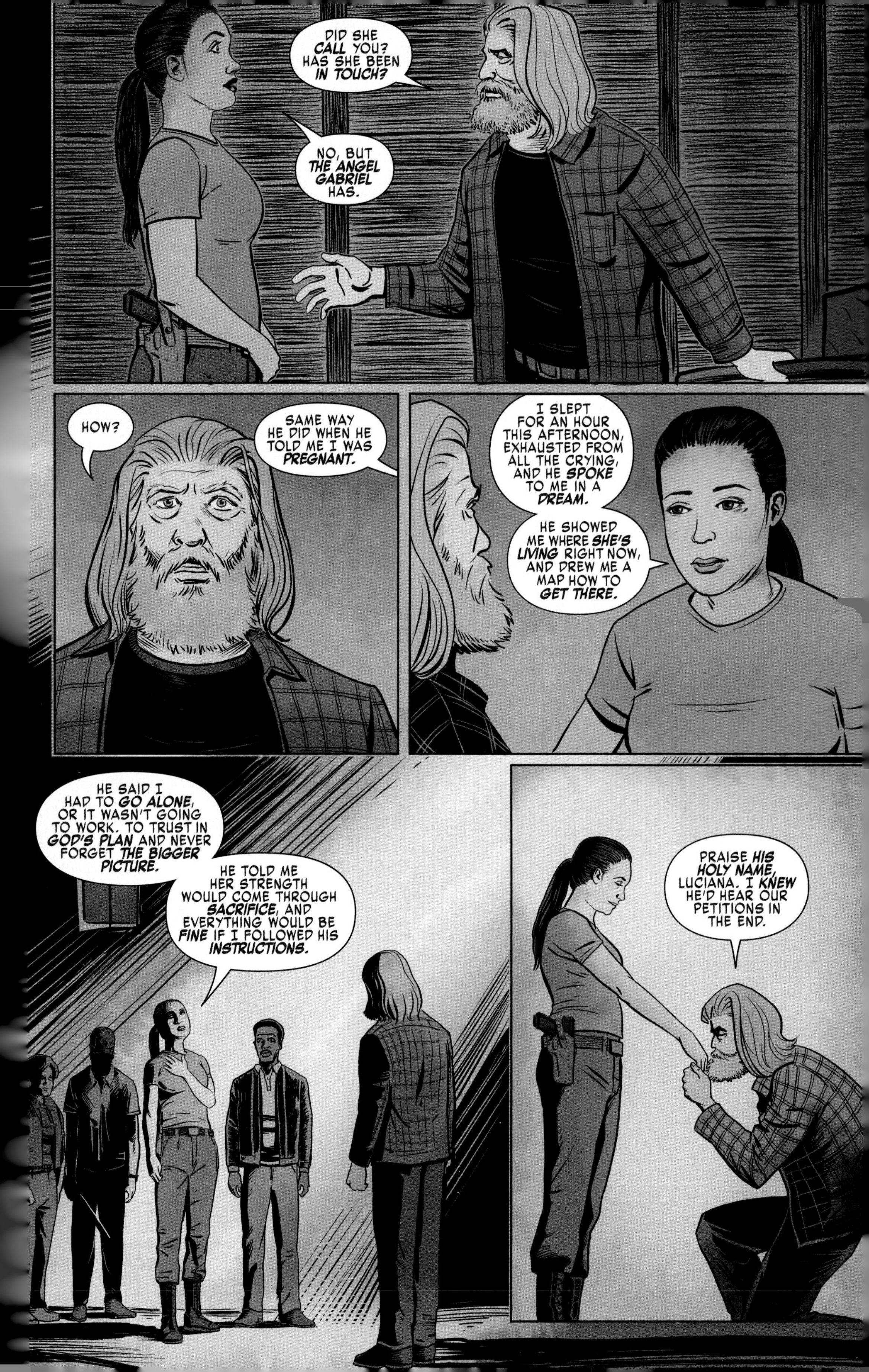
DID SHE CALL YOU? HAS SHE BEEN IN TOUCH?
NO, BUT THE ANGEL GABRIEL HAS.
HOW?
SAME WAY HE DID WHEN HE TOLD ME I WAS PREGNANT.
I SLEPT FOR AN HOUR THIS AFTERNOON, EXHAUSTED FROM ALL THE CRYING, AND HE SPOKE TO ME IN A DREAM.
HE SHOWED ME WHERE SHE'S LIVING RIGHT NOW, AND DREW ME A MAP HOW TO GET THERE.
HE SAID I HAD TO GO ALONE, OR IT WASN'T GOING TO WORK. TO TRUST IN GOD'S PLAN AND NEVER FORGET THE BIGGER PICTURE.
HE TOLD ME HER STRENGTH WOULD COME THROUGH SACRIFICE, AND EVERYTHING WOULD BE FINE IF I FOLLOWED HIS INSTRUCTIONS.
PRAISE HIS HOLY NAME, LUCIANA. I KNEW HE'D HEAR OUR PETITIONS IN THE END.

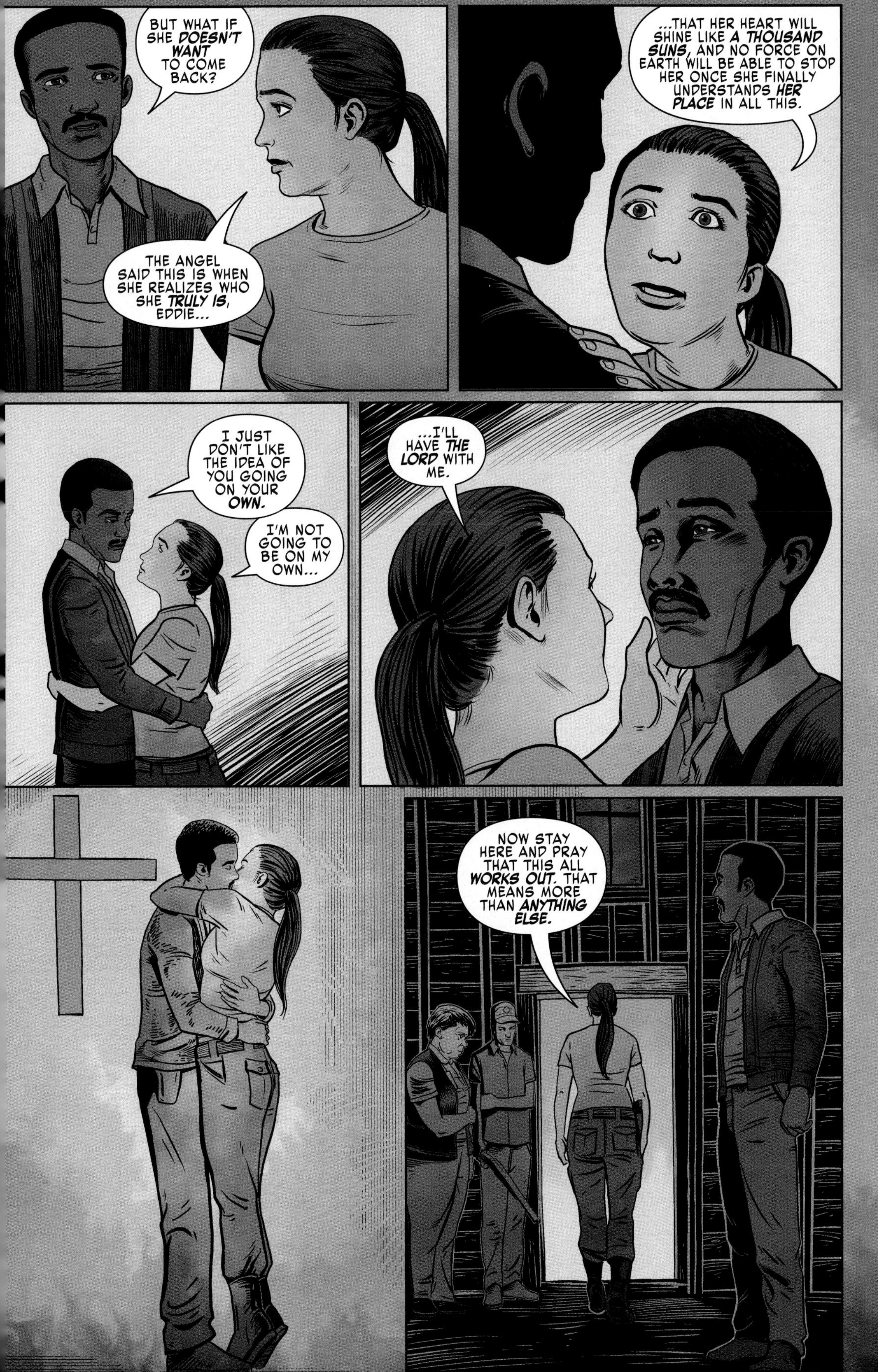
BUT WHAT IF SHE *DOESN'T WANT* TO COME BACK?
THE ANGEL SAID THIS IS WHEN SHE REALIZES WHO SHE *TRULY IS*, EDDIE...
...THAT HER HEART WILL SHINE LIKE *A THOUSAND SUNS*, AND NO FORCE ON EARTH WILL BE ABLE TO STOP HER ONCE SHE FINALLY UNDERSTANDS *HER PLACE* IN ALL THIS.
I JUST DON'T LIKE THE IDEA OF YOU GOING ON YOUR *OWN*.
I'M NOT GOING TO BE ON MY OWN...
...I'LL HAVE *THE LORD* WITH ME.
NOW STAY HERE AND PRAY THAT THIS ALL *WORKS OUT*. THAT MEANS MORE THAN *ANYTHING ELSE*.

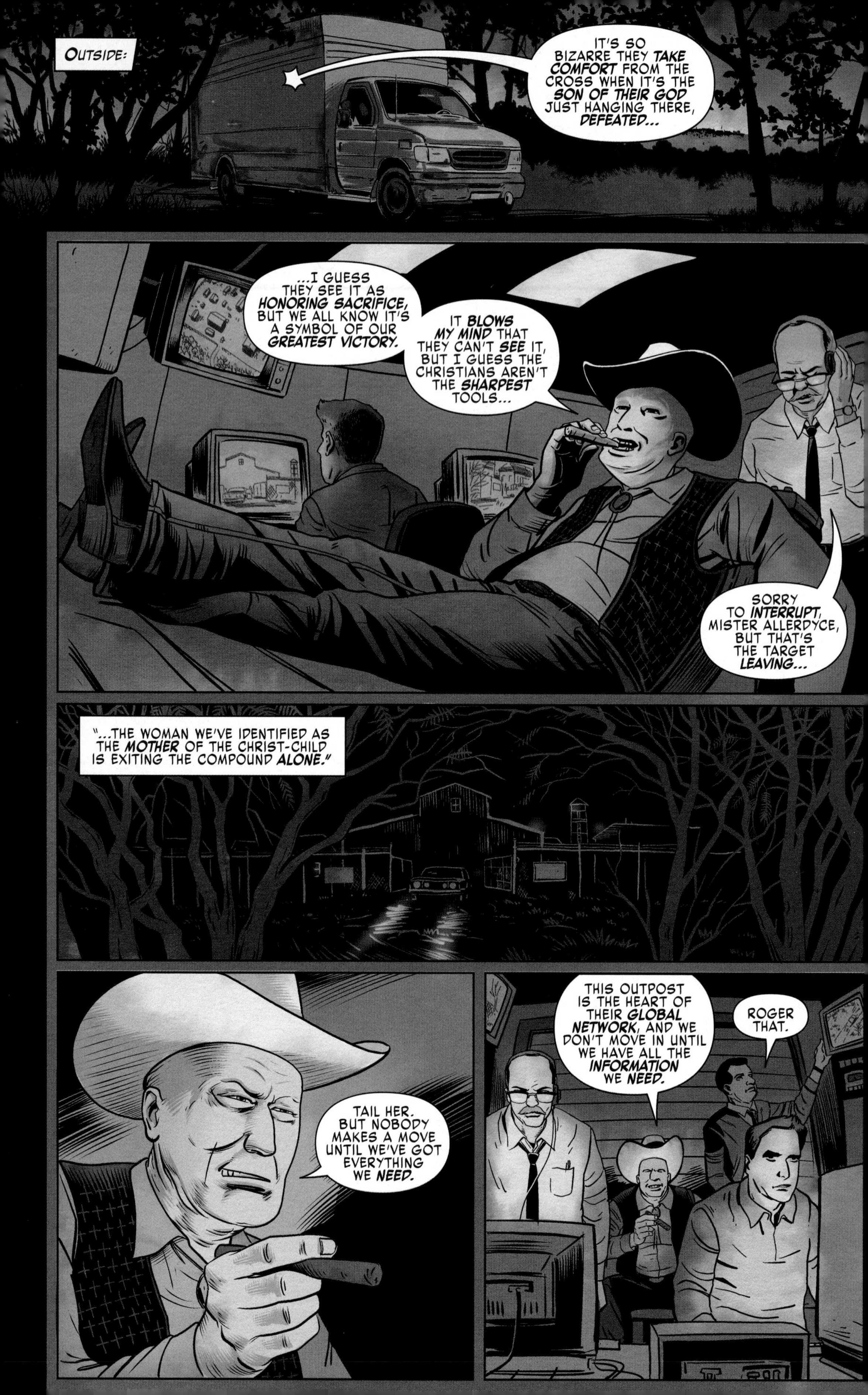
OUTSIDE:
IT'S SO BIZARRE THEY TAKE COMFORT FROM THE CROSS WHEN IT'S THE SON OF THEIR GOD JUST HANGING THERE, DEFEATED...
...I GUESS THEY SEE IT AS HONORING SACRIFICE, BUT WE ALL KNOW IT'S A SYMBOL OF OUR GREATEST VICTORY.
IT BLOWS MY MIND THAT THEY CAN'T SEE IT, BUT I GUESS THE CHRISTIANS AREN'T THE SHARPEST TOOLS...
SORRY TO INTERRUPT, MISTER ALLERDYCE, BUT THAT'S THE TARGET LEAVING...
"...THE WOMAN WE'VE IDENTIFIED AS THE MOTHER OF THE CHRIST-CHILD IS EXITING THE COMPOUND ALONE."
TAIL HER. BUT NOBODY MAKES A MOVE UNTIL WE'VE GOT EVERYTHING WE NEED.
THIS OUTPOST IS THE HEART OF THEIR GLOBAL NETWORK, AND WE DON'T MOVE IN UNTIL WE HAVE ALL THE INFORMATION WE NEED.
ROGER THAT.

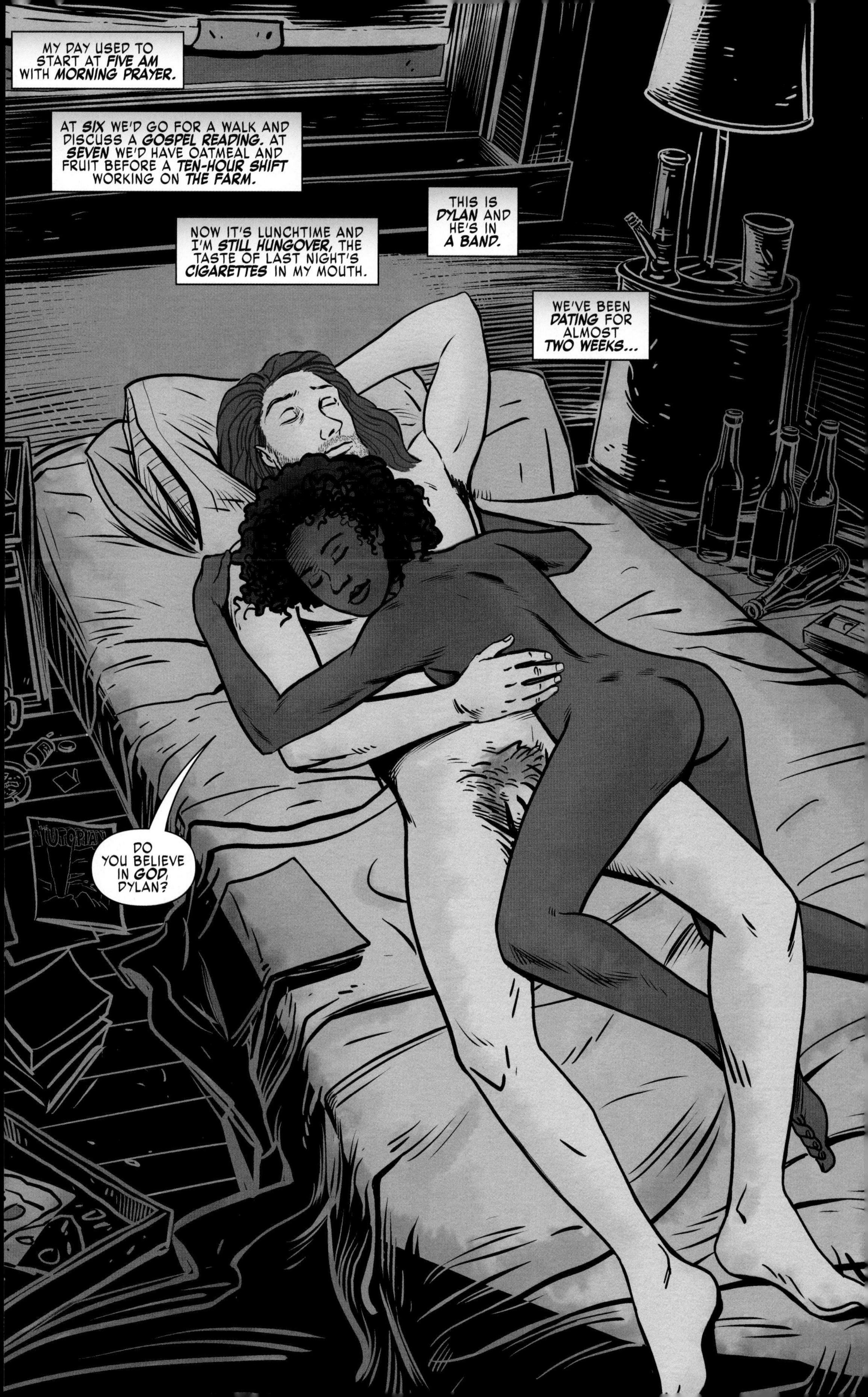
MY DAY USED TO START AT FIVE AM WITH MORNING PRAYER.
AT SIX WE'D GO FOR A WALK AND DISCUSS A GOSPEL READING. AT SEVEN WE'D HAVE OATMEAL AND FRUIT BEFORE A TEN-HOUR SHIFT WORKING ON THE FARM.
NOW IT'S LUNCHTIME AND I'M STILL HUNGOVER, THE TASTE OF LAST NIGHT'S CIGARETTES IN MY MOUTH.
THIS IS DYLAN AND HE'S IN A BAND.
WE'VE BEEN DATING FOR ALMOST TWO WEEKS...
DO YOU BELIEVE IN GOD, DYLAN?

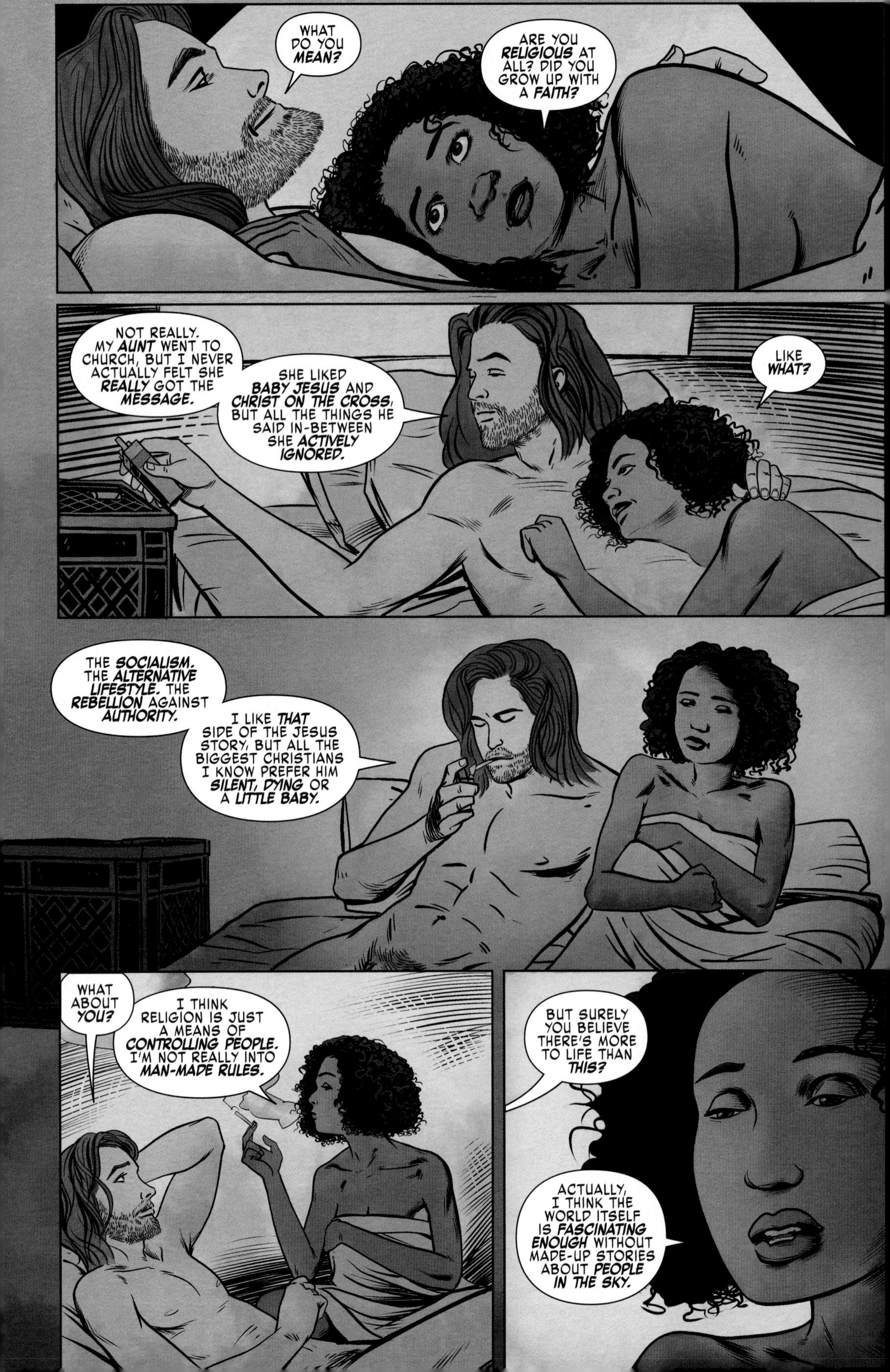
ARE YOU RELIGIOUS AT ALL? DID YOU GROW UP WITH A FAITH?
WHAT DO YOU MEAN?
NOT REALLY. MY AUNT WENT TO CHURCH, BUT I NEVER ACTUALLY FELT SHE REALLY GOT THE MESSAGE.
SHE LIKED BABY JESUS AND CHRIST ON THE CROSS; BUT ALL THE THINGS HE SAID IN-BETWEEN SHE ACTIVELY IGNORED.
LIKE WHAT?
THE SOCIALISM. THE ALTERNATIVE LIFESTYLE. THE REBELLION AGAINST AUTHORITY.
I LIKE THAT SIDE OF THE JESUS STORY, BUT ALL THE BIGGEST CHRISTIANS I KNOW PREFER HIM SILENT, DYING OR A LITTLE BABY.
WHAT ABOUT YOU?
I THINK RELIGION IS JUST A MEANS OF CONTROLLING PEOPLE. I'M NOT REALLY INTO MAN-MADE RULES.
BUT SURELY YOU BELIEVE THERE'S MORE TO LIFE THAN THIS?
ACTUALLY, I THINK THE WORLD ITSELF IS FASCINATING ENOUGH WITHOUT MADE-UP STORIES ABOUT PEOPLE IN THE SKY.

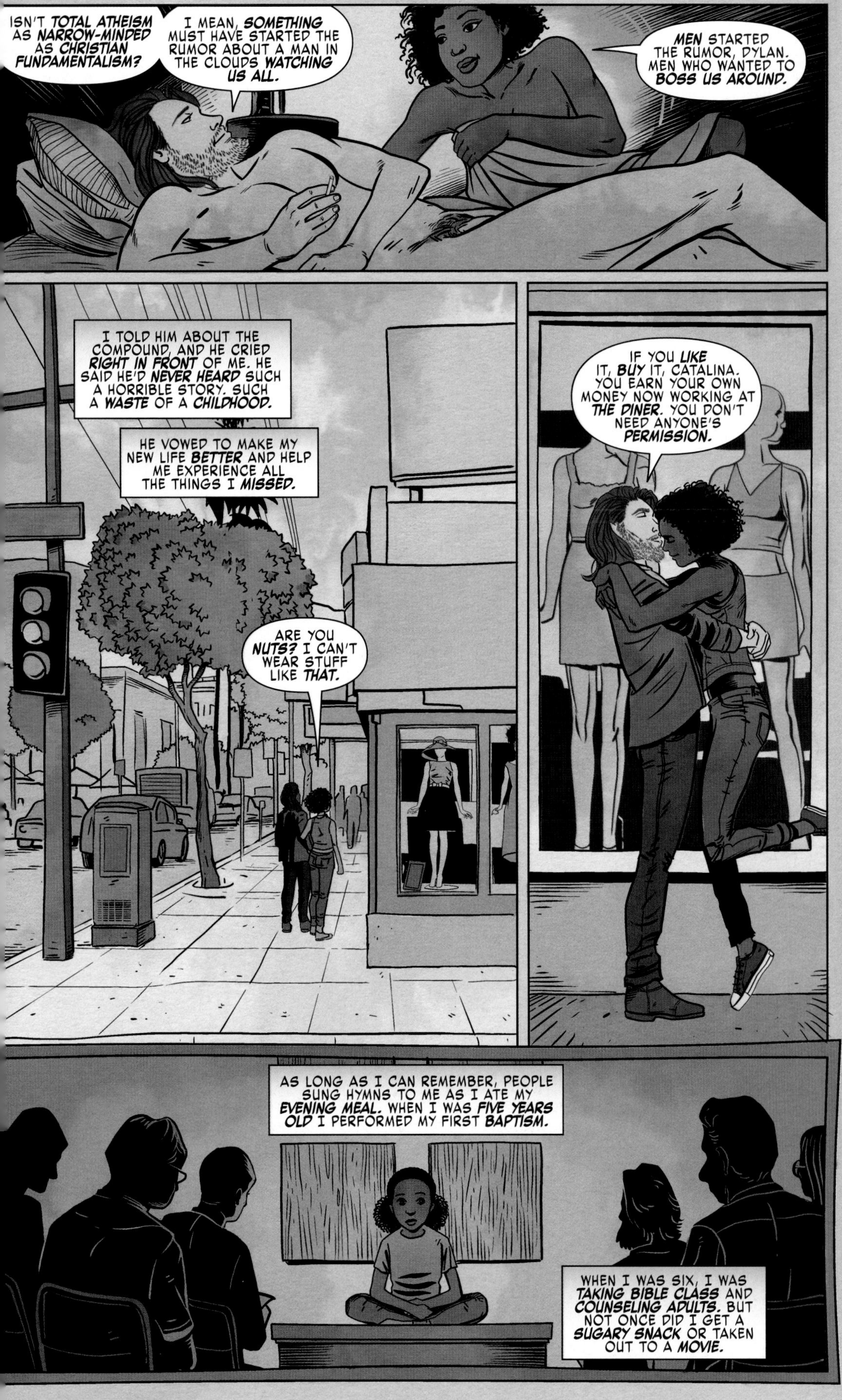
ISN'T TOTAL ATHEISM AS NARROW-MINDED AS CHRISTIAN FUNDAMENTALISM?
I MEAN, SOMETHING MUST HAVE STARTED THE RUMOR ABOUT A MAN IN THE CLOUDS WATCHING US ALL.
MEN STARTED THE RUMOR, DYLAN. MEN WHO WANTED TO BOSS US AROUND.
I TOLD HIM ABOUT THE COMPOUND, AND HE CRIED RIGHT IN FRONT OF ME. HE SAID HE'D NEVER HEARD SUCH A HORRIBLE STORY. SUCH A WASTE OF A CHILDHOOD.
HE VOWED TO MAKE MY NEW LIFE BETTER AND HELP ME EXPERIENCE ALL THE THINGS I MISSED.
ARE YOU NUTS? I CAN'T WEAR STUFF LIKE THAT.
IF YOU LIKE IT, BUY IT, CATALINA. YOU EARN YOUR OWN MONEY NOW WORKING AT THE DINER. YOU DON'T NEED ANYONE'S PERMISSION.
AS LONG AS I CAN REMEMBER, PEOPLE SUNG HYMNS TO ME AS I ATE MY EVENING MEAL. WHEN I WAS FIVE YEARS OLD I PERFORMED MY FIRST BAPTISM.
WHEN I WAS SIX, I WAS TAKING BIBLE CLASS AND COUNSELING ADULTS. BUT NOT ONCE DID I GET A SUGARY SNACK OR TAKEN OUT TO A MOVIE.

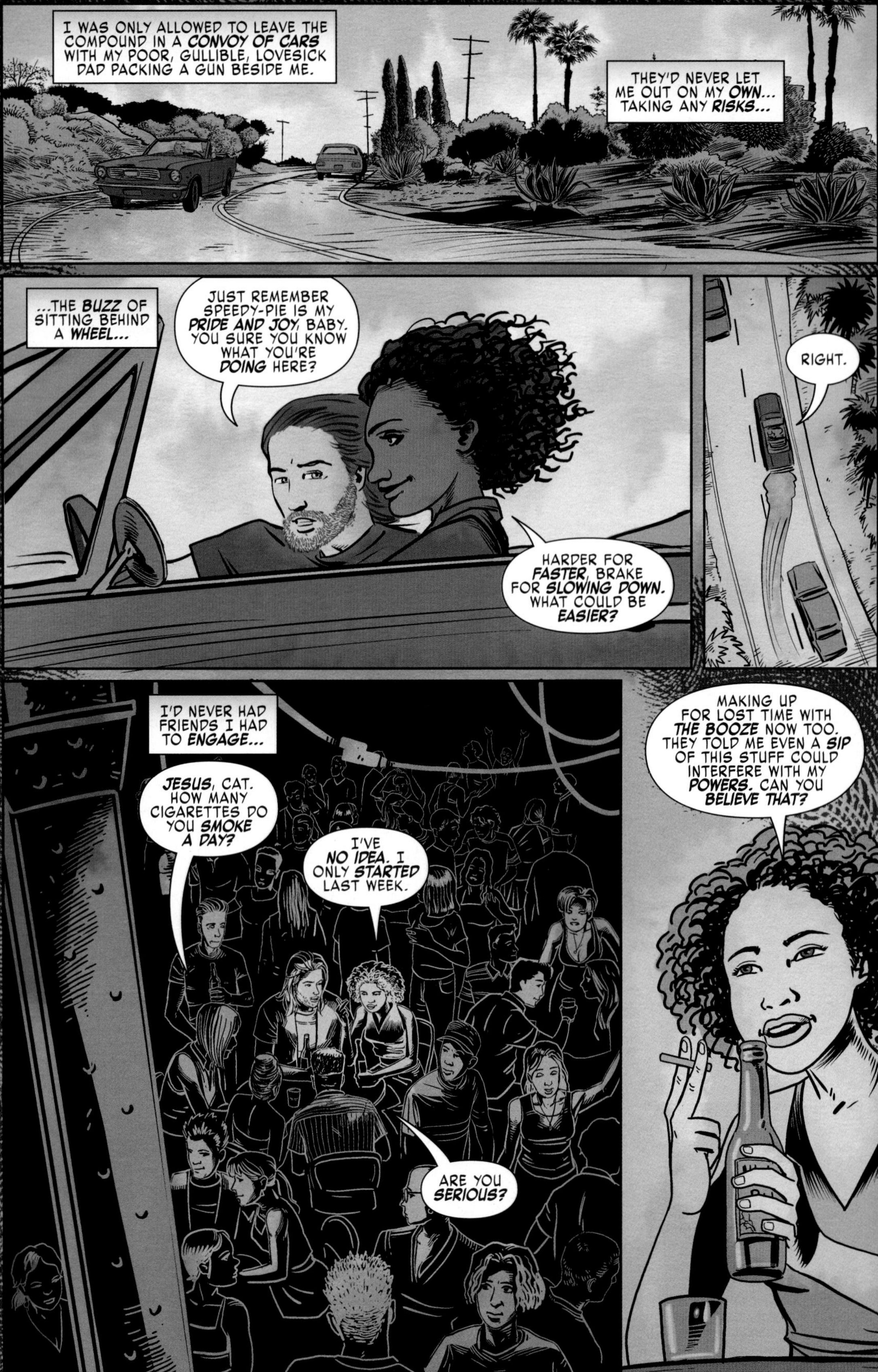
I WAS ONLY ALLOWED TO LEAVE THE COMPOUND IN A CONVOY OF CARS WITH MY POOR, GULLIBLE, LOVESICK DAD PACKING A GUN BESIDE ME.
THEY'D NEVER LET ME OUT ON MY OWN... TAKING ANY RISKS...
...THE BUZZ OF SITTING BEHIND A WHEEL...
JUST REMEMBER SPEEDY-PIE IS MY PRIDE AND JOY, BABY. YOU SURE YOU KNOW WHAT YOU'RE DOING HERE?
HARDER FOR FASTER, BRAKE FOR SLOWING DOWN. WHAT COULD BE EASIER?
RIGHT.
I'D NEVER HAD FRIENDS I HAD TO ENGAGE...
JESUS, CAT. HOW MANY CIGARETTES DO YOU SMOKE A DAY?
I'VE NO IDEA. I ONLY STARTED LAST WEEK.
ARE YOU SERIOUS?
MAKING UP FOR LOST TIME WITH THE BOOZE NOW TOO. THEY TOLD ME EVEN A SIP OF THIS STUFF COULD INTERFERE WITH MY POWERS. CAN YOU BELIEVE THAT?

C'MON, DYLAN. GET UP AND DANCE.

I WASN'T ALLOWED TO DO THIS GROWING UP, BUT I'D DO IT IN MY ROOM TO TOTAL SILENCE. ISN'T THAT CRAZY?

THEY CONTROLLED WHAT I USED TO SEE ON TV, SO I MADE UP TUNES IN MY HEAD INSTEAD.

YOU KNOW, YOU'RE REALLY SOMETHING SPECIAL, CATALINA. I'VE NEVER MET ANYONE LIKE YOU.

ACTUALLY, I'M NOTHING SPECIAL. THAT'S WHAT'S AMAZING.

I CAN'T PERFORM MIRACLES. I DON'T HAVE DISCIPLES. I DON'T HAVE THIS INCREDIBLE DESTINY...

...I'M REALLY JUST AN ORDINARY PERSON, AND I CAN'T STOP SMILING ABOUT IT.

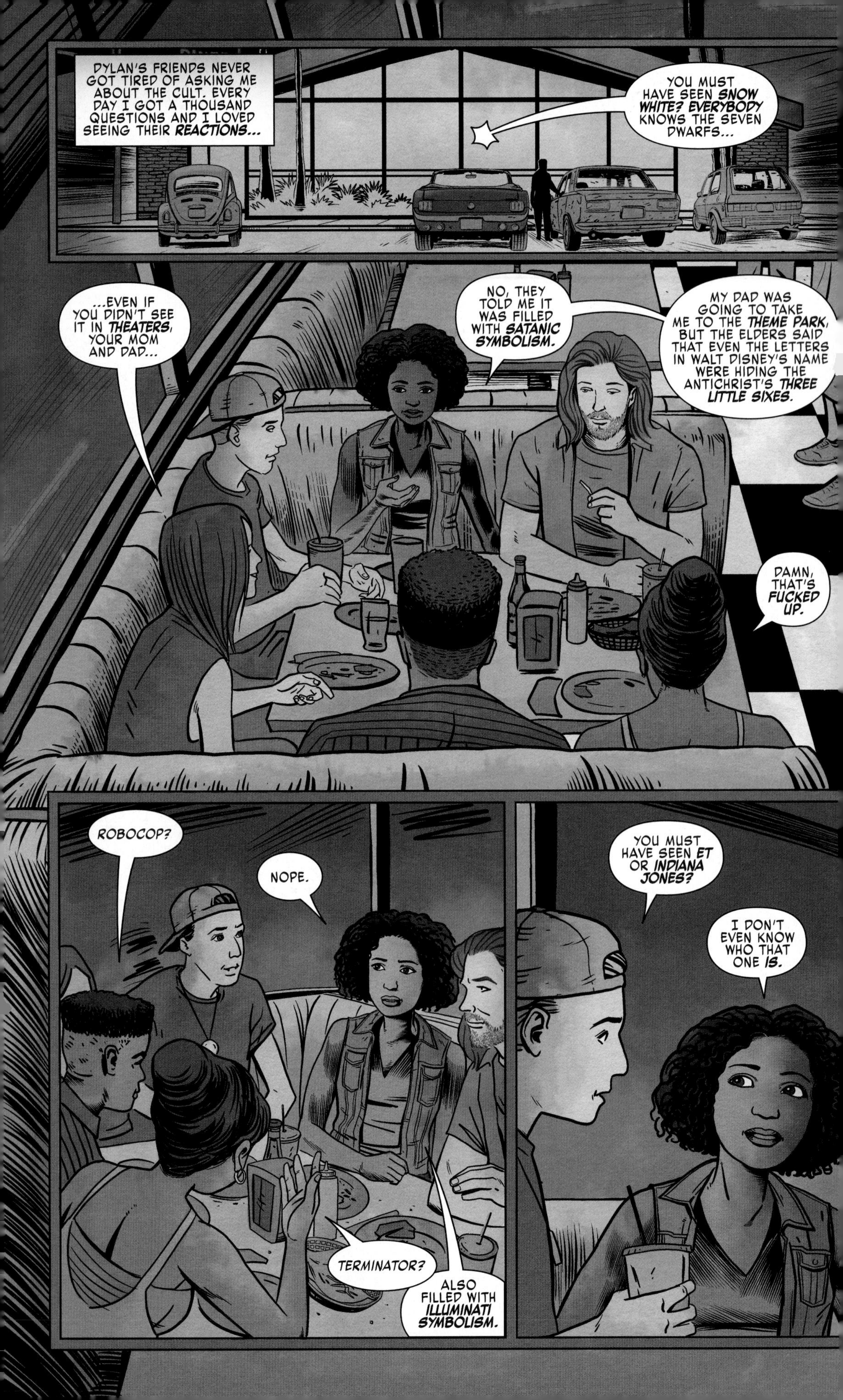
DYLAN'S FRIENDS NEVER GOT TIRED OF ASKING ME ABOUT THE CULT. EVERY DAY I GOT A THOUSAND QUESTIONS AND I LOVED SEEING THEIR REACTIONS...
YOU MUST HAVE SEEN SNOW WHITE? EVERYBODY KNOWS THE SEVEN DWARFS...
...EVEN IF YOU DIDN'T SEE IT IN THEATERS, YOUR MOM AND DAD...
NO, THEY TOLD ME IT WAS FILLED WITH SATANIC SYMBOLISM.
MY DAD WAS GOING TO TAKE ME TO THE THEME PARK, BUT THE ELDERS SAID THAT EVEN THE LETTERS IN WALT DISNEY'S NAME WERE HIDING THE ANTICHRIST'S THREE LITTLE SIXES.
DAMN, THAT'S FUCKED UP.
ROBOCOP?
NOPE.
TERMINATOR?
ALSO FILLED WITH ILLUMINATI SYMBOLISM.
YOU MUST HAVE SEEN ET OR INDIANA JONES?
I DON'T EVEN KNOW WHO THAT ONE IS.

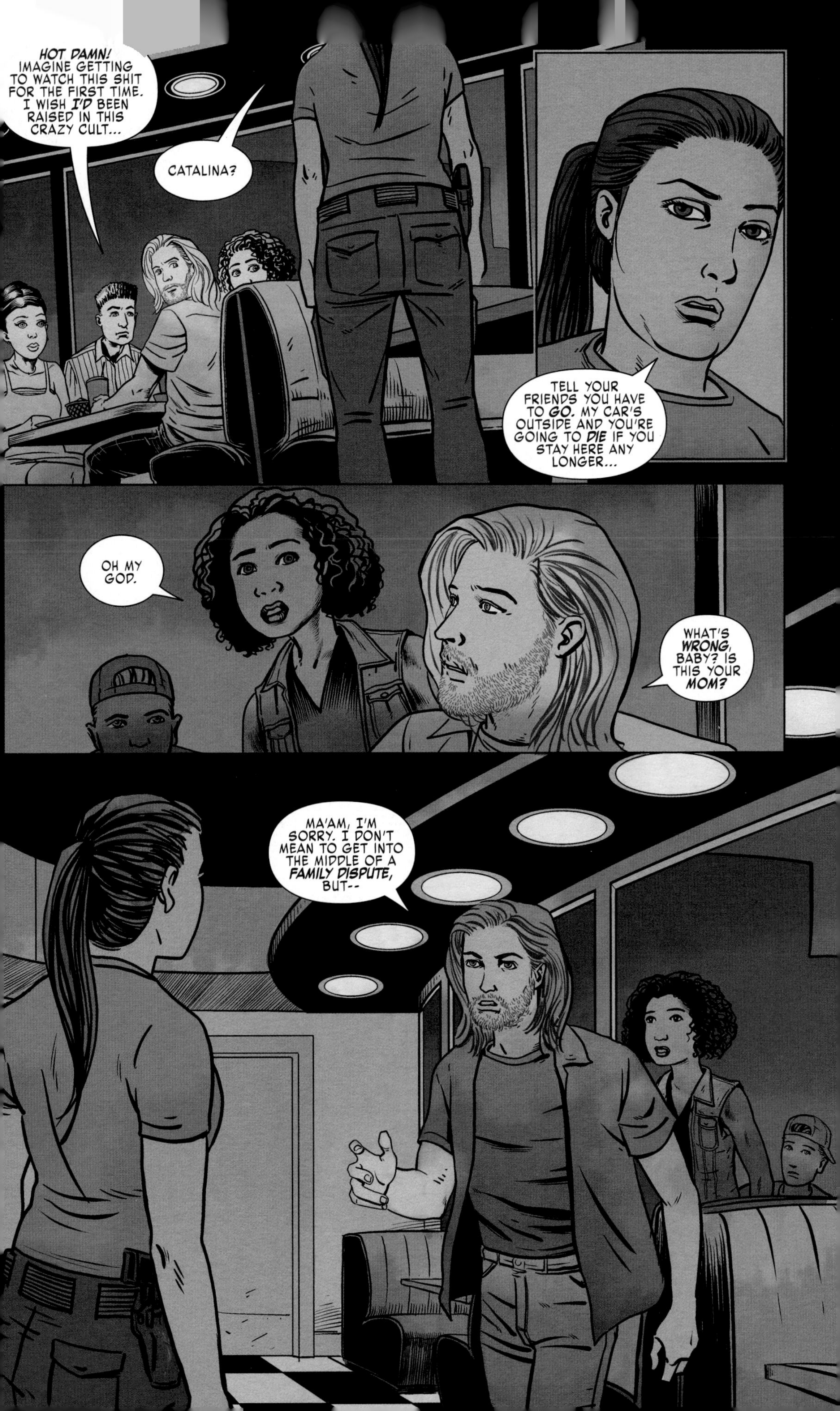
HOT DAMN! IMAGINE GETTING TO WATCH THIS SHIT FOR THE FIRST TIME. I WISH I'D BEEN RAISED IN THIS CRAZY CULT...
CATALINA?
TELL YOUR FRIENDS YOU HAVE TO GO. MY CAR'S OUTSIDE AND YOU'RE GOING TO DIE IF YOU STAY HERE ANY LONGER...
OH MY GOD.
WHAT'S WRONG, BABY? IS THIS YOUR MOM?
MA'AM, I'M SORRY. I DON'T MEAN TO GET INTO THE MIDDLE OF A FAMILY DISPUTE, BUT--

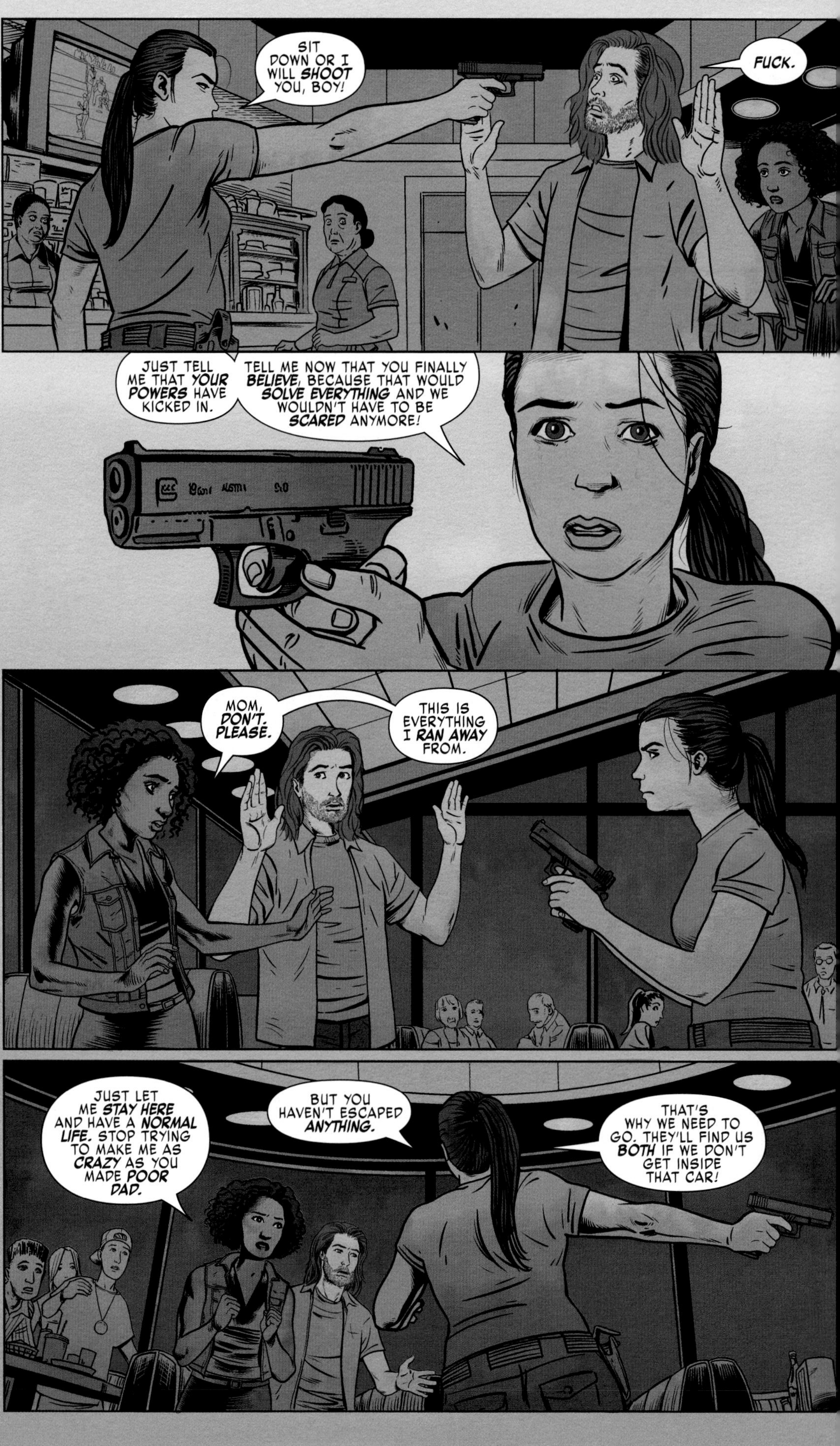
SIT DOWN OR I WILL SHOOT YOU, BOY!
FUCK.
JUST TELL ME THAT YOUR POWERS HAVE KICKED IN.
TELL ME NOW THAT YOU FINALLY BELIEVE, BECAUSE THAT WOULD SOLVE EVERYTHING AND WE WOULDN'T HAVE TO BE SCARED ANYMORE!
MOM, DON'T. PLEASE.
THIS IS EVERYTHING I RAN AWAY FROM.
JUST LET ME STAY HERE AND HAVE A NORMAL LIFE. STOP TRYING TO MAKE ME AS CRAZY AS YOU MADE POOR DAD.
BUT YOU HAVEN'T ESCAPED ANYTHING.
THAT'S WHY WE NEED TO GO. THEY'LL FIND US BOTH IF WE DON'T GET INSIDE THAT CAR!

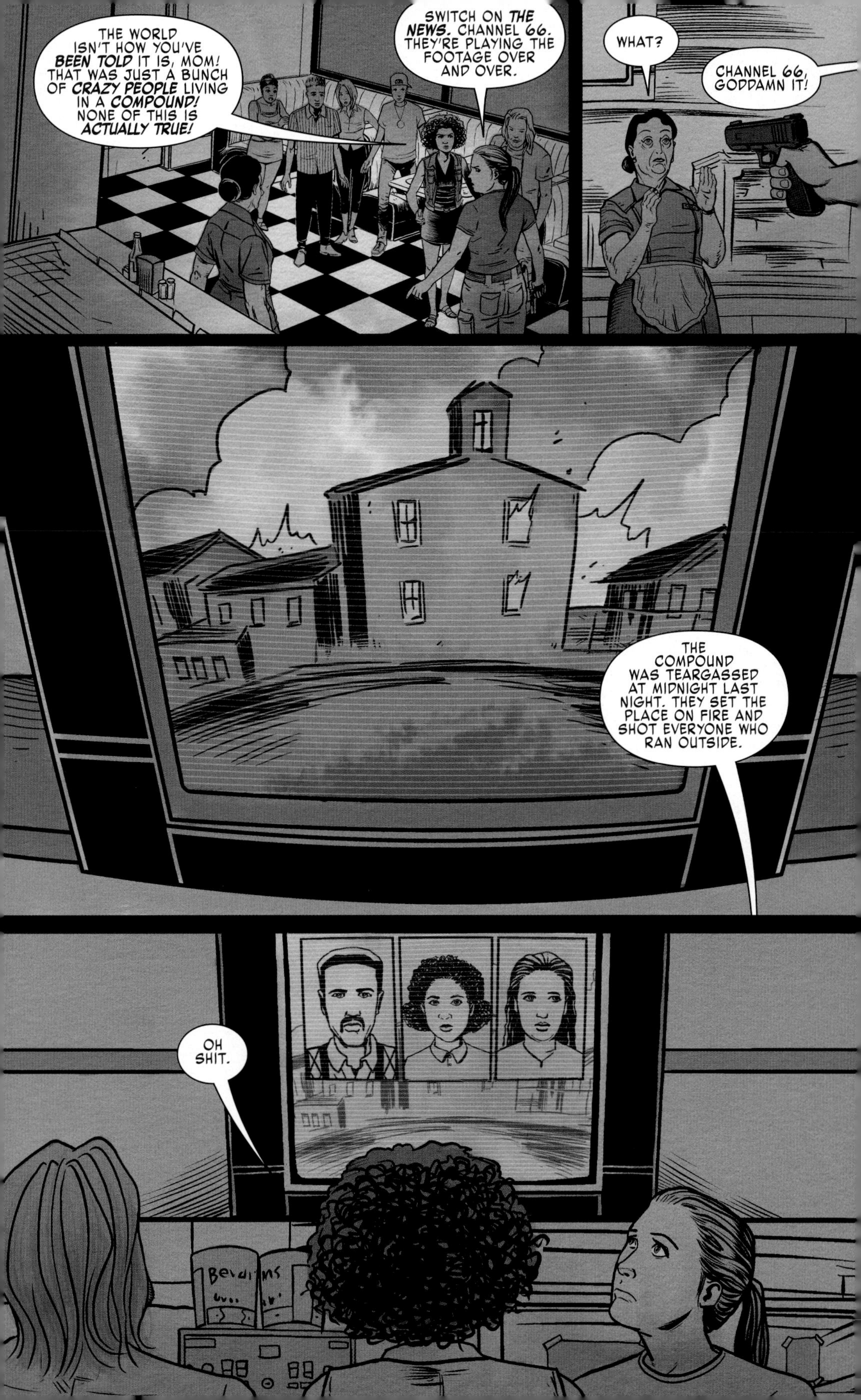
THE WORLD ISN'T HOW YOU'VE **BEEN TOLD** IT IS, MOM! THAT WAS JUST A BUNCH OF **CRAZY PEOPLE** LIVING IN A **COMPOUND!** NONE OF THIS IS **ACTUALLY TRUE!**
SWITCH ON **THE NEWS.** CHANNEL 66. THEY'RE PLAYING THE FOOTAGE OVER AND OVER.
WHAT?
CHANNEL 66, GODDAMN IT!
THE COMPOUND WAS TEARGASSED AT MIDNIGHT LAST NIGHT. THEY SET THE PLACE ON FIRE AND SHOT EVERYONE WHO RAN OUTSIDE.
OH SHIT.

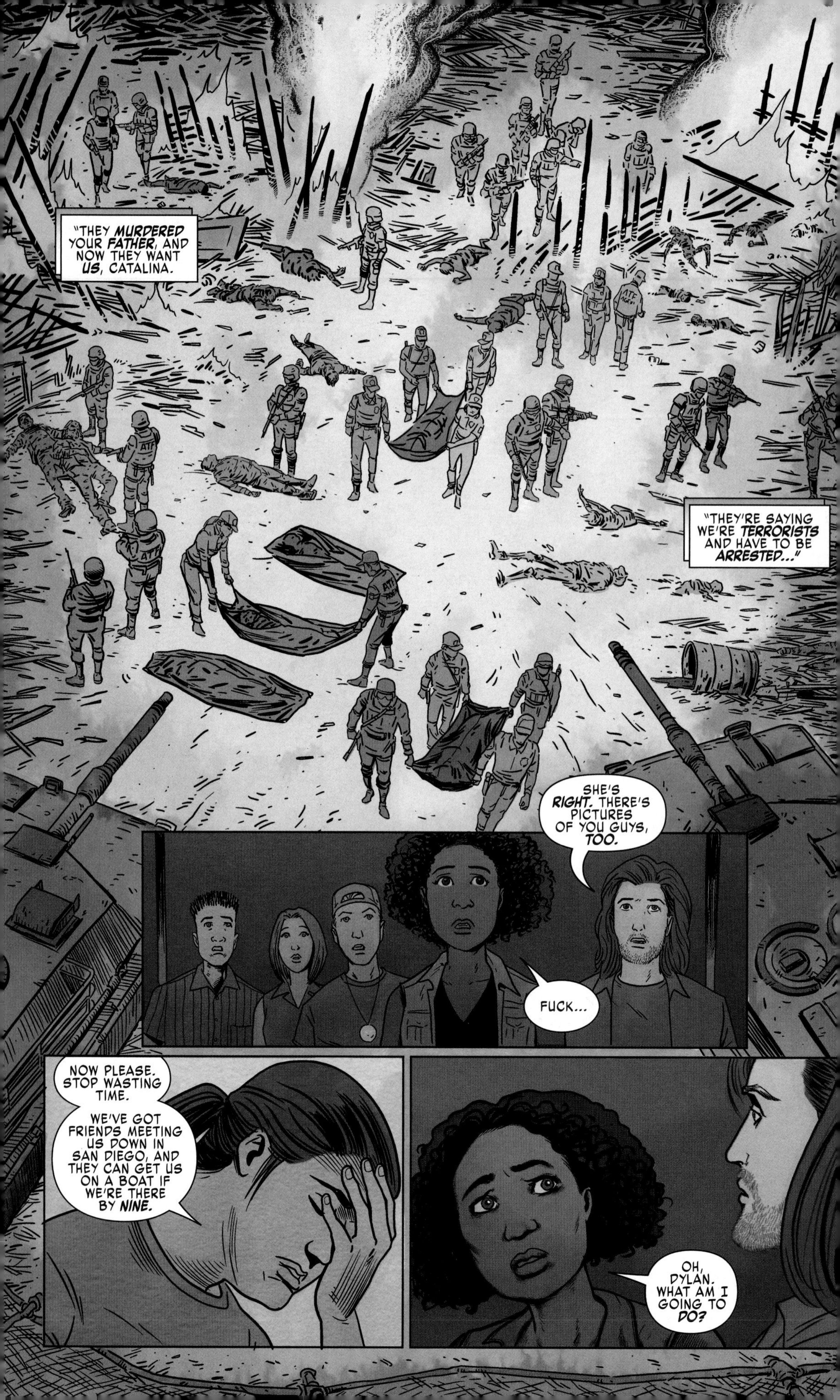
"THEY MURDERED YOUR FATHER, AND NOW THEY WANT US, CATALINA.
"THEY'RE SAYING WE'RE TERRORISTS AND HAVE TO BE ARRESTED..."
SHE'S RIGHT. THERE'S PICTURES OF YOU GUYS, TOO.
FUCK...
NOW PLEASE. STOP WASTING TIME.
WE'VE GOT FRIENDS MEETING US DOWN IN SAN DIEGO, AND THEY CAN GET US ON A BOAT IF WE'RE THERE BY NINE.
OH, DYLAN. WHAT AM I GOING TO DO?

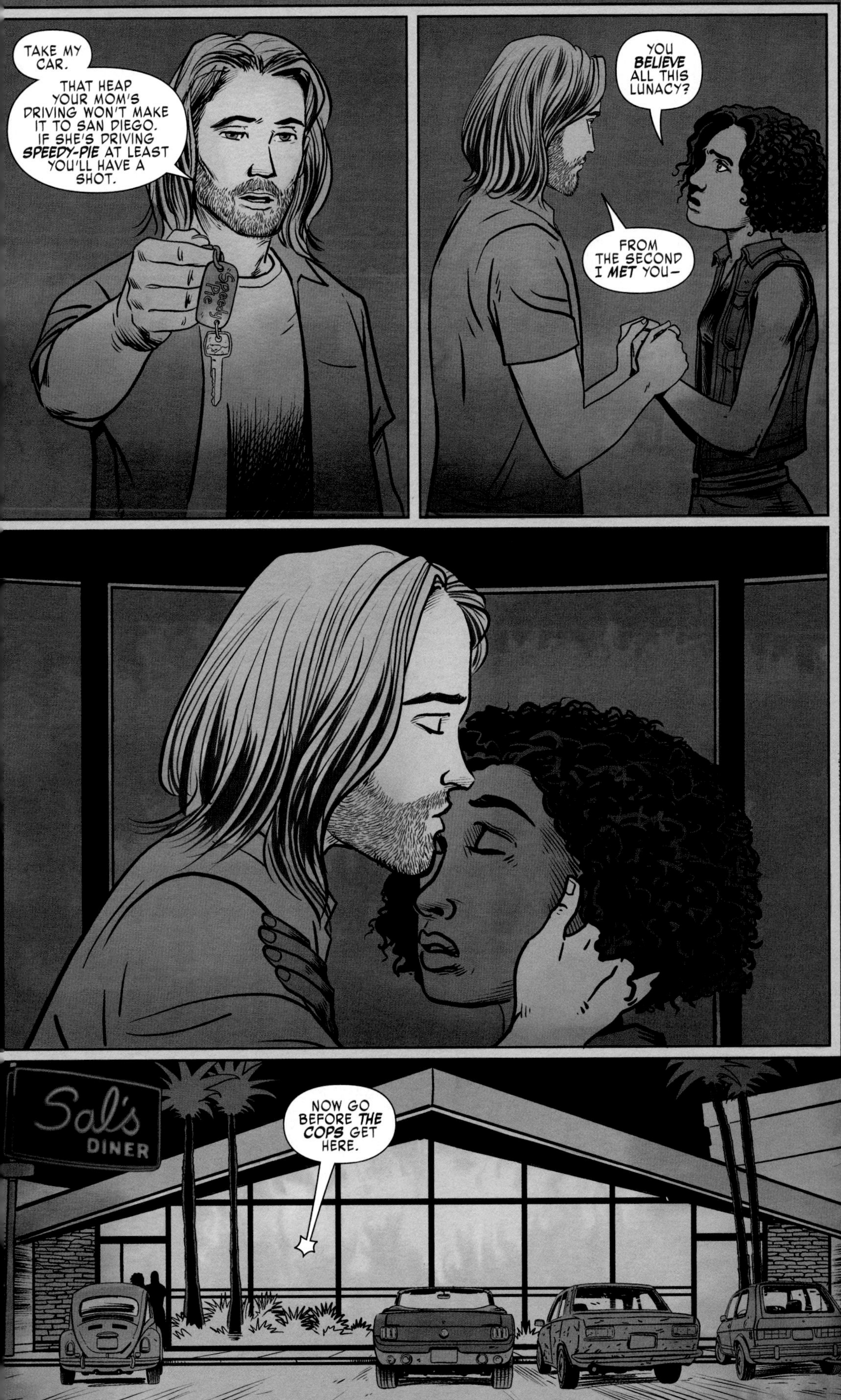

TAKE MY CAR.
THAT HEAP YOUR MOM'S DRIVING WON'T MAKE IT TO SAN DIEGO. IF SHE'S DRIVING SPEEDY-PIE AT LEAST YOU'LL HAVE A SHOT.
Speedy Pie
YOU BELIEVE ALL THIS LUNACY?
FROM THE SECOND I MET YOU—
Sal's DINER
NOW GO BEFORE THE COPS GET HERE.

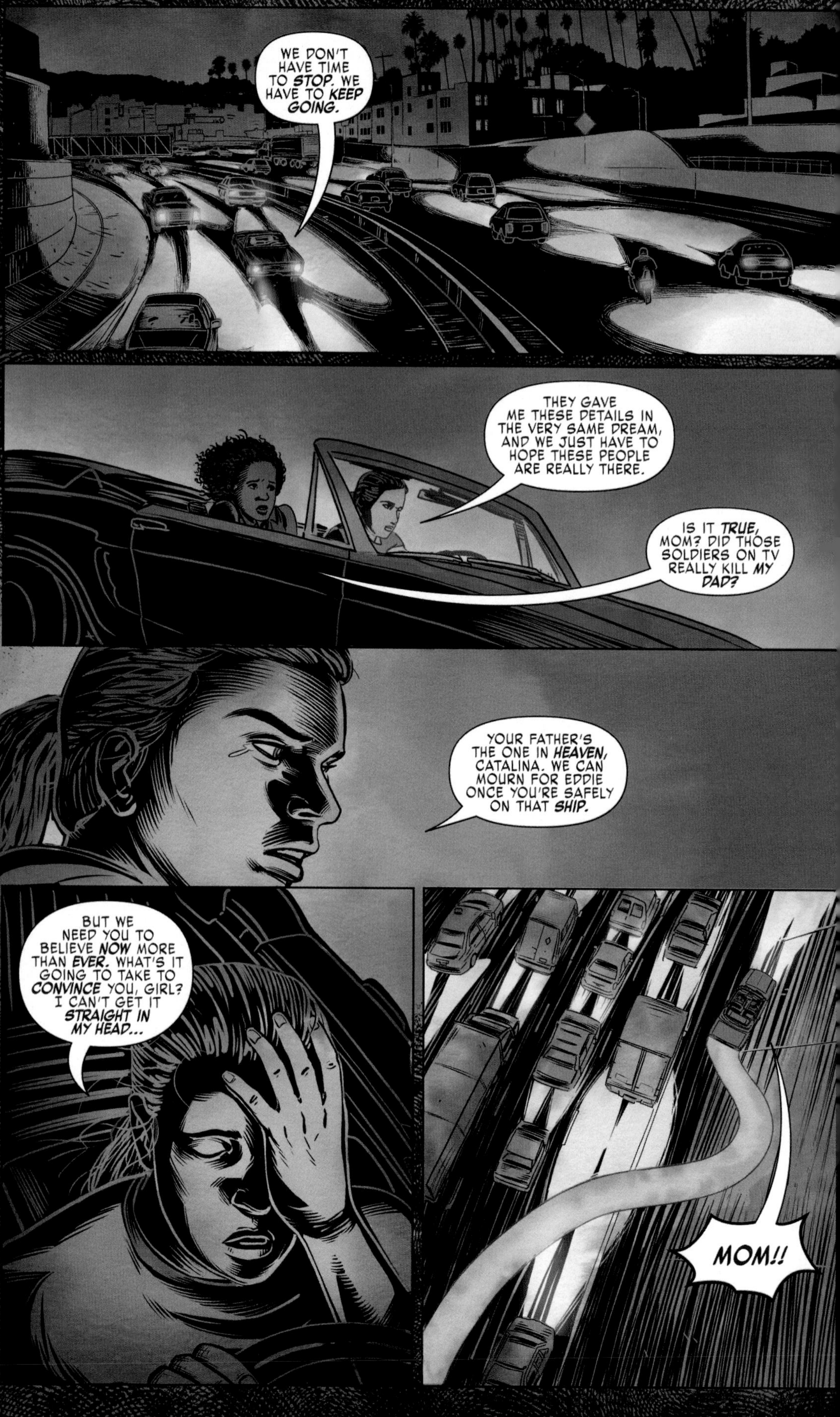
WE DON'T HAVE TIME TO STOP. WE HAVE TO KEEP GOING.
THEY GAVE ME THESE DETAILS IN THE VERY SAME DREAM, AND WE JUST HAVE TO HOPE THESE PEOPLE ARE REALLY THERE.
IS IT TRUE, MOM? DID THOSE SOLDIERS ON TV REALLY KILL MY DAD?
YOUR FATHER'S THE ONE IN HEAVEN, CATALINA. WE CAN MOURN FOR EDDIE ONCE YOU'RE SAFELY ON THAT SHIP.
BUT WE NEED YOU TO BELIEVE NOW MORE THAN EVER. WHAT'S IT GOING TO TAKE TO CONVINCE YOU, GIRL? I CAN'T GET IT STRAIGHT IN MY HEAD...
MOM!!

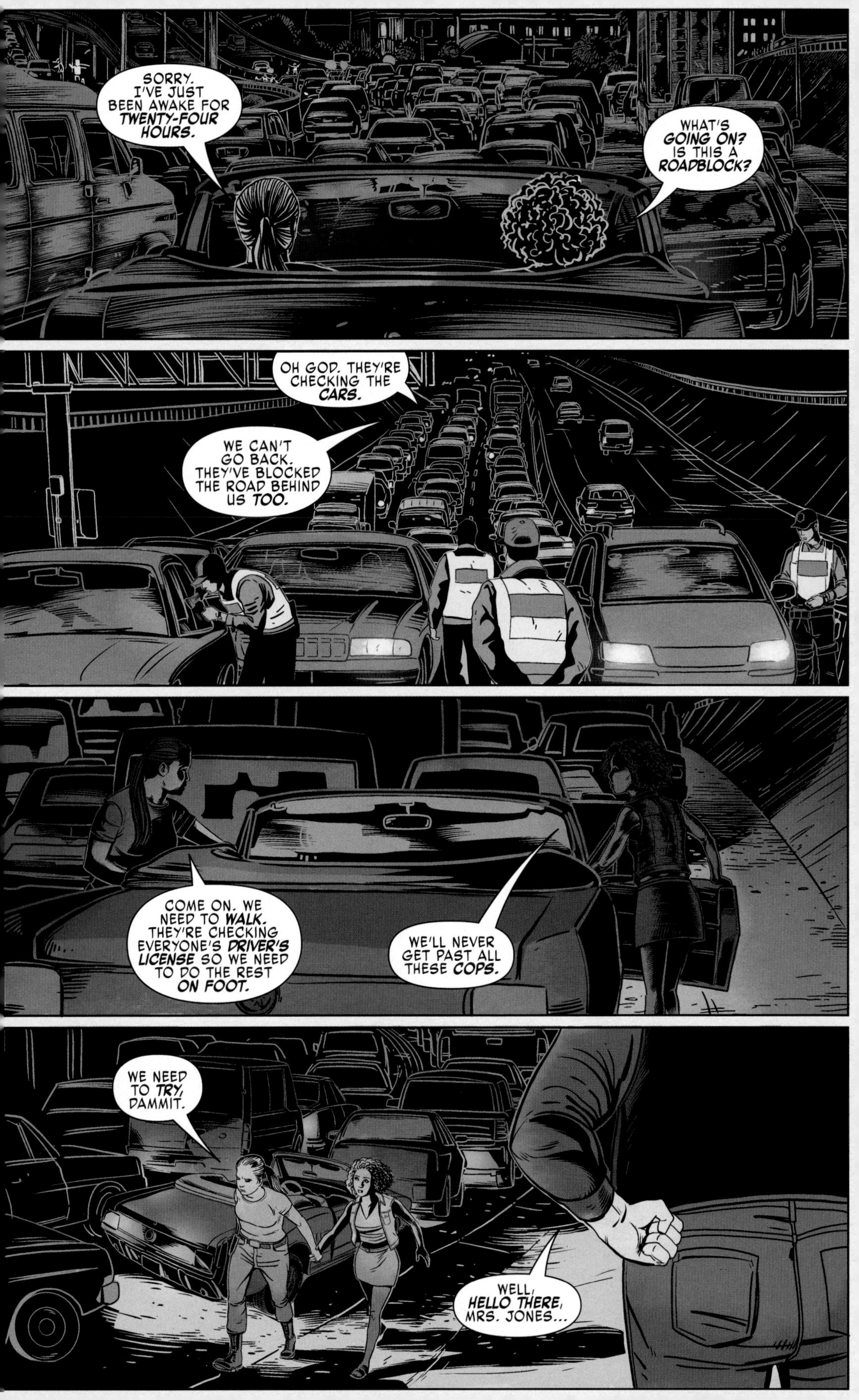
SORRY. I'VE JUST BEEN AWAKE FOR TWENTY-FOUR HOURS.
WHAT'S GOING ON? IS THIS A ROADBLOCK?
OH GOD. THEY'RE CHECKING THE CARS.
WE CAN'T GO BACK. THEY'VE BLOCKED THE ROAD BEHIND US TOO.
COME ON. WE NEED TO WALK. THEY'RE CHECKING EVERYONE'S DRIVER'S LICENSE SO WE NEED TO DO THE REST ON FOOT.
WE'LL NEVER GET PAST ALL THESE COPS.
WE NEED TO TRY, DAMMIT.
WELL, HELLO THERE, MRS. JONES...

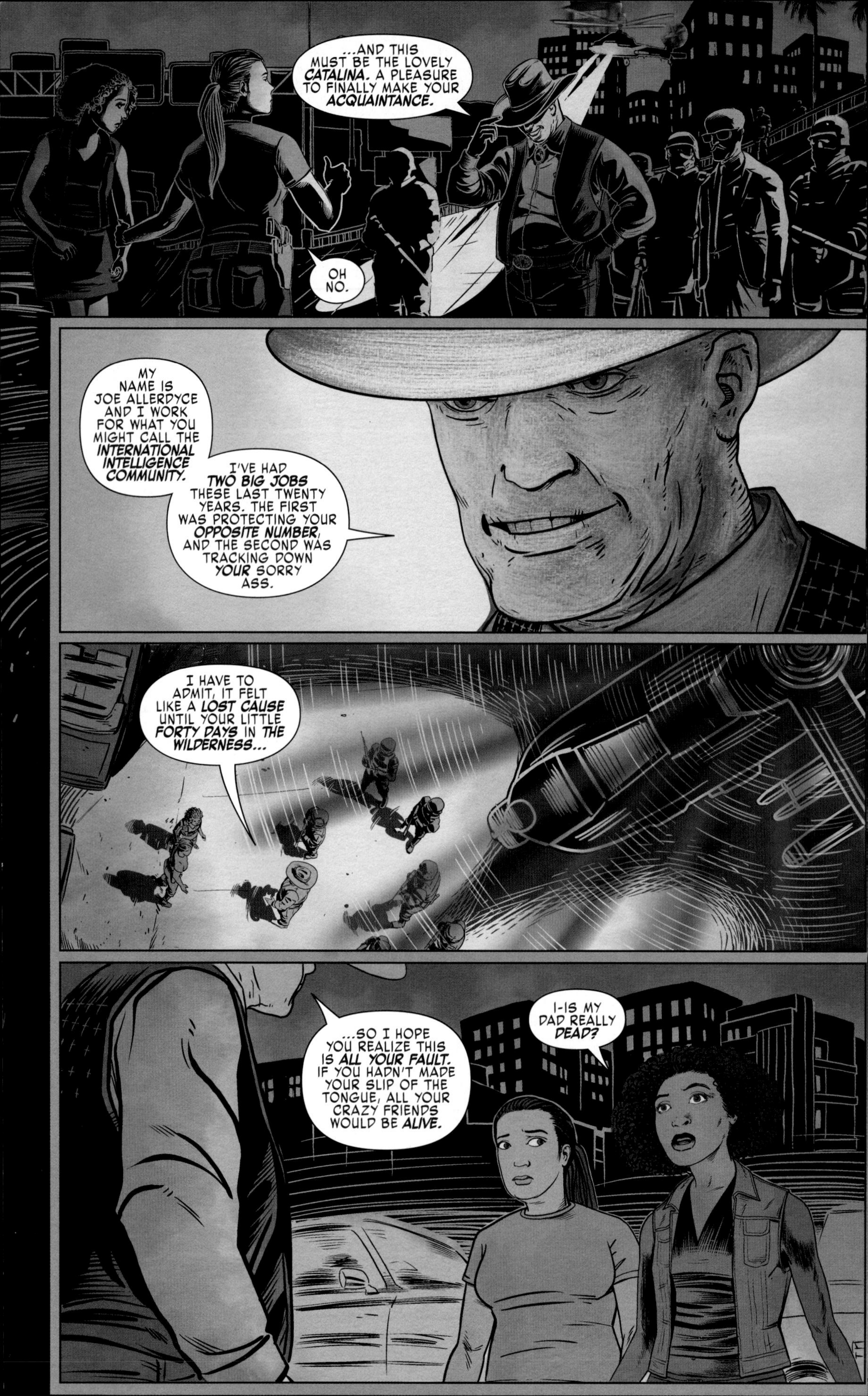
...AND THIS MUST BE THE LOVELY CATALINA. A PLEASURE TO FINALLY MAKE YOUR ACQUAINTANCE.
OH NO.
MY NAME IS JOE ALLERDYCE AND I WORK FOR WHAT YOU MIGHT CALL THE INTERNATIONAL INTELLIGENCE COMMUNITY.
I'VE HAD TWO BIG JOBS THESE LAST TWENTY YEARS. THE FIRST WAS PROTECTING YOUR OPPOSITE NUMBER, AND THE SECOND WAS TRACKING DOWN YOUR SORRY ASS.
I HAVE TO ADMIT, IT FELT LIKE A LOST CAUSE UNTIL YOUR LITTLE FORTY DAYS IN THE WILDERNESS...
...SO I HOPE YOU REALIZE THIS IS ALL YOUR FAULT. IF YOU HADN'T MADE YOUR SLIP OF THE TONGUE, ALL YOUR CRAZY FRIENDS WOULD BE ALIVE.
I-IS MY DAD REALLY DEAD?

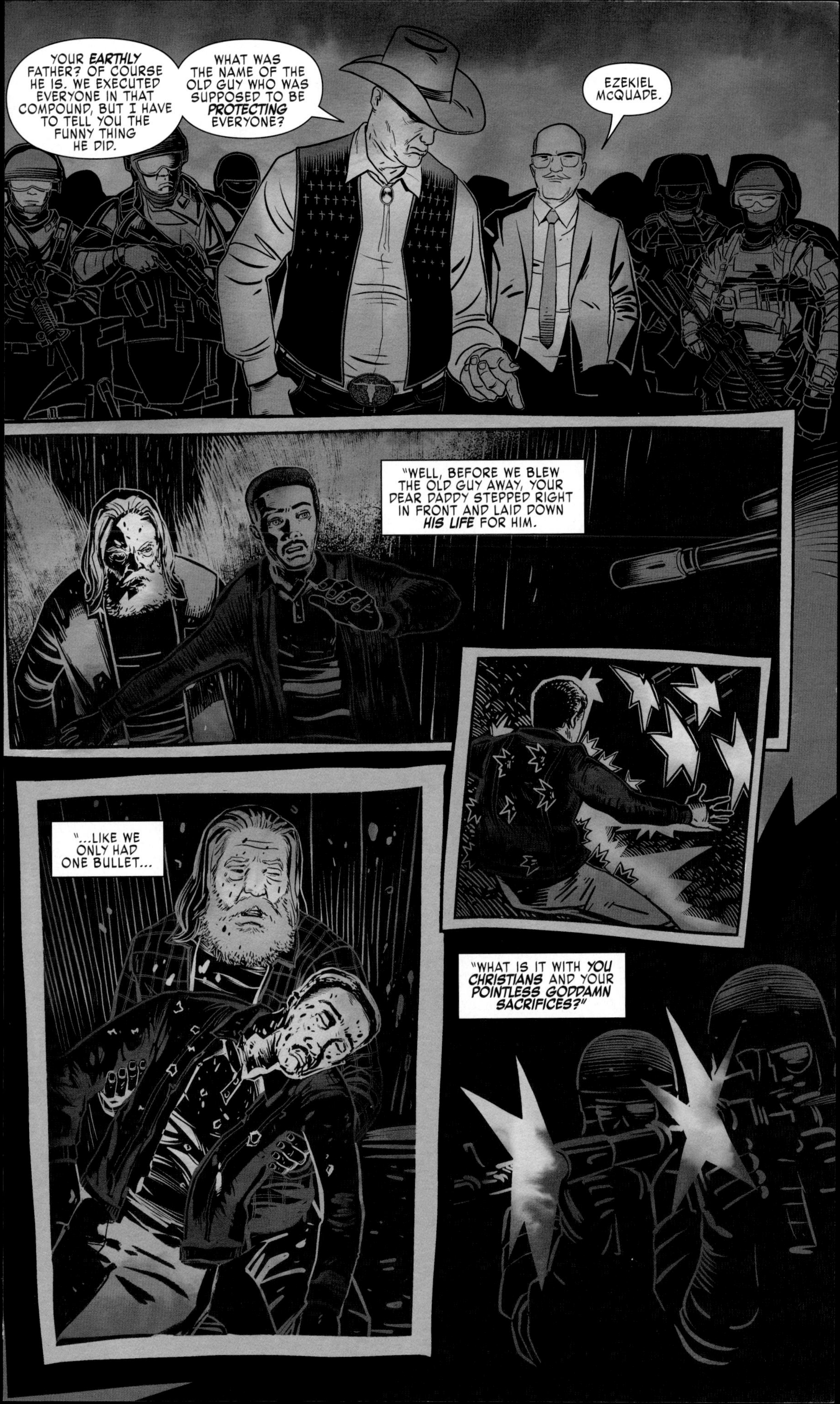
YOUR EARTHLY FATHER? OF COURSE HE IS. WE EXECUTED EVERYONE IN THAT COMPOUND, BUT I HAVE TO TELL YOU THE FUNNY THING HE DID.
WHAT WAS THE NAME OF THE OLD GUY WHO WAS SUPPOSED TO BE PROTECTING EVERYONE?
EZEKIEL McQUADE.
"WELL, BEFORE WE BLEW THE OLD GUY AWAY, YOUR DEAR DADDY STEPPED RIGHT IN FRONT AND LAID DOWN HIS LIFE FOR HIM.
"...LIKE WE ONLY HAD ONE BULLET...
"WHAT IS IT WITH YOU CHRISTIANS AND YOUR POINTLESS GODDAMN SACRIFICES?"

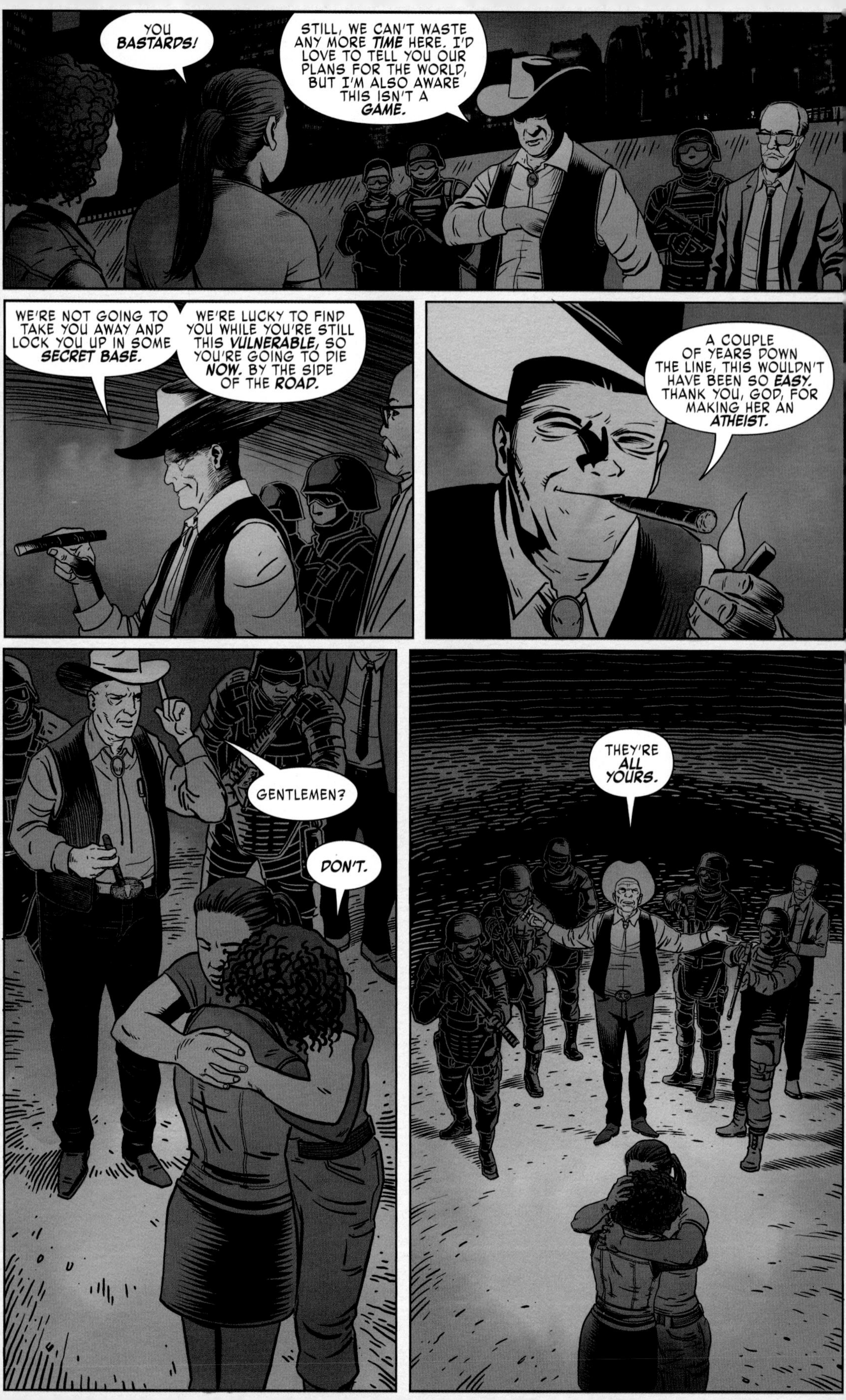
YOU BASTARDS!
STILL, WE CAN'T WASTE ANY MORE TIME HERE. I'D LOVE TO TELL YOU OUR PLANS FOR THE WORLD, BUT I'M ALSO AWARE THIS ISN'T A GAME.
WE'RE NOT GOING TO TAKE YOU AWAY AND LOCK YOU UP IN SOME SECRET BASE.
WE'RE LUCKY TO FIND YOU WHILE YOU'RE STILL THIS VULNERABLE, SO YOU'RE GOING TO DIE NOW. BY THE SIDE OF THE ROAD.
A COUPLE OF YEARS DOWN THE LINE, THIS WOULDN'T HAVE BEEN SO EASY. THANK YOU, GOD, FOR MAKING HER AN ATHEIST.
GENTLEMEN?
DON'T.
THEY'RE ALL YOURS.

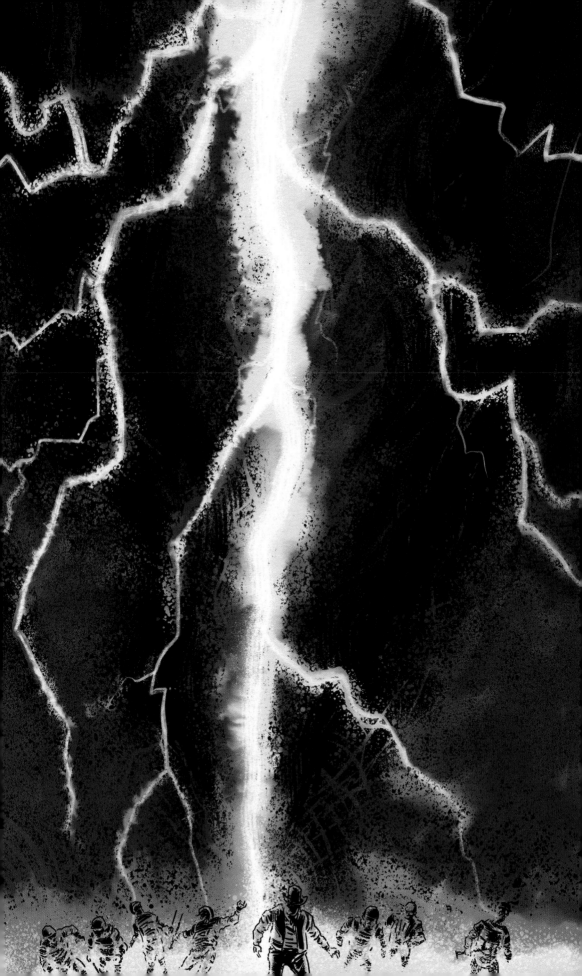

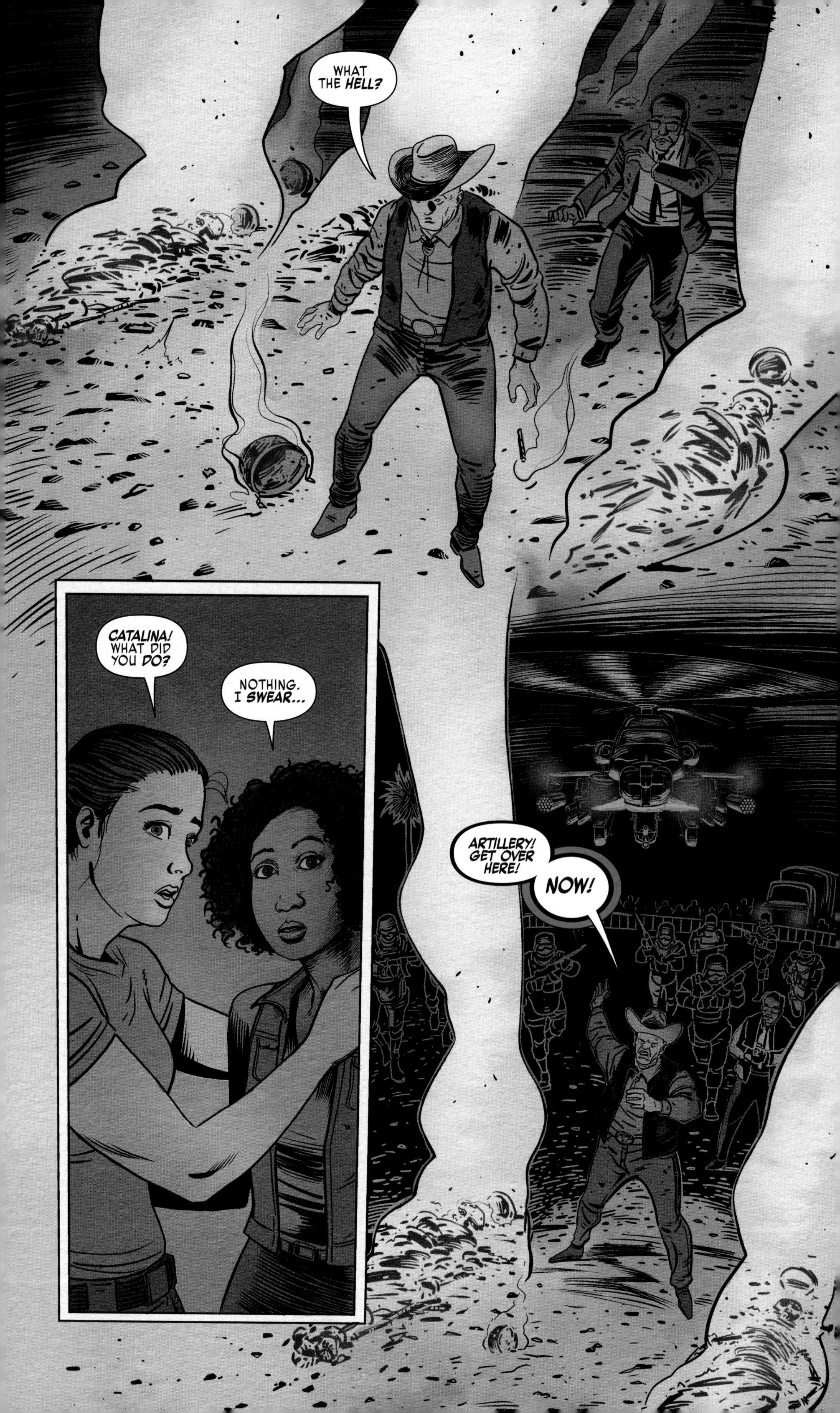
WHAT THE HELL?
CATALINA! WHAT DID YOU DO?
NOTHING. I SWEAR...
ARTILLERY! GET OVER HERE!
NOW!

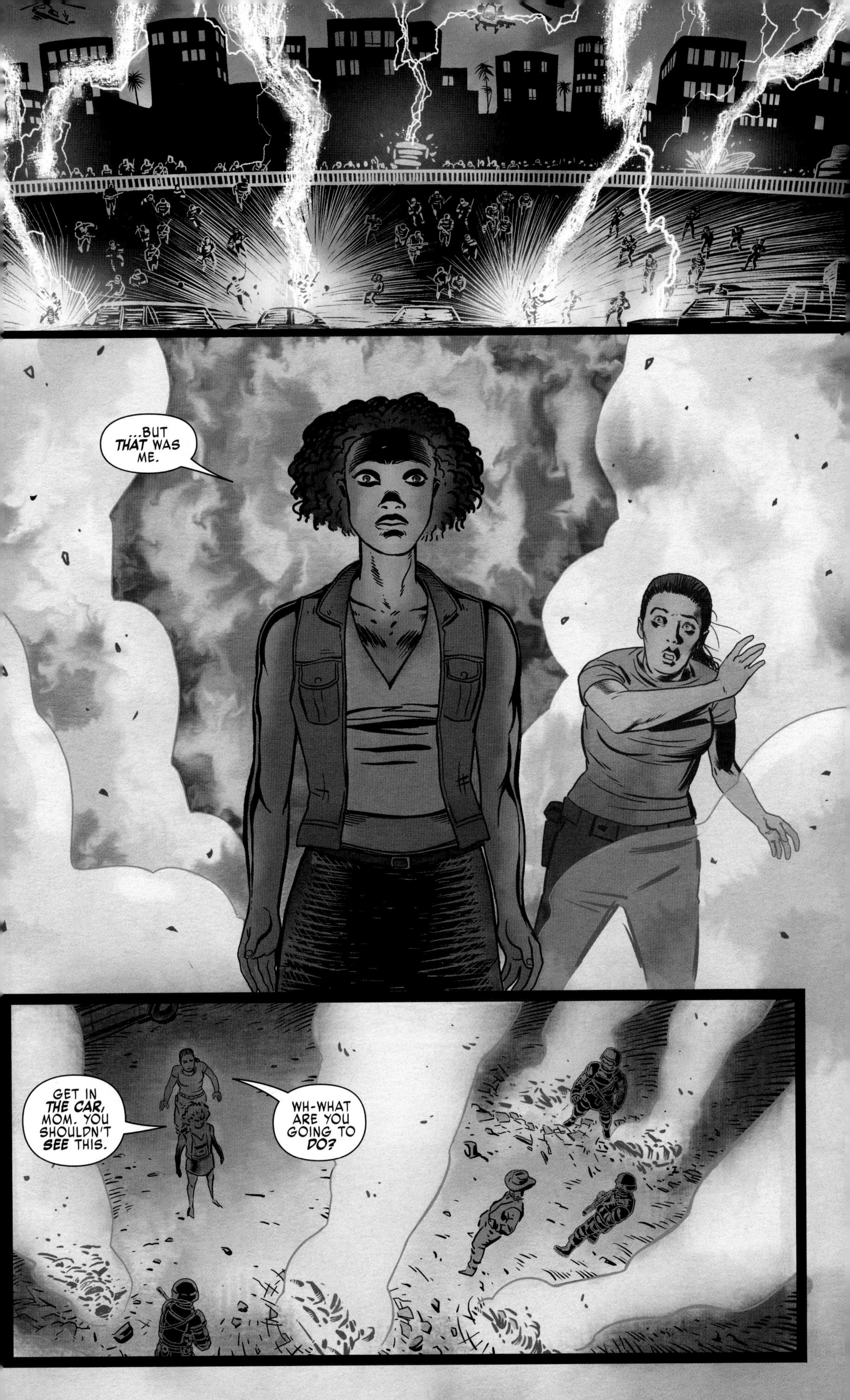
...BUT THAT WAS ME.
GET IN THE CAR, MOM. YOU SHOULDN'T SEE THIS.
WH-WHAT ARE YOU GOING TO DO?

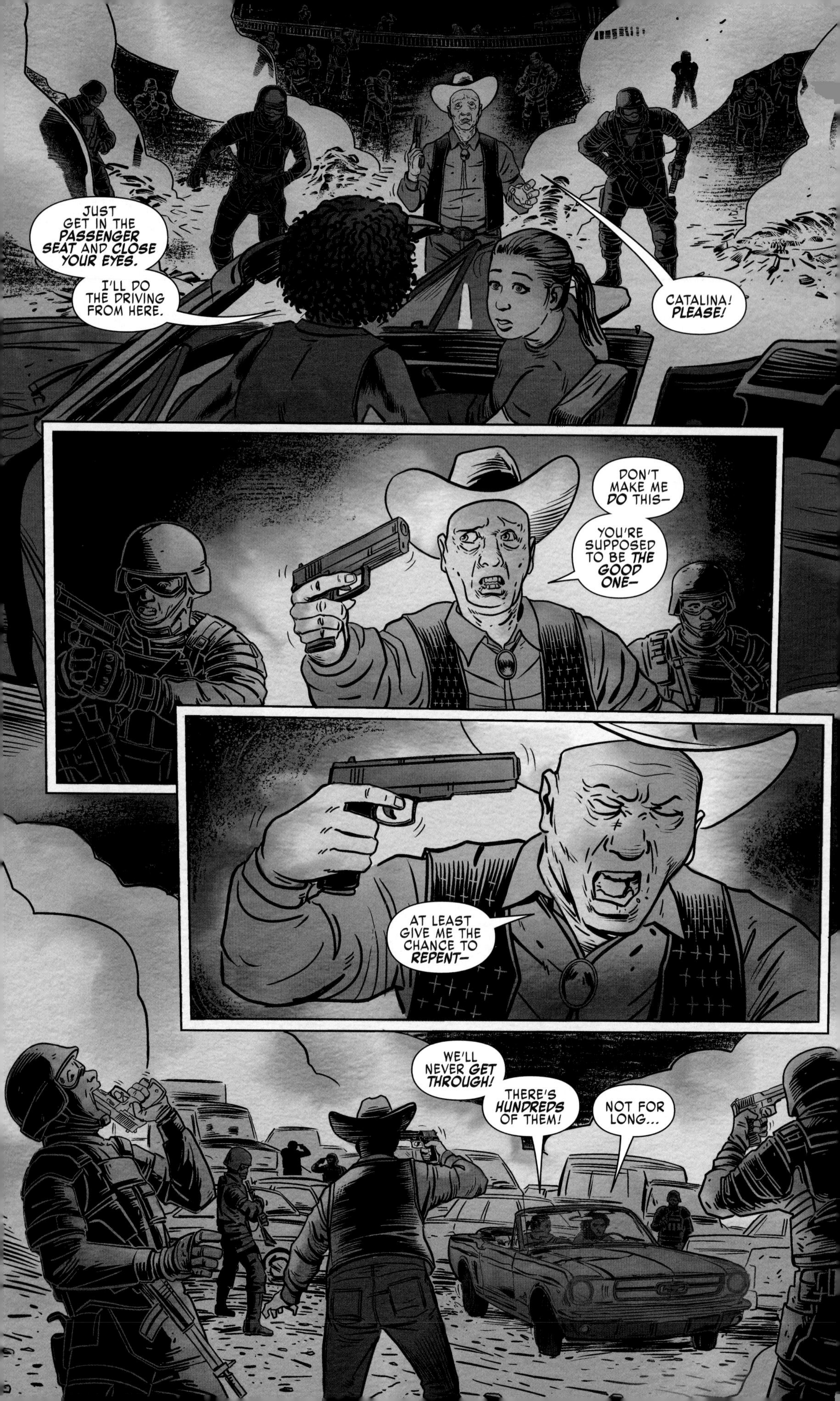
JUST GET IN THE PASSENGER SEAT AND CLOSE YOUR EYES.
I'LL DO THE DRIVING FROM HERE.
CATALINA! PLEASE!
DON'T MAKE ME DO THIS–
YOU'RE SUPPOSED TO BE THE GOOD ONE–
AT LEAST GIVE ME THE CHANCE TO REPENT–
WE'LL NEVER GET THROUGH!
THERE'S HUNDREDS OF THEM!
NOT FOR LONG...

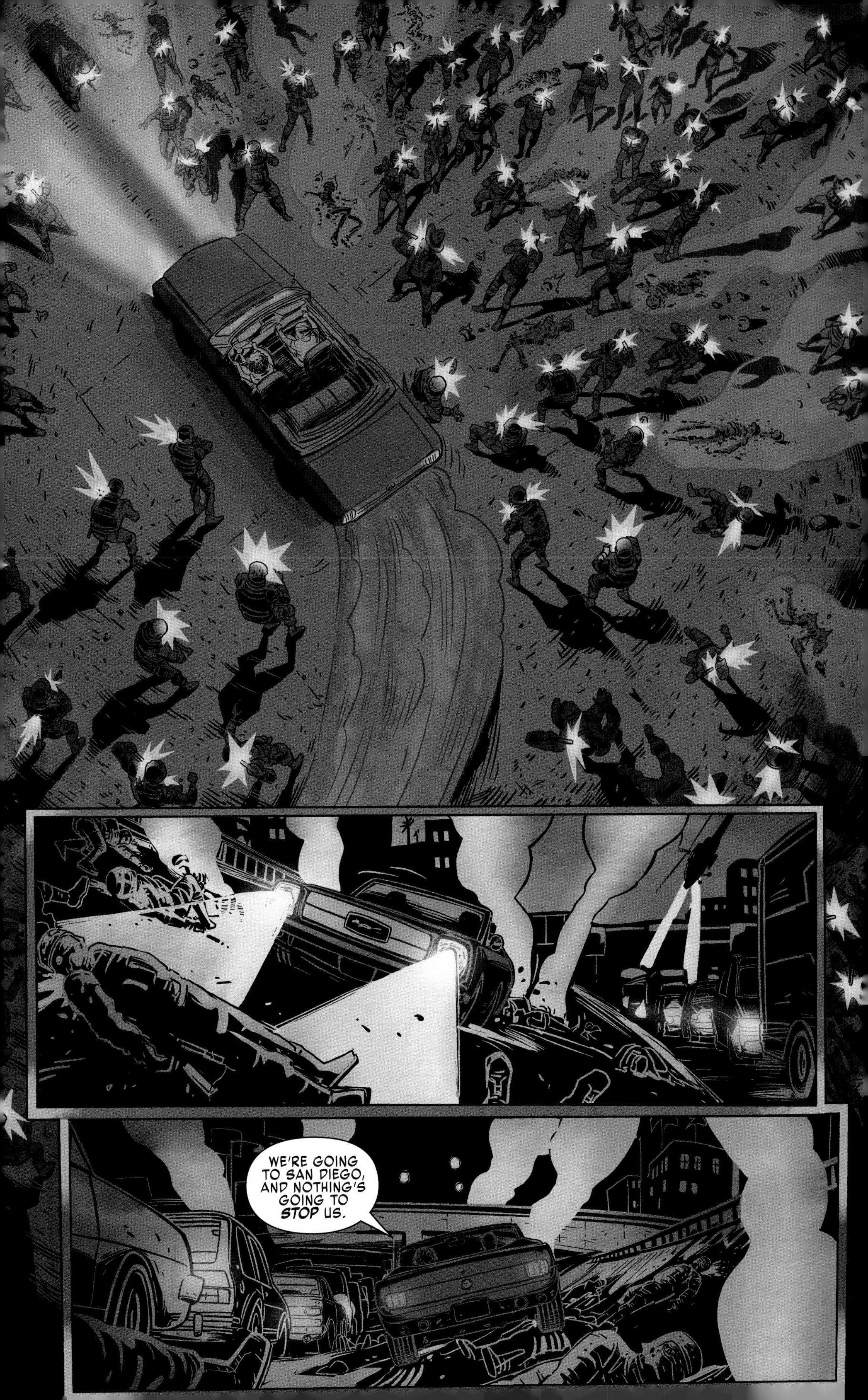
WE'RE GOING TO SAN DIEGO, AND NOTHING'S GOING TO STOP US.

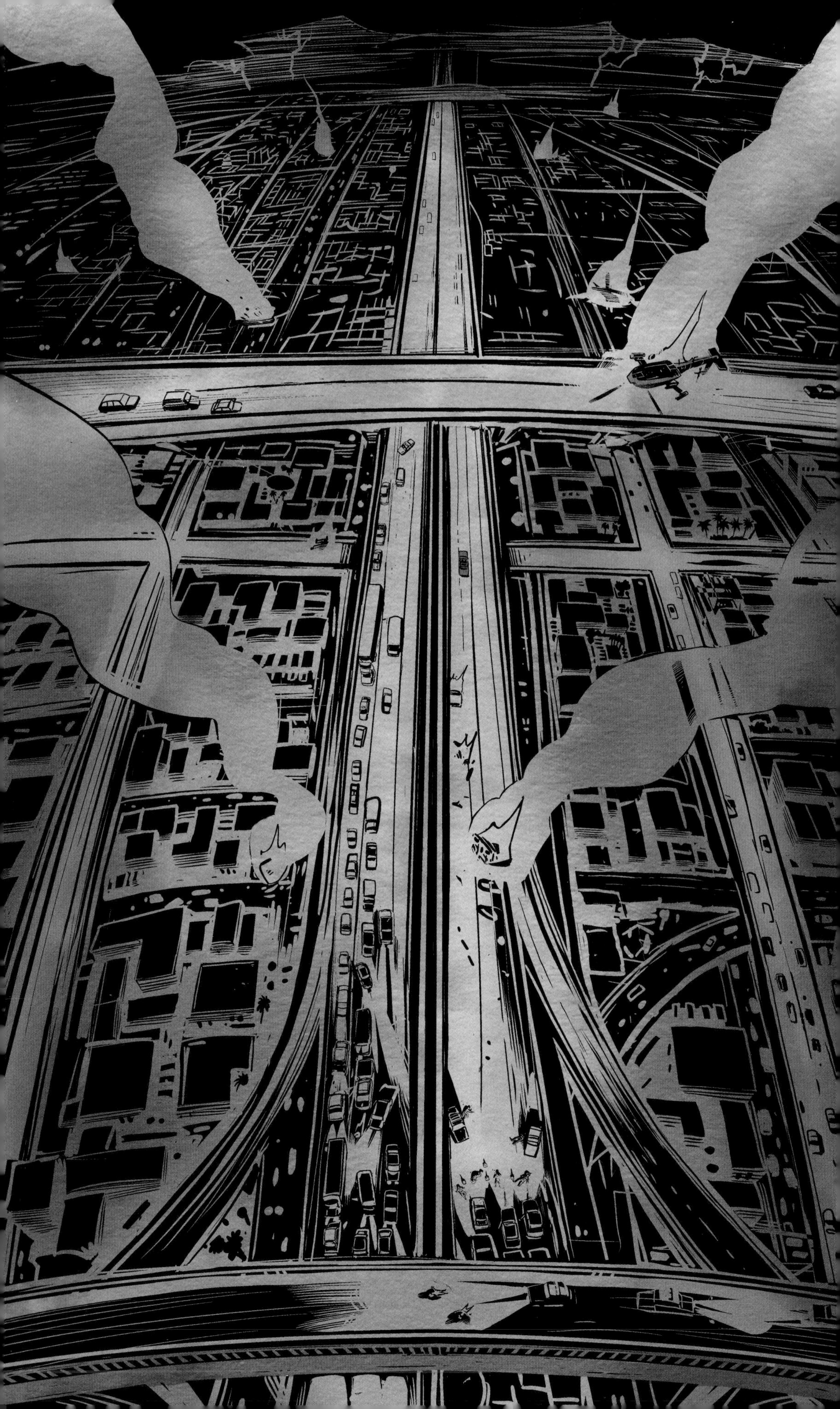

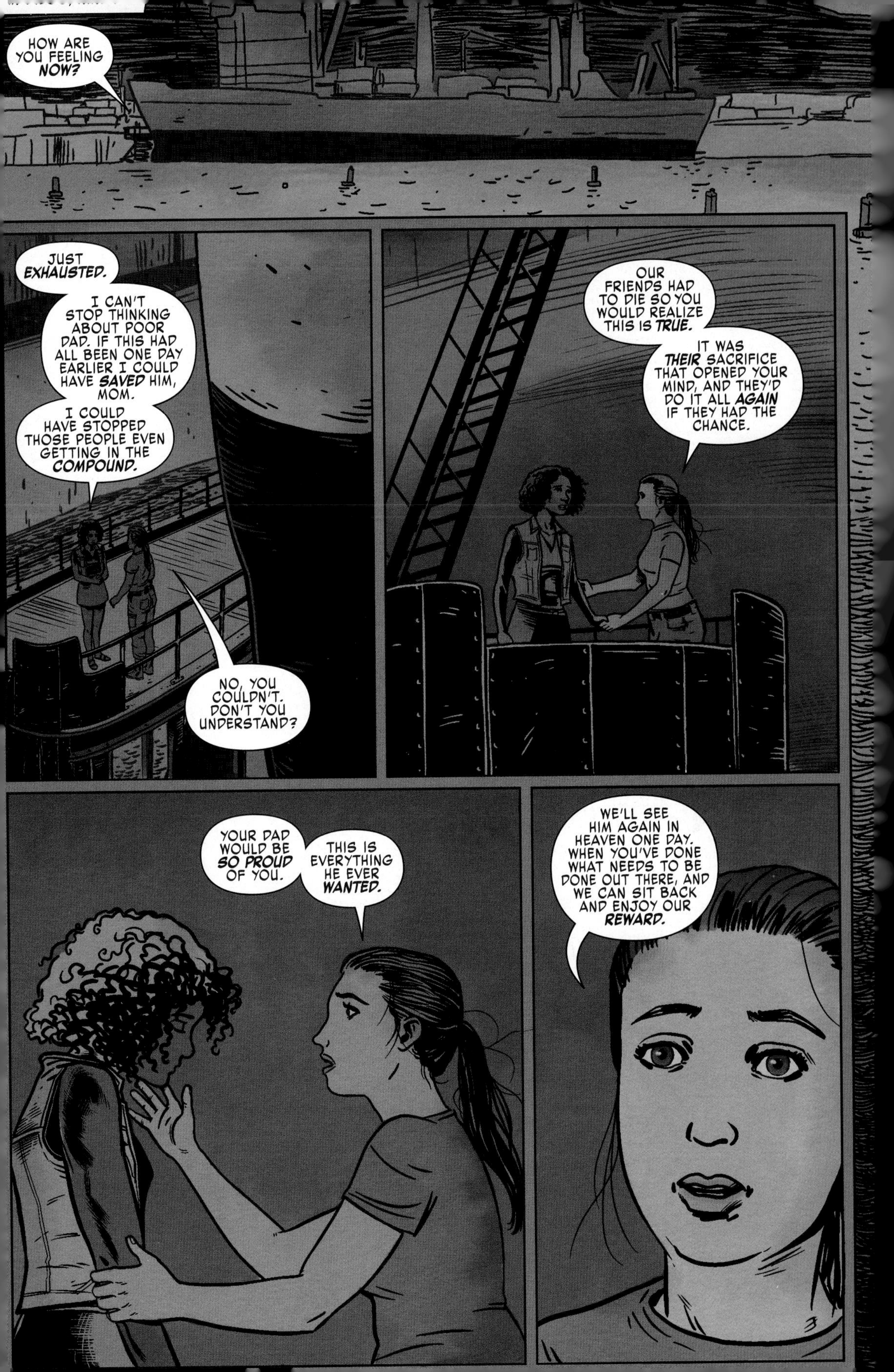
HOW ARE YOU FEELING NOW?
JUST EXHAUSTED.
I CAN'T STOP THINKING ABOUT POOR DAD. IF THIS HAD ALL BEEN ONE DAY EARLIER I COULD HAVE SAVED HIM, MOM.
I COULD HAVE STOPPED THOSE PEOPLE EVEN GETTING IN THE COMPOUND.
NO, YOU COULDN'T. DON'T YOU UNDERSTAND?
OUR FRIENDS HAD TO DIE SO YOU WOULD REALIZE THIS IS TRUE.
IT WAS THEIR SACRIFICE THAT OPENED YOUR MIND, AND THEY'D DO IT ALL AGAIN IF THEY HAD THE CHANCE.
YOUR DAD WOULD BE SO PROUD OF YOU.
THIS IS EVERYTHING HE EVER WANTED.
WE'LL SEE HIM AGAIN IN HEAVEN ONE DAY. WHEN YOU'VE DONE WHAT NEEDS TO BE DONE OUT THERE, AND WE CAN SIT BACK AND ENJOY OUR REWARD.

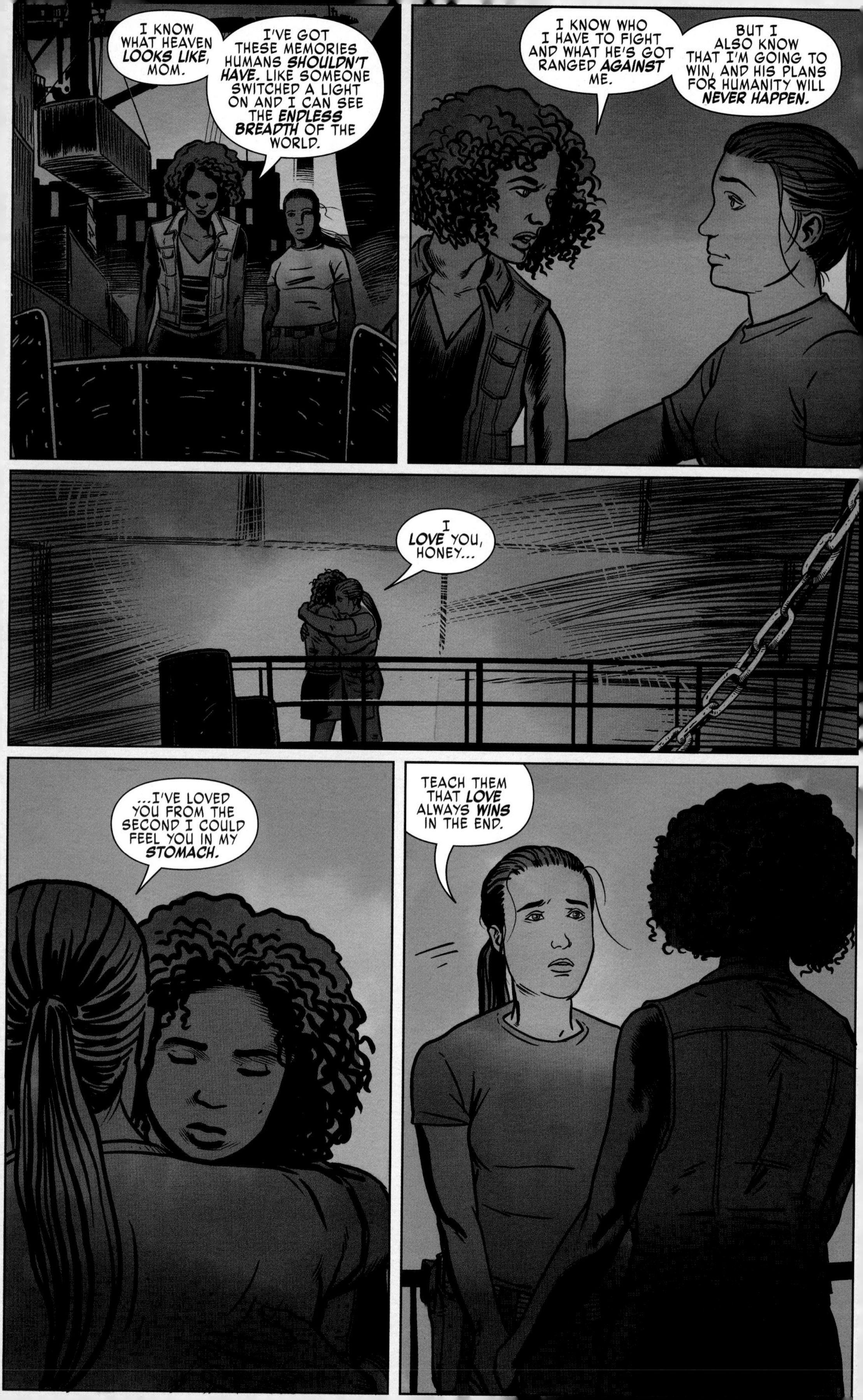

I KNOW WHAT HEAVEN LOOKS LIKE, MOM.
I'VE GOT THESE MEMORIES HUMANS SHOULDN'T HAVE. LIKE SOMEONE SWITCHED A LIGHT ON AND I CAN SEE THE ENDLESS BREADTH OF THE WORLD.
I KNOW WHO I HAVE TO FIGHT AND WHAT HE'S GOT RANGED AGAINST ME.
BUT I ALSO KNOW THAT I'M GOING TO WIN, AND HIS PLANS FOR HUMANITY WILL NEVER HAPPEN.
I LOVE YOU, HONEY...
...I'VE LOVED YOU FROM THE SECOND I COULD FEEL YOU IN MY STOMACH.
TEACH THEM THAT LOVE ALWAYS WINS IN THE END.

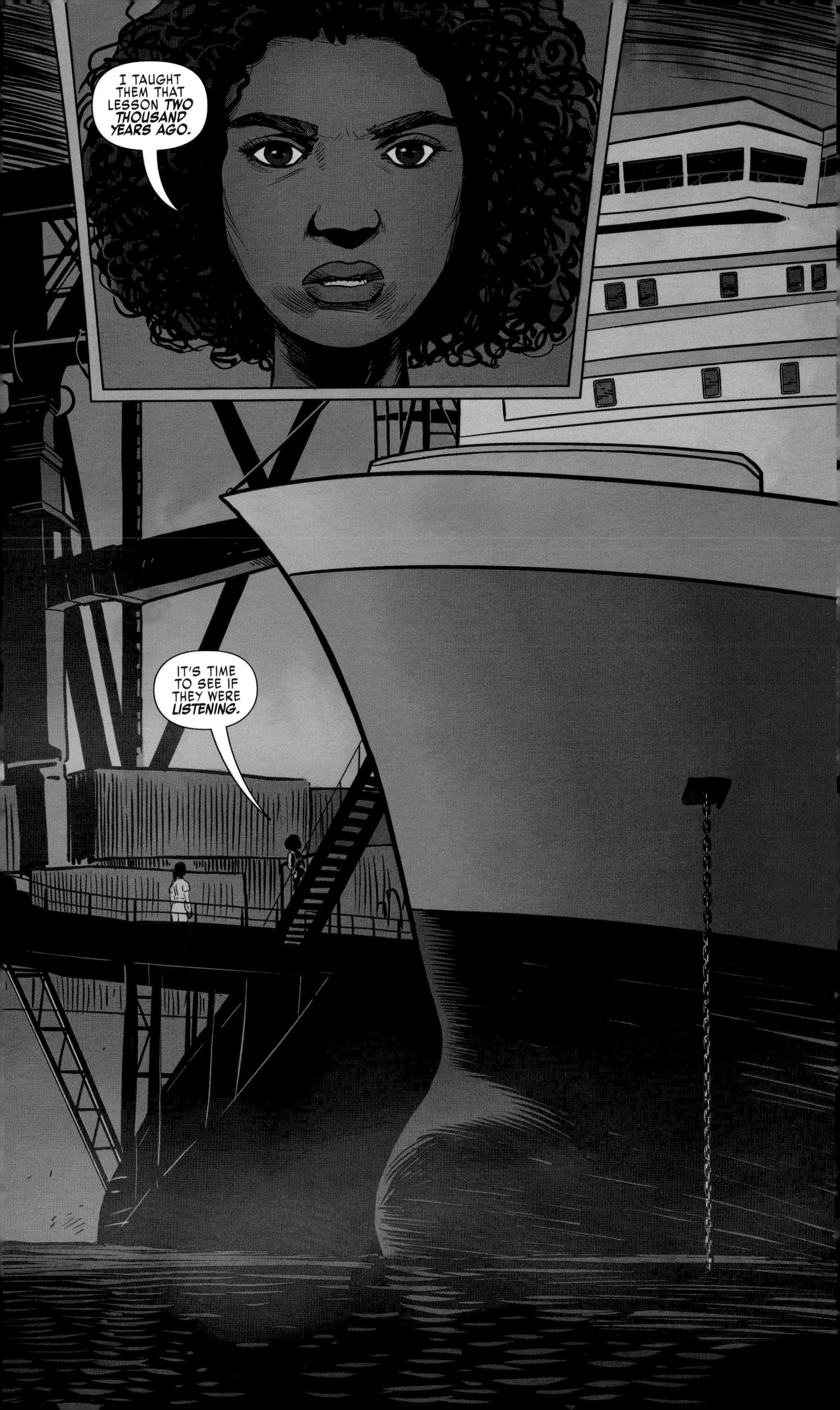
I TAUGHT THEM THAT LESSON TWO THOUSAND YEARS AGO.
IT'S TIME TO SEE IF THEY WERE LISTENING.

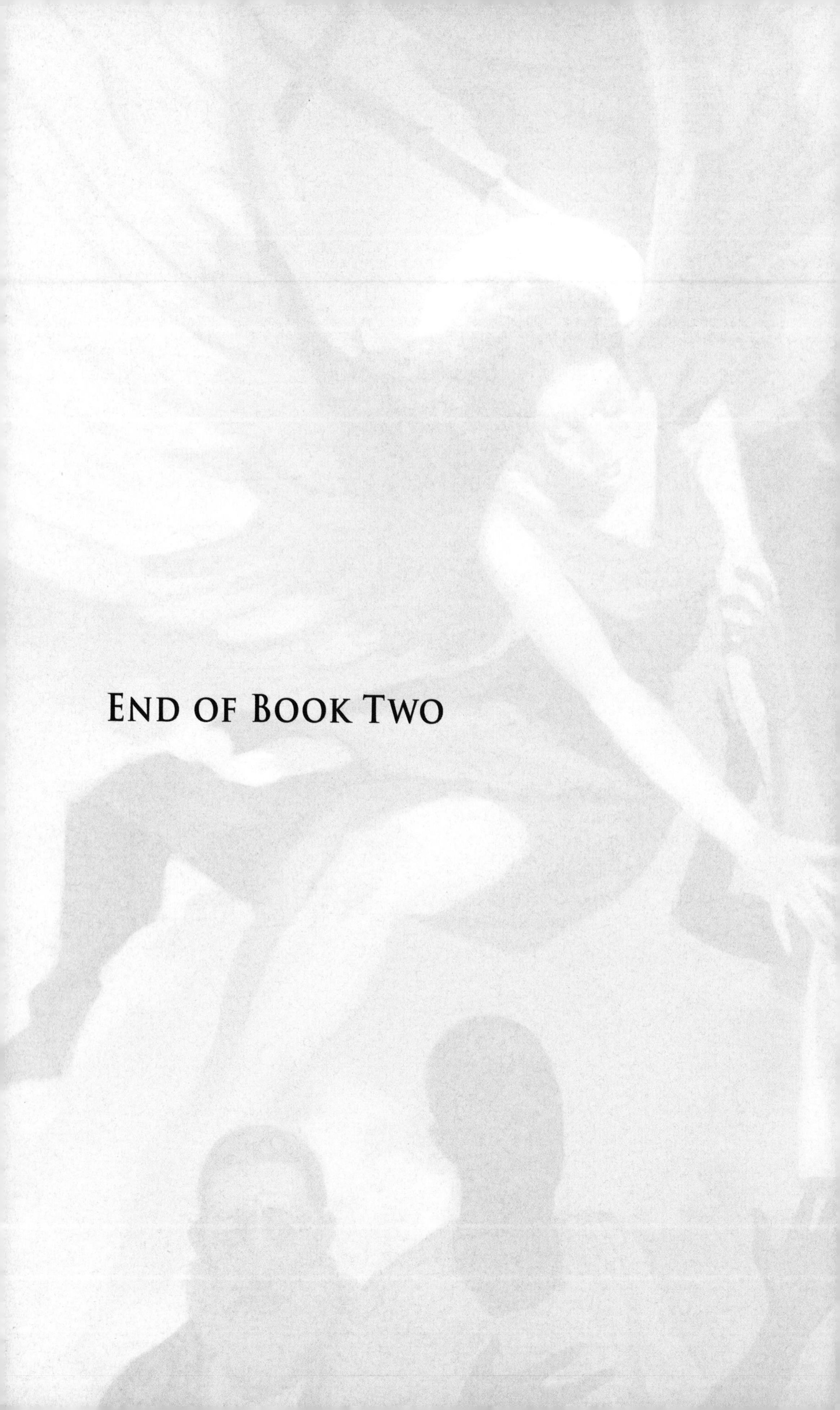

End of Book Two

FRANK QUITELY

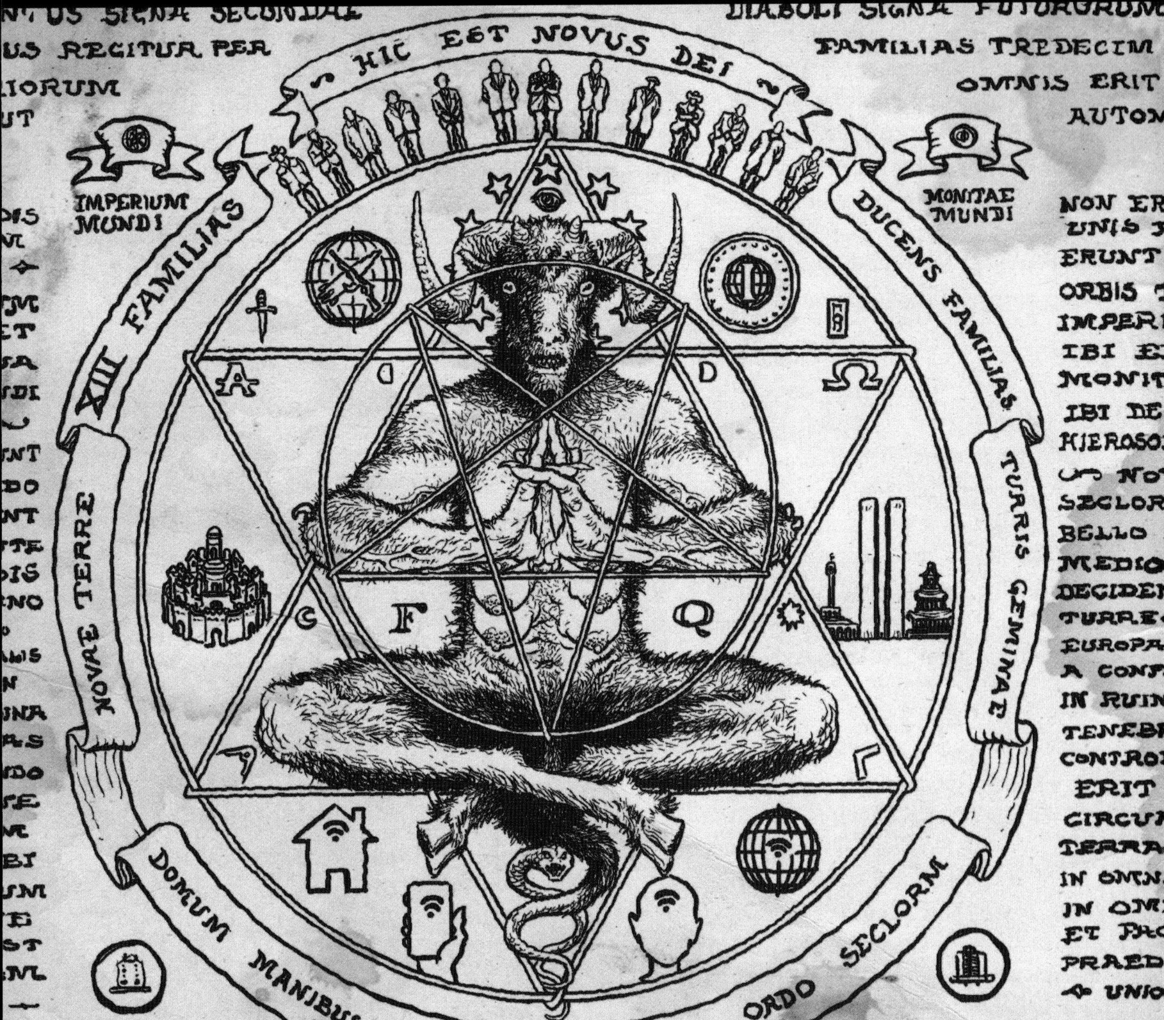

THE SECOND COMING OF MILLAR AND GROSS

Sixteen Years Later

Mark Millar: So here we are, back together again after 16 years! Did you think the sequel would ever really happen? Are you pleased we got this out there, before the REAL Jesus comes back?

Peter Gross: Somehow, I always had faith it would happen. Even when reason tried to convince me otherwise. It's been a great exercise in just being patient and waiting for something to arrive when it's meant to. On the other hand, I have no faith in the real Jesus ever making a comeback (laughs).

MM: If I learned anything from the New Testament it's never count him out! It's funny though, because the book almost happened so many times, then something else ended up happening and I kept getting distracted -- whether it was finishing The Ultimates, or starting Civil War, or disappearing and creating Millarworld. Every time I was about to write the next one I got diverted, but I'm going to call divine intervention here, because I think I subconsciously finessed the story over the years into something I was really happy with. When I was doing maths at school a teacher once gave me the most amazing advice, and it was to leave an equation you were having trouble with and jump onto the next question. When you come back half an hour later your subconscious will have solved the problem. Stories work like that too. Do you remember the various versions we discussed over the years? All the different potential takes?

PG: I love that we have Catalina in the story now, instead of two dudes, which I think was the original plan. It shows some evolution on our part, and in the zeitgeist of the world. It's amazing how much culture can change in a short time, and story choices that seem obvious now didn't come up back then. I think this is a better story for it, and I think in some ways, it's meant to be. The other thing I noticed over the course of starting this in 2004 and coming back to it in 2019 is that Conservatives were in charge during both those times. Maybe something about that gets your juices flowing for this story?

MM: Ha! That's really interesting, because I hadn't noticed that. But I have always noticed that comic books tend to do a little better in conservative administrations. W Bush and Reagan gave us characters to react against. The Clintons and the Obamas (and soft Conservatives like Ford and George HW Bush) are less cartoonish and there's more shades of grey. Alan Moore and Frank Miller were the comic-book antagonists for Thatcher and Reagan, and I don't think that's an accident. That's a really good point. Catalina, by the way, was something I'd been mulling over for a while because I wanted to play around with preconceptions, but I worried it was a little too obvious in a way. Like that old story where a man wakes up from dying on the operating table and when he's asked what God looked like he tells everyone she's black. I didn't know if in some ways going the traditional biblical route would be the more surprising, but it was Leopoldo Gout (the producer of the Netflix show) who talked me into choosing the Catalina option over a very long call between Scotland and New York, where

he's living now. In hindsight, I think he was absolutely right and I know it's the direction he has planned for the show too, though he wants to make that section of the story more global and set her on a different continent entirely from what we've done here.

PG: I'm dying to see how the show will be different from the comic—and it's interesting that it was talking with Leopoldo that crystallized Catalina for you. I like that the synergy between the show and the comic affect each other, but they'll both be their own things. Over the years, working with different writers, I've developed the ability to work on stories without knowing what the end is going to be. It keeps me interested in them as I work on them, even though I have to walk the line of knowing enough to not screw something up in the art. I was totally surprised when I found out who Jodie really was in the first volume of American Jesus, and I'm totally clueless what's going to happen in Volume 3 when Catalina and Jodie face off against each other. I'm expecting some twists and turns there. But my point is, I try to balance being an insider creator and audience member at the same time, so I can use that perspective, which is essentially different than the writer's perspective -- assuming *you* know where the story is going next! (laughs). I even sort of intentionally forget upcoming things that I may have been told. Probably frustrating to a writer when the artist can't seem to remember some big far-off plot point.

MM: That's hilarious. I didn't know that. There's a very famous comic artist I know who doesn't read the dialogue in the actual scripts he's drawing so he can still be surprised when he gets the book in the store (laughs.) This blew my mind because relying on panel descriptions alone means you miss all the nuance from dialogue, but he didn't seem to have a problem with it and, weirdly, no readers have ever complained. As a writer, I used to make a plot up as I went along for the same reason, that idea of being constantly surprised, but working in film taught me how great it is to have your structure all worked out in the most watertight way so I do everything on a board now and just break the whole story down over however many issues I need. It makes the job so much easier and the endings always work out great this way too, because you can reverse engineer everything you need. For example, in this particular volume we needed a getaway car for the girls and this let me set up Speedy Pie in issue two and a driving lesson for Catalina in issue three. I knew I wanted Eddie to make the sacrifice that made Catalina realize her true potential, and so I knew I wanted to get the little moment in at the beginning of the issue when it says the crucifix is simultaneously the greatest failure and the greatest sacrifice in Christian history, depending on your perspective. Interestingly, our first book (Chosen) was one of the few occasions back in the old days where I knew the ending before I knew the opening, and I think that's why it's so well put together. The third and final volume, I literally have the opening and closing scenes, everything else is a little more amorphous, before I stand at my big board for two weeks and block it all out.

PG: Back in the olden days of comics when I first started at DC and pages were still lettered on the art boards, I got some pages to ink where the letterer had lettered the wrong pages of script onto art that clearly didn't fit. There were balloons pointing to nowhere! The pages were basically ruined and had to be re-inked on vellum. When I was inking some highly detailed and very light pencilled pages by Phil Jimenez, the letterer would pencil in his guidelines. Letter, then erase the lines and accidentally erase some of the surrounding art. I had to guess some of it. We've come a long way. And despite my desire as an artist to remain clueless, whenever I'm writing or collaborating on the story plotting, I love knowing what the endings and the major beats are, and then let the story surprise you on the way. My most favorite thing is when a character takes over and determines his or her own path through to that end—or even demands a different twist to the ending. It's like they have a life and will of their own.

MM: That's the maddest thing I've ever heard in my life. That's more like doing a jigsaw! I know what you mean about the characters leading the way. Sometimes you have to switch off and use The Force. The plot is your entire map, but only when it's being guided by the character. I love sitting plotting, it's the most rewarding part of the job, but if the character is being forced into a scene or to act a certain way it all falls apart. Usually sitting drawing the character for a while and letting your subconscious take over allows the story to choose the right path. Do we sound mental? If anyone's got this far I assume they're with us for the ride now. But yeah, Jodie's back at the wheel for the final volume and I've been sketching a little of that out, scenes coming together.

PG: I can't wait to read it! I can't imagine what it's like to be writing the comic and guiding the work on the adaptation too. How much do you think each affects the other? Especially in this case, where you'll be writing the conclusion at the same time the show is being written. Has that happened on any of your other projects?

MM: I'm generally done by the time an adaptation is being written, and I've rarely done sequels, so it tends not to change things too much, but I must confess when I was writing the later Kick-Ass volumes I could see Aaron and Chloe, and it was distracting because the thing had become something else by that point. But you have to shut all that out. I'm writing the final book of Jupiter's Legacy right now, and you honestly just have to forget it's a Netflix series too and crack on with the book. If you tried to ride two horses you'd just fall off, so when I'm giving notes on an adaptation I try to keep the comic work as far away from it as possible. As far as American Jesus goes, the big change is that they've added a lot of new material. The first book is only three issues, which works out at around 90 minutes of a movie. When Matthew Vaughn and I were entertaining the idea of doing this, before I sent him Kick-Ass, he said that was going to be the challenge. He tends to work in a very compressed way, and thought we'd have to really flesh stuff out to get to the two-hour mark. In a six-hour show, as Leopoldo and Everardo Gout are doing right now, there's a lot of new material in there, but it's all so beautiful. It's just completely poetic and, like all good adaptations, I think it brings more to the table. Fans will love it because the experience is just so rich. And the other change, of course, is that most of the action has moved from '80s America to a remote town in Mexico by the sea. When the guys were pitching me this, they sent me this amazing mood book of colours and all the backdrops they wanted to use. It was just beautiful. If these were movie sets it would cost 200 million dollars, but it's all just sitting there in real life and almost looks like an alien world in places. It's just totally authentic. I think they're doing something very special with this show, and the fact that it's Spanish language is really exciting. Netflix's theory is that this material will resonate most powerfully in Catholic, Spanish-speaking countries, so the logic is very clever. They really are very smart, those streaming people!

PG: They are indeed.

MM: Here's a thought, Peter. Do you feel your art style has changed at all in these sixteen years? I think it looks incredibly consistent with what came before and it's great having Jeanne and Cory back too. The trick will be to make sure that nobody gets hit by a bus between now and the third volume, because I want a big hardcover that looks the same all the way through. Drive carefully!

PG: I won't leave the house until it's done! In terms of style, I'm starting to think that the more it changes, the more it stays the same. I think my style is different—certainly a lot of my thinking and approach is very different, and hopefully more accomplished, but the end result is still me, and connects easily with the original series. The weird thing is, in the last five years or so, I've developed a severe hand tremor, and had two hand surgeries. I can't even draw on paper anymore; some days I can't even address an envelope by hand. So everything I do is digital now, where I can zoom the art up so large that it minimizes my tremor. And Clip Studio Paint has a stabilizer that turns my shaky line into a straight one. So my working method is totally different than before, and it took a while to get comfortable with it. I was lucky that American Jesus (along with the Millarworld company) was sold to Netflix right after my last hand surgery, and it meant I was able to take a year off to recover and relearn how to draw. As part of my retraining, I started re-inking my first comic, *Empire Lanes*, And doing that, I sort of travelled through my life as a comic artist and reconnected with my thinking back then and my joy in drawing. I pretty much rebuilt myself from the ground up and became Digital Peter. Then I jumped straight into this volume of American Jesus. Even though I have relearned how to draw digitally, I found out I also had to relearn how to be productive. The first issue of this took a long time, and it was only by the end of the volume that I really felt like I was getting normal speed again. Thanks for being patient with it all! And interestingly enough, Jeanne colored this all digitally too, whereas the original was done in watercolor on paper.

MM: My God. That's like a superhero origin story. You were basically Tony Stark in that Afghanistan cave building your prototype Iron Man suit!!

PG: That's closer to true than you can imagine—I had a machinist make custom mounts and robot arms so I can swing my massive drawing display around and use it like a lap desk. People are a little startled when they first see my studio!

MM: Do you remember all the various incarnations the American Jesus movie adaptations have taken over the years? I can't remember how much of this was in our first conversation at the back of Book One, but there was the hugely famous Hollywood producer who told me it was the best book she'd read in years, but could we take Jesus out of it because that might irritate some people. There was Matthew Vaughn as I mentioned, who was really into it for a while, and later suggested we do it as a musical, which might not be as crazy as it sounds. He'd just heard Cameron Mackintosh was a billionaire from musicals and he phoned me up, totally inspired (laughs). A couple of different TV people came in for it too, and one had a very good take, but nothing ever really got off the ground or felt right. A big European studio was also very interested, really liking the book and actually flying up to Scotland to meet me at some point, but the sequel ideas made their eyes swivel. I think the plan I had at the time would have cost around five hundred million so we parted ways (laughs), their budget idea was more like five or ten per picture.

PG: I was always sure the material would end up scaring away any prospective producers—especially after your stories about taking Jesus out and the musical idea --though I would have loved to see that, obviously. I think you even mentioned Brad Pitt's production company showing some interest at one point. We did actually have a couple of offers and contracts on the table at different points, but they didn't finalize for one reason or another. Was there any choice that would have been an absolute mistake?

MM: Oh, yes. The very nice producers who thought this could be the next Twilight, which I almost got talked into, as I really like the guys a lot. This was back when Twilight was massive and still being read under the covers by 12-year-old girls everywhere. Their idea was a kind of Sexy Jesus and Sexy Antichrist as teen heartthrobs, both in the same town and sort of STARING at each other across the high-school, very much modelled after Team Edward and Team Whatever the other guy was called. I remember at the time doing a lot of meetings like this, where people would suggest working with me on something and half the time I thought I was getting Punk'd. I swear to God I'd sometimes look around for a camera (laughs).

PG: I'm just so happy that we ended up at Netflix, I've learned to be very patient when it comes to media adaptations and never count on anything until the check clears! I kept thinking the Netflix deal would fall apart, even after we signed contracts. I remember you sending an email to me as I was driving home from a week camping off the grid and you said "Check your bank account!" I signed on and saw and transaction with Netflix for $8.99 (my monthly subscription), and then below it another Netflix with a deposit for a life-changing amount! One of the great moments of my life. Couldn't believe that our 1/3 finished story from 14 years before was suddenly paying off big time.

MM: Haha. I love the idea of the $8.99 in there. You must have almost had a stroke! But yeah, you have to kiss a lot of frogs before you find your prince sometimes, and I'm really happy here too. I guess it's like all those terrible names thrown around to play Superman before they eventually lucked out with Christopher Reeve. I think there were just a few near-misses here before landing with the Gout Brothers. Netflix saw the potential in the material immediately, and most importantly they understood it. It's a weird thing sending your baby off to be adopted by someone else. I've been lucky on everything so far, but the worry is that it ends up with Ed Gein as opposed to Ma and Pa Kent. But this is great, and even though I've never worked harder in my life I'm loving it.

PG: I'm just in it for the fun ride at this point. I'm enjoying everything about this!

MM: Here's a question I'm not sure I've asked before, but do you BELIEVE in the mythology we've been putting together here, or is this just another fictional story to you, like Superman or Batman? Basically, do you believe there's something at the basis of Christianity, and do you think things are going to play out in a way anything close to resembling this book?

PG: I believe in the vast power of stories, but I don't feel the need for these stories to also have to be real, Not to push another book of mine, but it was what my series *The Unwritten* (with Mike Carey) was about. I think most of the misery in the world is caused by people who insist that stories must be true—and then try to force others to also believe and live by the rules of their stories. There's shades of that going on all around us now, where facts become fake news, and that opens the door for any lie to become true if it's repeated enough. So take all the teachings you want from any religious or secular story that inspires you—change your life based on it if you want; but respect everyone else's right to pick their own stories. I guess in my world, Batman and Spider-Man are potentially just as powerful and legit as the Bible or any other religious work.

MM: What about the more 'out-there' stuff we've touched on in this book? Does the conspiracy angle resonate with you at all, this notion that we're all ruled by an international cabal of Satanists? Likely or unlikely?

PG: I have to confess that when I read Angel's worldview in his conversation with Luciana, it painted a pretty chilling and convincing picture, and I thought, "Is Mark just writing this, or does he believe it?" I don't even want to go down the rabbit hole with that stuff, because I think we all have a primordial connection to the idea of conspiracies. I think it's easier to just remain convinced that it's all stories as I said before (laughs).

MM: Yeah, you're going to hell, pal. I've got my bases covered with church on Sunday, so I'll put in a good word!

PG: How long have you had this story in your head?

MM: It's funny you say that, because every story I've ever written has been percolating most of my life. All our influences date back to when we first form memories, and all my favorite things as a kid wind up in my adult work, whether it's Superman or Buster Crabbe movies or James Bond or, in this case, The Omen. Sometimes you just want to do something like you wanted it to be when you were a kid. For example, I assumed The Final Conflict was going to be Jesus Vs Sam Neill, but it slightly copped out by just giving us that in the final couple of minutes, as much as I love that movie and as fantastic as Sam Neill is in it. I've seen other Antichrist things over the years, but nothing's ever really done what we've done here, and since I'm obsessed with global conspiracy stories it's been really exciting to weave all this in here, too. Being a Catholic, the mythology is very powerful for me, and I've touched on this in a couple of stories, but one of the very earliest things I ever came up with I pitched to my teacher as a sequel to the bible and I called it Bible 2. I told her the first one had been a massive bestseller and if even half of those people picked up the sequel I'd make a lot of money. I was maybe thirteen at the time and I guess this was my original story.

PG: Can you give me a clue to what horribly difficult and time consuming thing you're going to make me draw in the next one?

MM: Heaven versus hell? The Apocalypse on planet Earth? Everyone who ever lived rising from the grave for the Day of Judgement? Piece of cake (laughs).

PG: (Deep sigh...)

MARK MILLAR is a *New York Times*-bestselling author, Hollywood producer, and now president of his own division at Netflix.

His DC Comics work includes the seminal *Superman: Red Son*. At Marvel Comics, he created *The Ultimates*, which was selected by *Time Magazine* as the comic book of the decade, and described by screenwriter Zak Penn as his major inspiration for *The Avengers* movie.

Millar also created *Wolverine: Old Man Logan* and *Civil War*. *Civil War* was the basis of the *Captain America: Civil War* movie, and *Old Man Logan* was the inspiration for Fox's *Logan*. Mark has been an executive producer on all adaptations of his books, and worked as a creative consultant to Fox Studios on their Marvel slate of movies.

Millar's creator-owned books *Kick-Ass*, *Wanted*, and *Kingsman: The Secret Service* have all been adapted into hugely successful Hollywood franchises.

When he sold his publishing company to Netflix in 2017, Millar also signed on to exclusively create comics, TV series, and movies for the streaming service. Adaptations of *Jupiter's Legacy*, *The Magic Order*, *Reborn*, *Sharkey the Bounty Hunter*, *American Jesus*, *Empress*, and *Super Crooks* are among those currently being made right now with *Jupiter's Legacy* the first to be streamed.

His much-anticipated autobiography, *Broccoli*, will be published next year.

PETER GROSS is an Eisner-nominated and *New York Times*-bestselling comic artist. He started his career with the creator-owned series *Empire Lanes*, and went on to illustrate three of DC/Vertigo's longest running series: *Books Of Magic, Lucifer* (now a Netflix series), and *The Unwritten* (co-created with Mike Carey).

Peter was one of the initial artists to join up with Mark Millar on the original launch of Millarworld, illustrating *American Jesus: Chosen*. Other recent work includes *The Highest House* and *The Dollhouse Family*.

Peter lives in Minneapolis, Minnesota with his wife Jeanne McGee, who is also the colorist on *American Jesus*. They have one daughter and one cat. He's happy to be back working on the *American Jesus* sequels and looks forward to the Netflix series.

JEANNE MCGEE was born and raised in San Francisco and currently lives in Minneapolis, Minnesota with her husband Peter Gross. She works in a variety of mediums, including printmaking, drawing, and textile design. When she is not coloring comics, you can find her carving and printing stamps onto wood, paper, and fabric.

You can see more of Jeanne's work at jeannemcgee.com

CORY PETIT is an artist living in Brooklyn, New York with his semi-famous stray cat, Fluff.

He's a twenty-year vet of the comic book industry, who got his lettering powers when bitten by a radioactive raccoon. You have seen his work on such titles as *Avengers*, *Wolverine*, *Superman*, *Guardians of the Galaxy*, *X-Men*, *Alias*...and a few others.

MELINA MIKULIC is a Master of Arts, and graduated from the Faculty of Design in Zagreb, Croatia, where she was born. As a graphic designer, she is primarily engaged in design for print, with a growing interest in illustration and interactive media. She now lives in Rijeka.

RACHAEL FULTON is a writer, journalist, and comic book editor from Scotland. She spent the last four years working as editor for Mark Millar at Millarworld, and later at Netflix's Mark Millar Division. Within that time, she was series editor on *Empress*, *Jupiter's Legacy*, *Reborn*, *Kick-Ass: The New Girl*, *Hit-Girl*, *Kingsman: The Red Diamond*, *The Magic Order*, *Prodigy*, *Sharkey The Bounty Hunter*, *Space Bandits*, *Chrononauts 2*, *American Jesus 2*, as well as other reprints. She lives in rural Scotland with her family and cat, Skwee. She tweets from the handle @Rachael_Fulton. *American Jesus: The New Messiah* is her last book for Netflix.

NET

FROM THE MIND OF

Huck
MARK MILLAR
RAFAEL ALBUQUERQUE
DAVE McCAIG
ART BY RAFAEL ALBUQUERQUE

THE MAGIC ORDER
MARK MILLAR
OLIVIER COIPEL
BOOK ONE
ART BY OLIVIER COIPEL

MARK MILLAR · GORAN PARLOV
STARLIGHT
ART BY GORAN PARLOV

MARK MILLAR
WILFREDO TORRES · DAVIDE GIANFELICE
JUPITER'S CIRCLE
BOOK ONE
ART BY
WILFREDO TORRES

MILLAR · TORRES · SPROUSE
JUPITER'S CIRCLE
ART BY WILFREDO TORRES
& CHRIS SPROUSE

MARK MILLAR · FRANK QUITELY
JUPITER'S LEGACY
BOOK ONE
ART BY FRANK QUITELY

MARK MILLAR · FRANK QUITELY
JUPITER'S LEGACY
BOOK TWO
ART BY FRANK QUITELY

REBORN
BOOK ONE
MARK MILLAR · GREG CAPULLO
ART BY GREG CAPULLO

Prodigy.
Mark Millar
Rafael Albuquerque
THE EVIL EARTH
ART BY RAFAEL ALBUQUERQUE

MARK MILLAR & LEINIL YU
SUPERIOR
FROM THE WRITER OF KICK-ASS
ART BY LEINIL YU

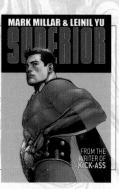

MARK MILLAR

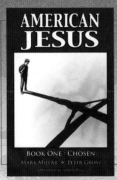

AMERICAN JESUS
BOOK ONE : CHOSEN
MARK MILLAR ✣ PETER GROSS

ART BY PETER GROSS

MARK MILLAR • MATTEO SCALERA
SPACE BANDITS

ART BY MATTEO SCALERA

MARK MILLAR • SIMONE BIANCHI
SHARKEY
THE BOUNTY HUNTER

ART BY SIMONE BIANCHI

EMPRESS
BOOK ONE
MARK MILLAR
STUART IMMONEN
WADE VON GRAWBADGER & IVE SVORCINA

ART BY STUART IMMONEN

MARK MILLAR LEINIL YU
SUPER CROOKS
THE HEIST

ART BY LEINIL YU

MILLAR & McNIVEN'S
NEMESIS

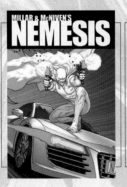

ART BY STEVE MCNIVEN

WANTED
MARK MILLAR • JG JONES • PAUL MOUNTS

ART BY JG JONES &
PAUL MOUNTS

MILLAR MURPHY
CHRONONAUTS

ART BY SEAN MURPHY

MILLAR • CANETE
CHRONONAUTS
FUTURESHOCK

ART BY ERIC CANETE

MARK MILLAR DUNCAN FEGREDO
MPH

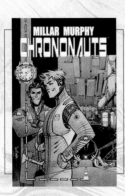

ART BY DUNCAN FEGREDO

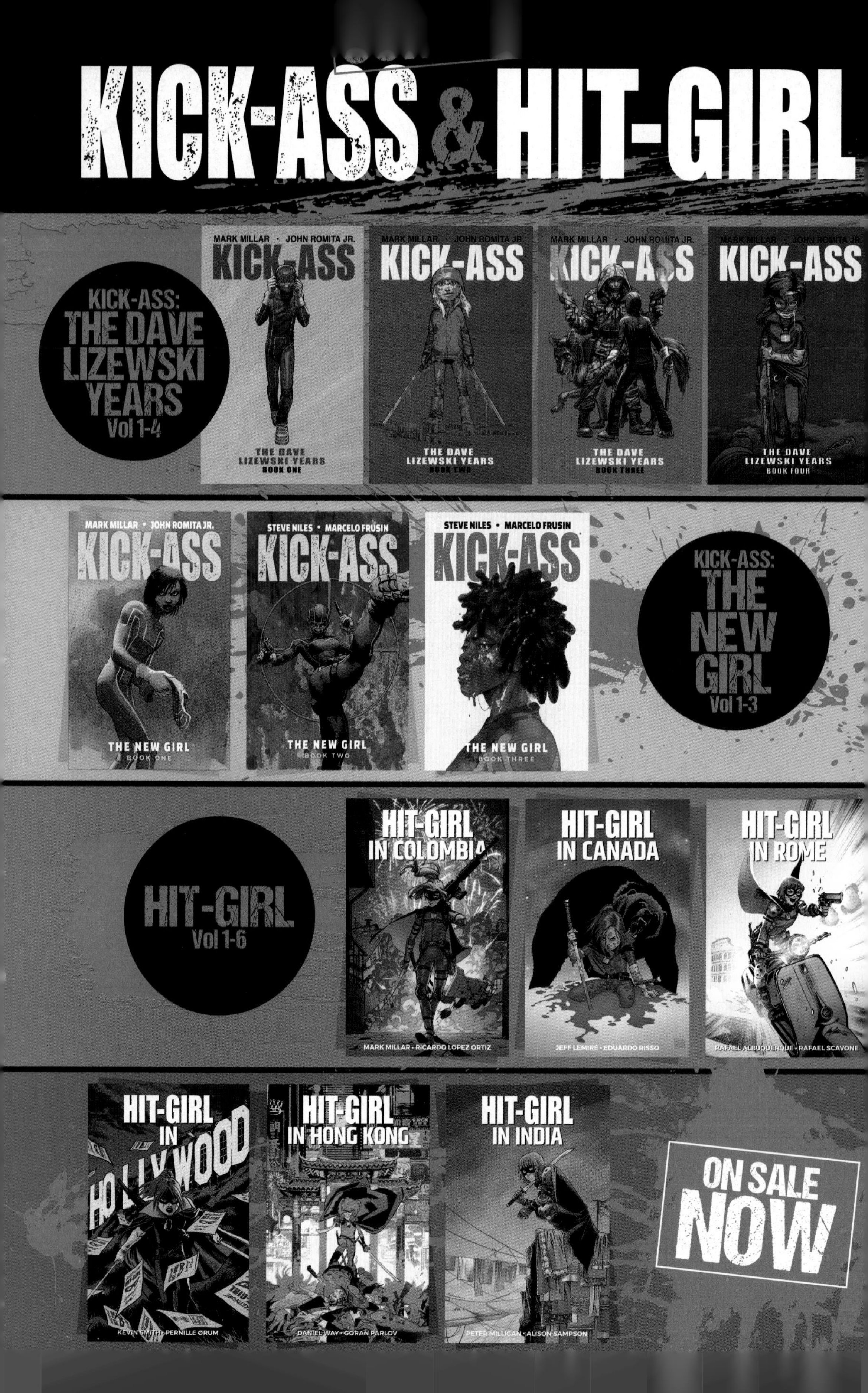
KICK-ASS & HIT-GIRL
KICK-ASS: THE DAVE LIZEWSKI YEARS
Vol 1-4
MARK MILLAR • JOHN ROMITA JR.
KICK-ASS
THE DAVE LIZEWSKI YEARS
BOOK ONE
MARK MILLAR • JOHN ROMITA JR.
KICK-ASS
THE DAVE LIZEWSKI YEARS
BOOK TWO
MARK MILLAR • JOHN ROMITA JR.
KICK-ASS
THE DAVE LIZEWSKI YEARS
BOOK THREE
MARK MILLAR • JOHN ROMITA JR.
KICK-ASS
THE DAVE LIZEWSKI YEARS
BOOK FOUR
MARK MILLAR • JOHN ROMITA JR.
KICK-ASS
THE NEW GIRL
BOOK ONE
STEVE NILES • MARCELO FRUSIN
KICK-ASS
THE NEW GIRL
BOOK TWO
STEVE NILES • MARCELO FRUSIN
KICK-ASS
THE NEW GIRL
BOOK THREE
KICK-ASS: THE NEW GIRL
Vol 1-3
HIT-GIRL
Vol 1-6
HIT-GIRL IN COLOMBIA
MARK MILLAR • RICARDO LOPEZ ORTIZ
HIT-GIRL IN CANADA
JEFF LEMIRE • EDUARDO RISSO
HIT-GIRL IN ROME
RAFAEL ALBUQUERQUE • RAFAEL SCAVONE
HIT-GIRL IN HOLLYWOOD
KEVIN SMITH • PERNILLE ØRUM
HIT-GIRL IN HONG KONG
DANIEL WAY • GORAN PARLOV
HIT-GIRL IN INDIA
PETER MILLIGAN • ALISON SAMPSON
ON SALE NOW